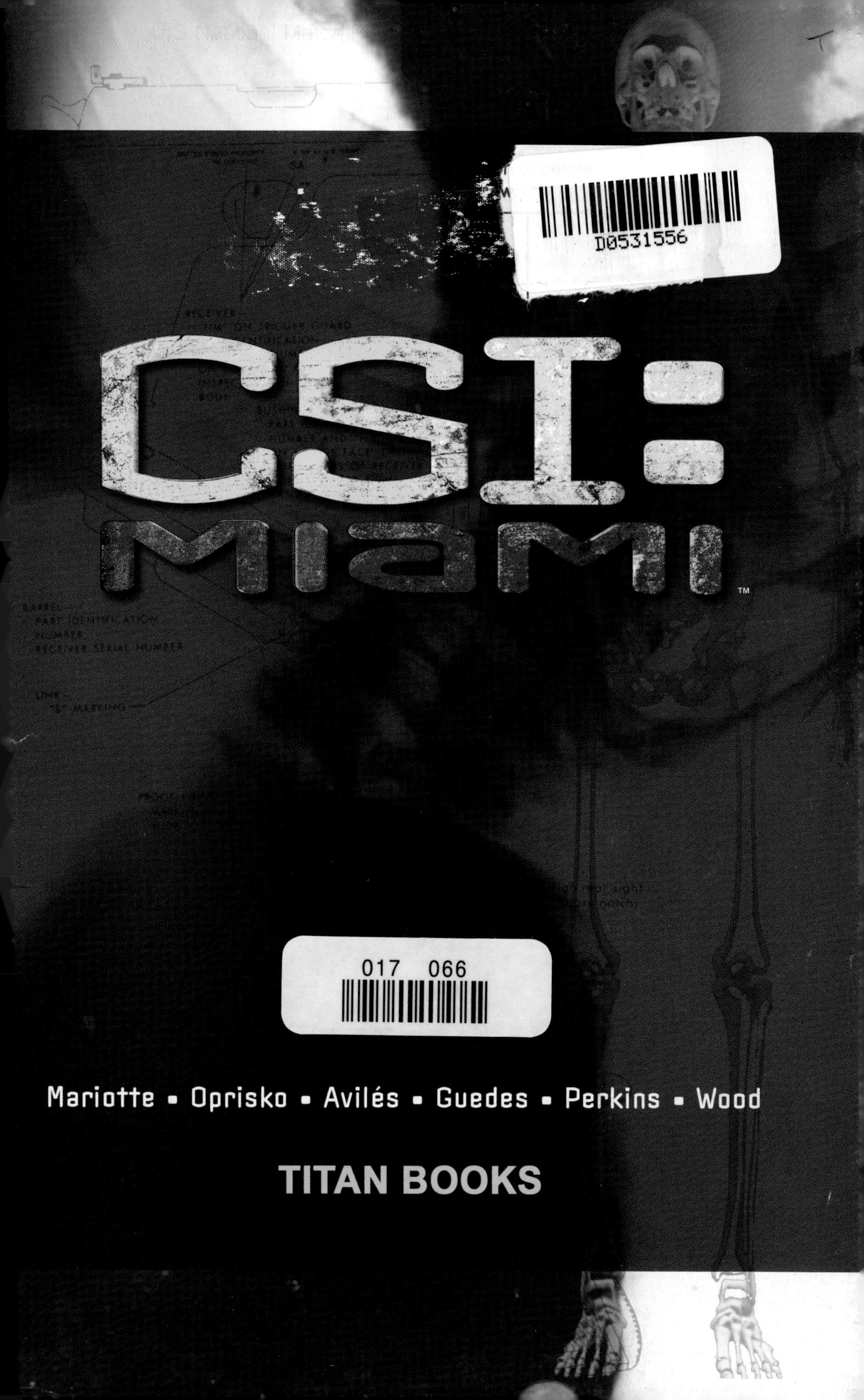

CSI: MIAMI™
Mariotte • Oprisko • Avilés • Guedes • Perkins • Wood
TITAN BOOKS

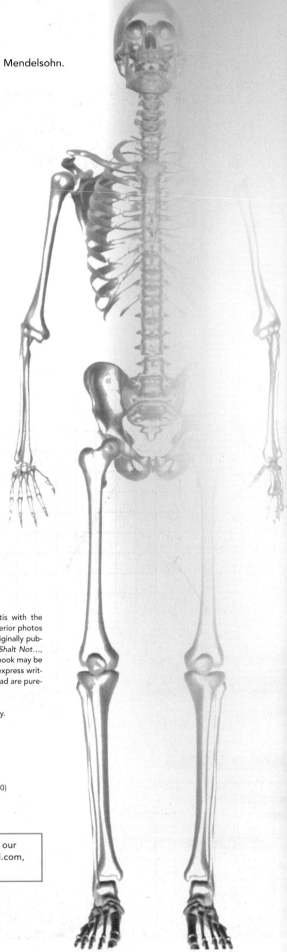

CSI: MIAMI

Created by Anthony E. Zuiker, Ann Donahue & Carol Mendelsohn.

ISBN 1 84576 003 4

"SMOKING GUN"

Written by JEFF MARIOTTE
Pencils by JOSÉ AVILÉS
Inks by JAVI BIT & JUAN C. HIDALGO
Colours by FRAN GAMBOA
Painted artwork by ASHLEY WOOD
Lettering by CINDY CHAPMAN

"THOU SHALT NOT..."

Written by KRIS OPRISKO
Art by RENATO GUEDES
Painted artwork by ASHLEY WOOD
Lettered by ROBBIE ROBBINS

"BLOOD/MONEY"

Written by KRIS OPRISKO
Art by RENATO GUEDES
Painted artwork by STEVEN PERKINS
Lettered by ROBBIE ROBBINS

Edited by JEFF MARIOTTE & KRIS OPRISKO
Design by CINDY CHAPMAN & ROBBIE ROBBINS

Published by
Titan Books
A division of Titan Publishing Group Ltd.
144 Southwark St
London SE1 0UP

First edition: January 2005

10 9 8 7 6 5 4 3 2 1

A CIP catalogue record for this title is available from the British Library.

Printed in Italy.

Also available from Titan Books:
***CSI: Crime Scene Investigation* – Serial** (ISBN: 1 84023 771 6)
***CSI: Crime Scene Investigation* – Bad Rap** (ISBN: 1 84023 799 6)
***CSI: Crime Scene Investigation* – Demon House** (ISBN: 1 84023 936 0)

What did you think of this book? We love to hear from our readers. Please email us at: readerfeedback@titanemail.com, or write to us at the above address.

You can also visit us at www.titanbooks.com

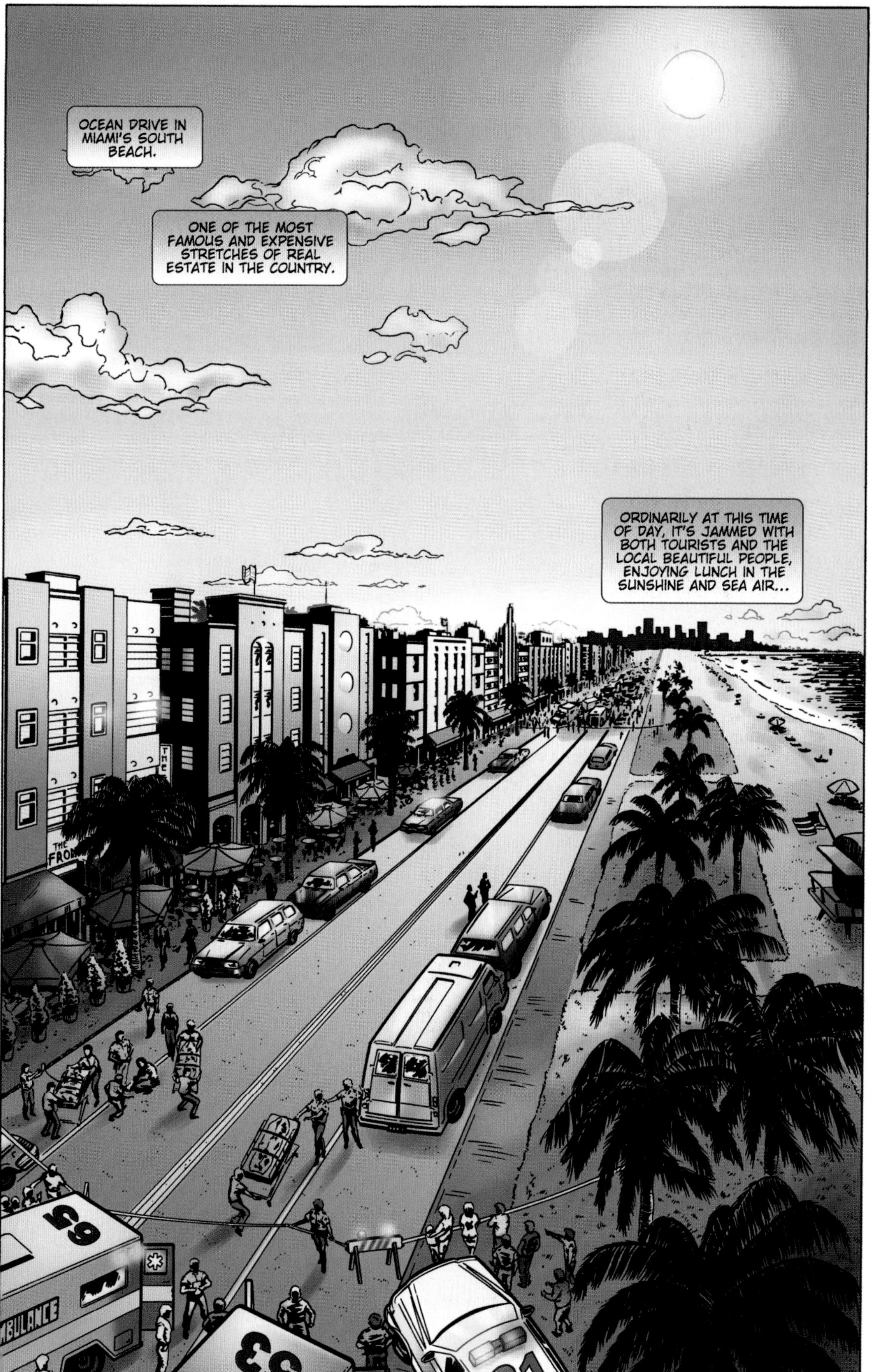
OCEAN DRIVE IN MIAMI'S SOUTH BEACH.
ONE OF THE MOST FAMOUS AND EXPENSIVE STRETCHES OF REAL ESTATE IN THE COUNTRY.
ORDINARILY AT THIS TIME OF DAY, IT'S JAMMED WITH BOTH TOURISTS AND THE LOCAL BEAUTIFUL PEOPLE, ENJOYING LUNCH IN THE SUNSHINE AND SEA AIR...
65
AMBULANCE
53
21

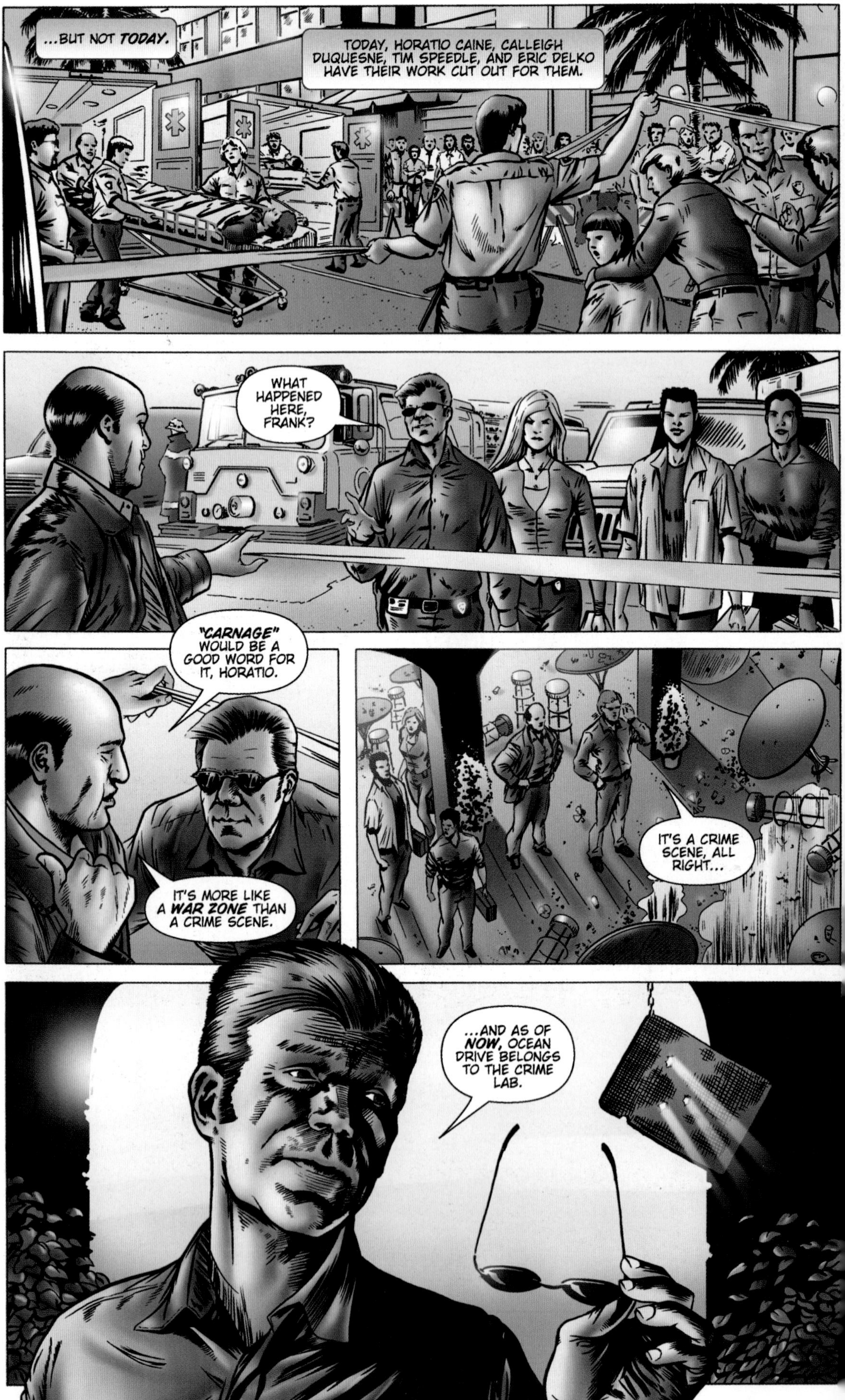
...BUT NOT TODAY.
TODAY, HORATIO CAINE, CALLEIGH DUQUESNE, TIM SPEEDLE, AND ERIC DELKO HAVE THEIR WORK CUT OUT FOR THEM.
WHAT HAPPENED HERE, FRANK?
"CARNAGE" WOULD BE A GOOD WORD FOR IT, HORATIO.
IT'S MORE LIKE A WAR ZONE THAN A CRIME SCENE.
IT'S A CRIME SCENE, ALL RIGHT...
...AND AS OF NOW, OCEAN DRIVE BELONGS TO THE CRIME LAB.

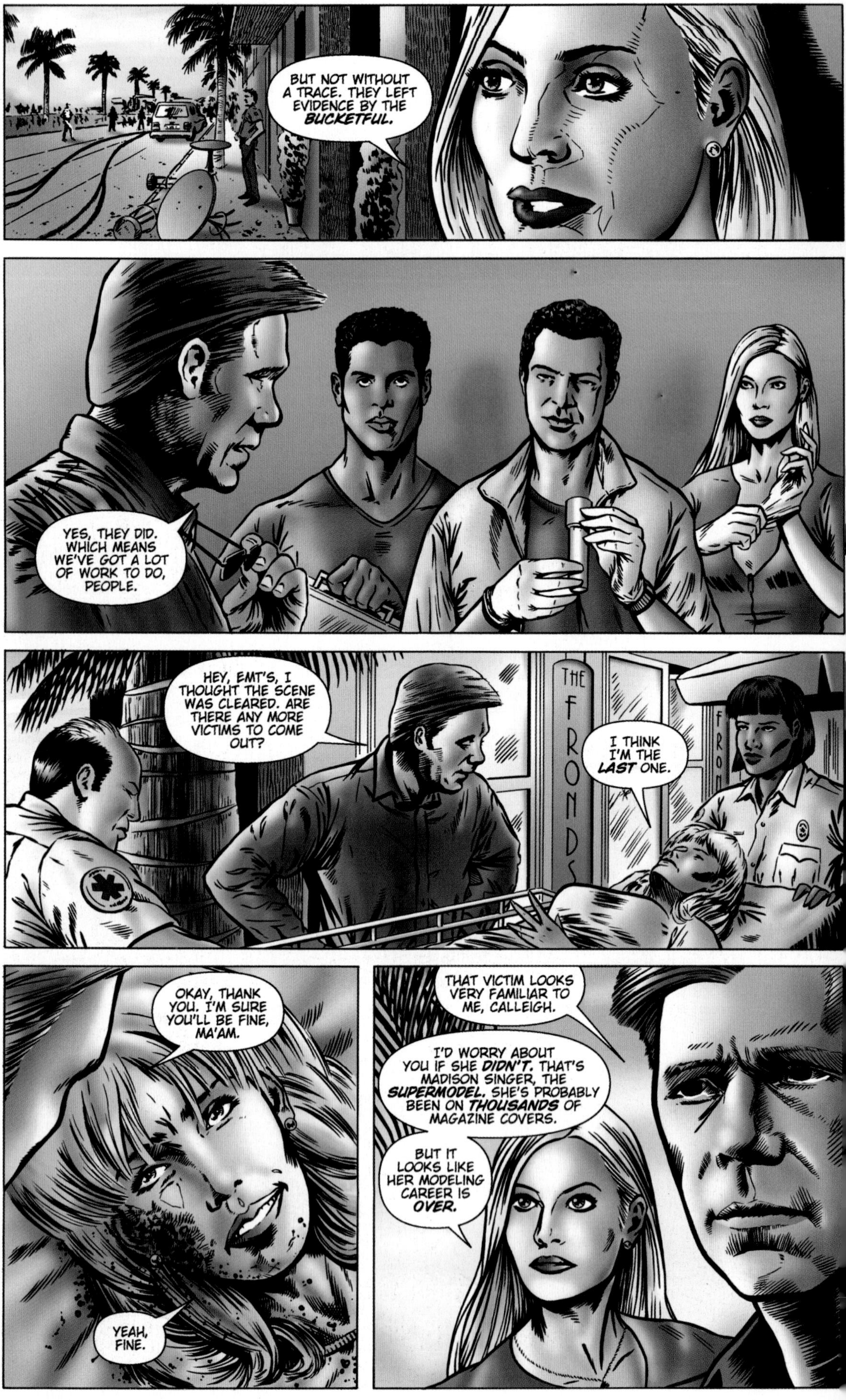
BUT NOT WITHOUT A TRACE. THEY LEFT EVIDENCE BY THE ***BUCKETFUL.***
YES, THEY DID. WHICH MEANS WE'VE GOT A LOT OF WORK TO DO, PEOPLE.
HEY, EMT'S, I THOUGHT THE SCENE WAS CLEARED. ARE THERE ANY MORE VICTIMS TO COME OUT?
THE FRONDS
I THINK I'M THE ***LAST*** ONE.
OKAY, THANK YOU. I'M SURE YOU'LL BE FINE, ***MA'AM.***
YEAH, FINE.
THAT VICTIM LOOKS VERY FAMILIAR TO ME, CALLEIGH.
I'D WORRY ABOUT YOU IF SHE ***DIDN'T.*** THAT'S MADISON SINGER, THE ***SUPERMODEL.*** SHE'S PROBABLY BEEN ON ***THOUSANDS*** OF MAGAZINE COVERS.
BUT IT LOOKS LIKE HER MODELING CAREER IS ***OVER.***

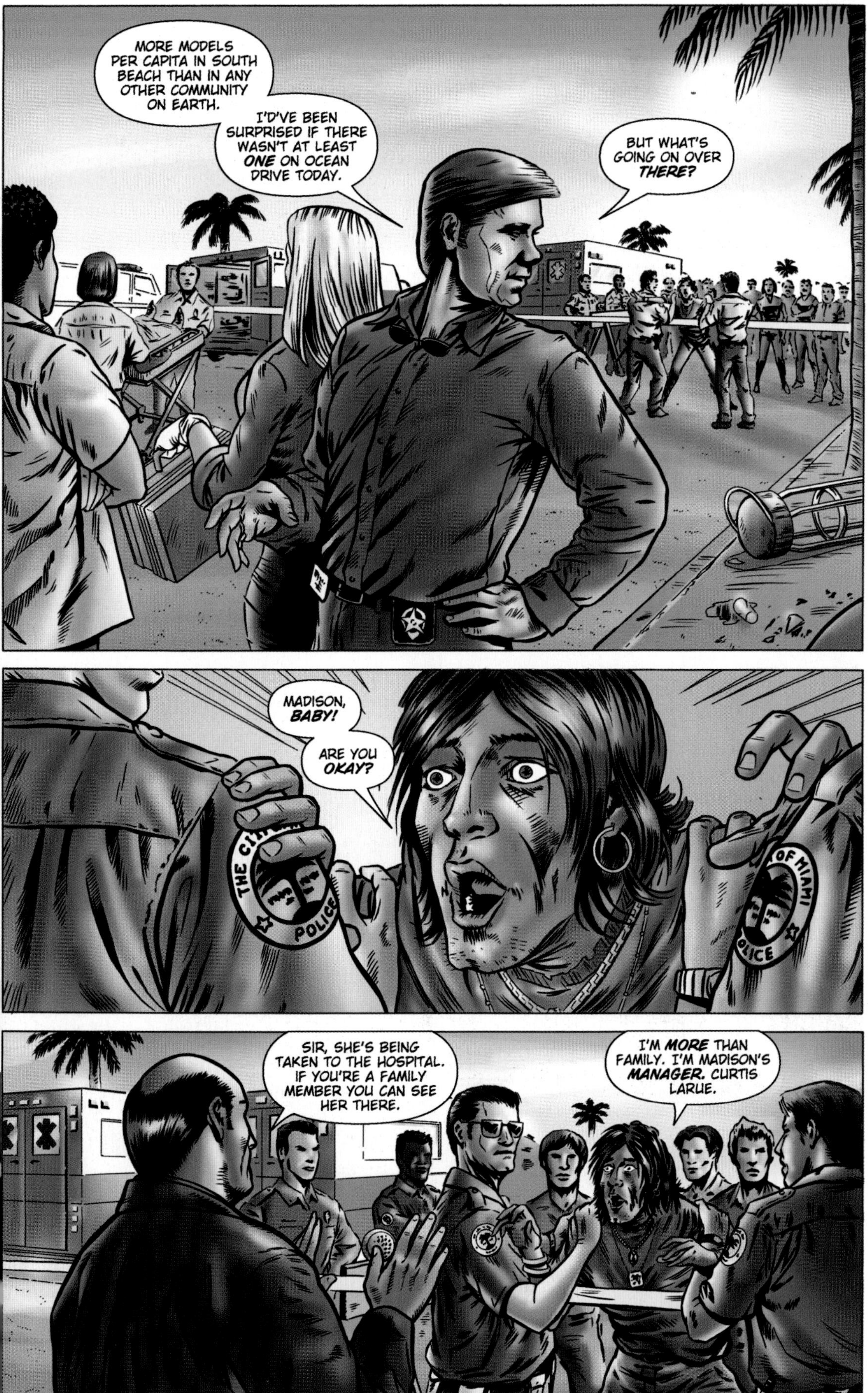
MORE MODELS PER CAPITA IN SOUTH BEACH THAN IN ANY OTHER COMMUNITY ON EARTH.
I'D'VE BEEN SURPRISED IF THERE WASN'T AT LEAST *ONE* ON OCEAN DRIVE TODAY.
BUT WHAT'S GOING ON OVER *THERE?*
MADISON, *BABY!*
ARE YOU *OKAY?*
SIR, SHE'S BEING TAKEN TO THE HOSPITAL. IF YOU'RE A FAMILY MEMBER YOU CAN SEE HER THERE.
I'M *MORE* THAN FAMILY. I'M MADISON'S *MANAGER.* CURTIS LARUE.

I WAS SUPPOSED TO MEET MADISON FOR LUNCH. TRAFFIC ON THE DAMN MACARTHUR CAUSEWAY HELD ME UP. NOW LOOK!

WILL SHE BE *OKAY?*

I'M A *DETECTIVE*, MR. LARUE, NOT A DOCTOR.

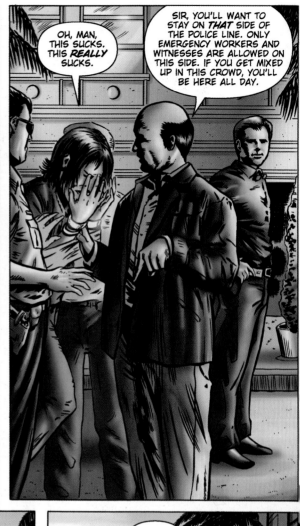

OH, MAN, THIS SUCKS. THIS *REALLY* SUCKS.

SIR, YOU'LL WANT TO STAY ON *THAT* SIDE OF THE POLICE LINE. ONLY EMERGENCY WORKERS AND WITNESSES ARE ALLOWED ON THIS SIDE. IF YOU GET MIXED UP IN THIS CROWD, YOU'LL BE HERE ALL DAY.

I HEAR YOU, PAL. GUESS I'LL SEE MADISON AT THE HOSPITAL, THEN.

THAT'D BE BEST.

OKAY, FOLKS. DRAMA'S OVER...

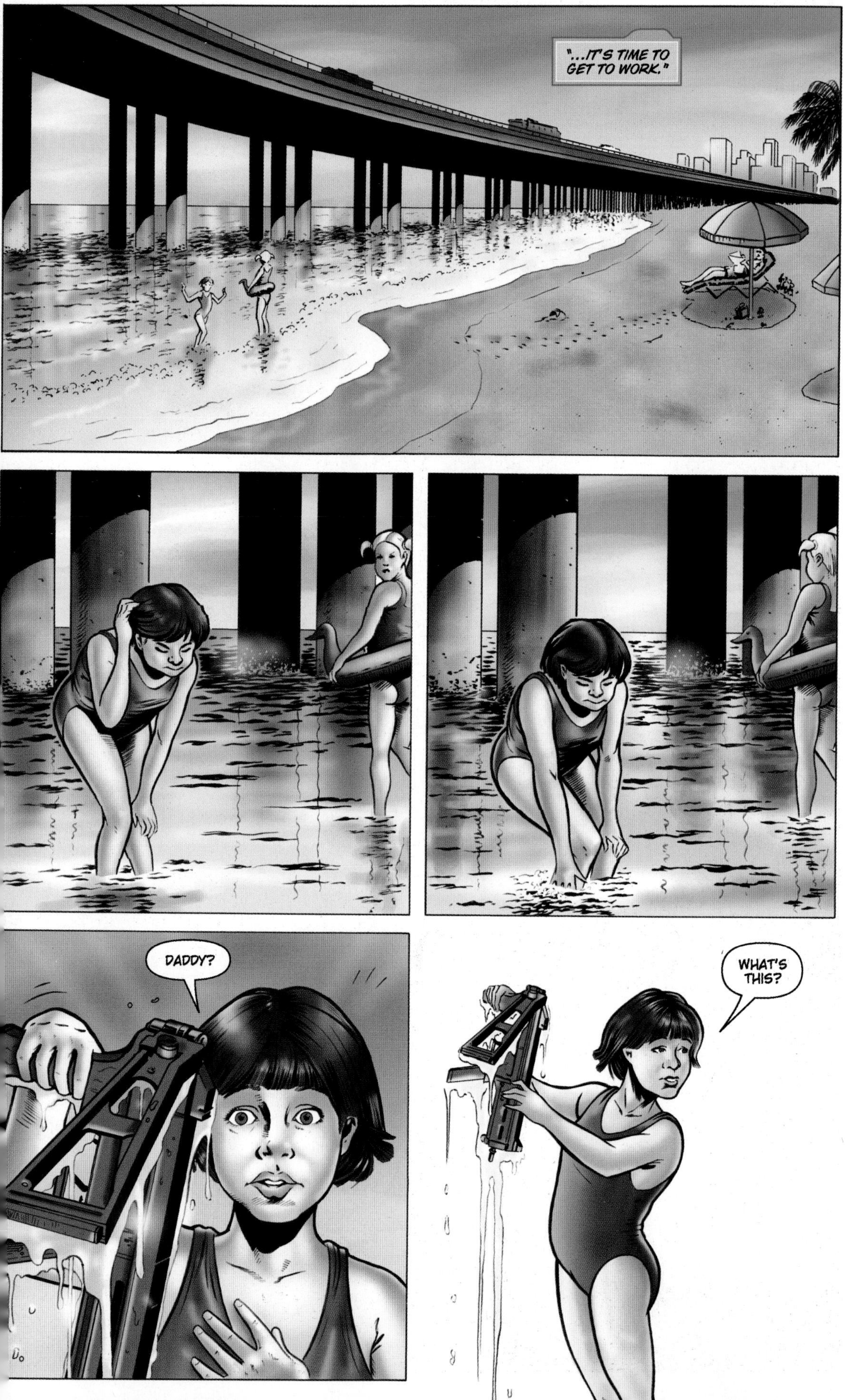
"...IT'S TIME TO GET TO WORK."
DADDY?
WHAT'S THIS?

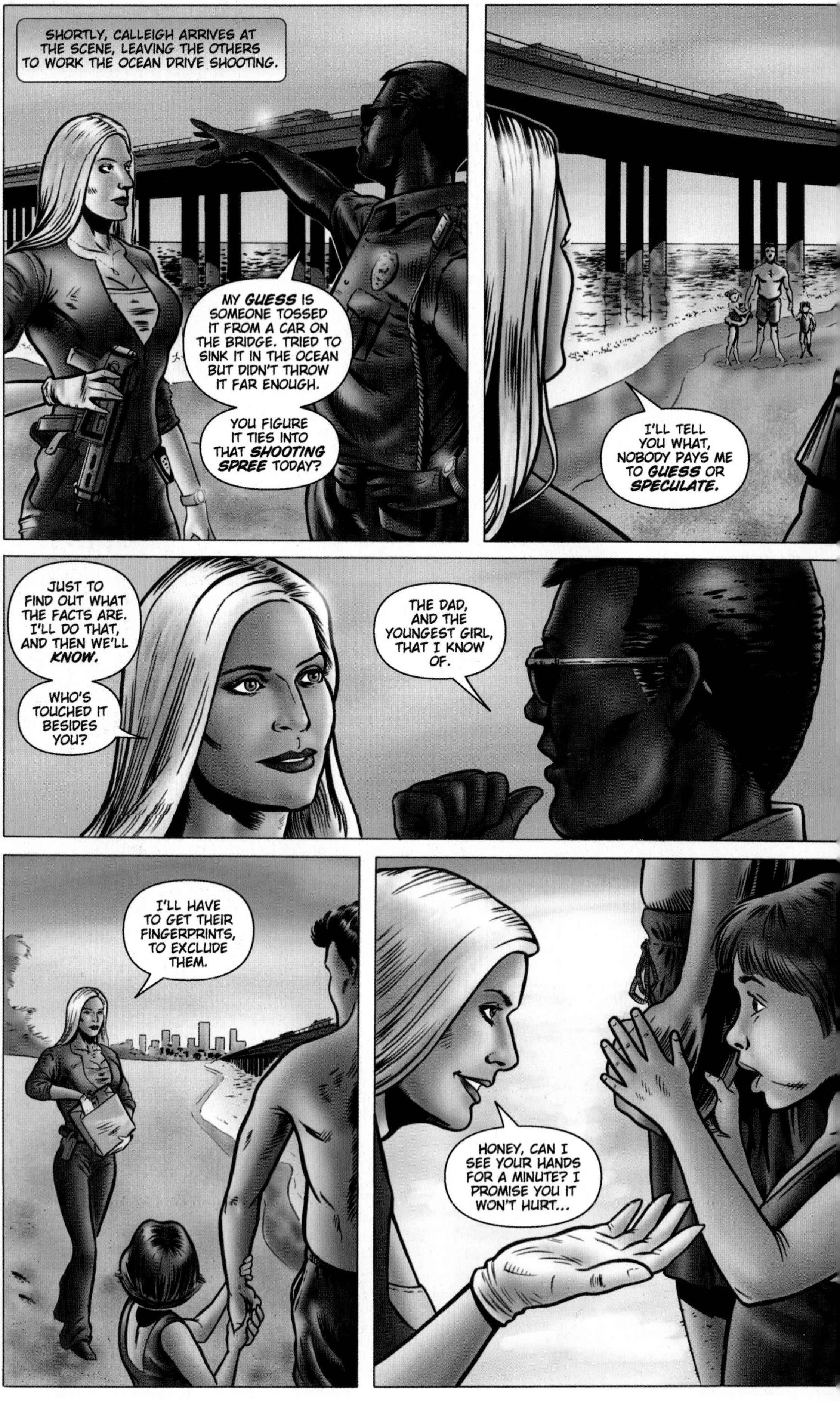

SHORTLY, CALLEIGH ARRIVES AT THE SCENE, LEAVING THE OTHERS TO WORK THE OCEAN DRIVE SHOOTING.
MY GUESS IS SOMEONE TOSSED IT FROM A CAR ON THE BRIDGE. TRIED TO SINK IT IN THE OCEAN BUT DIDN'T THROW IT FAR ENOUGH.
YOU FIGURE IT TIES INTO THAT SHOOTING SPREE TODAY?
I'LL TELL YOU WHAT, NOBODY PAYS ME TO GUESS OR SPECULATE.
JUST TO FIND OUT WHAT THE FACTS ARE. I'LL DO THAT, AND THEN WE'LL KNOW.
WHO'S TOUCHED IT BESIDES YOU?
THE DAD, AND THE YOUNGEST GIRL, THAT I KNOW OF.
I'LL HAVE TO GET THEIR FINGERPRINTS, TO EXCLUDE THEM.
HONEY, CAN I SEE YOUR HANDS FOR A MINUTE? I PROMISE YOU IT WON'T HURT...

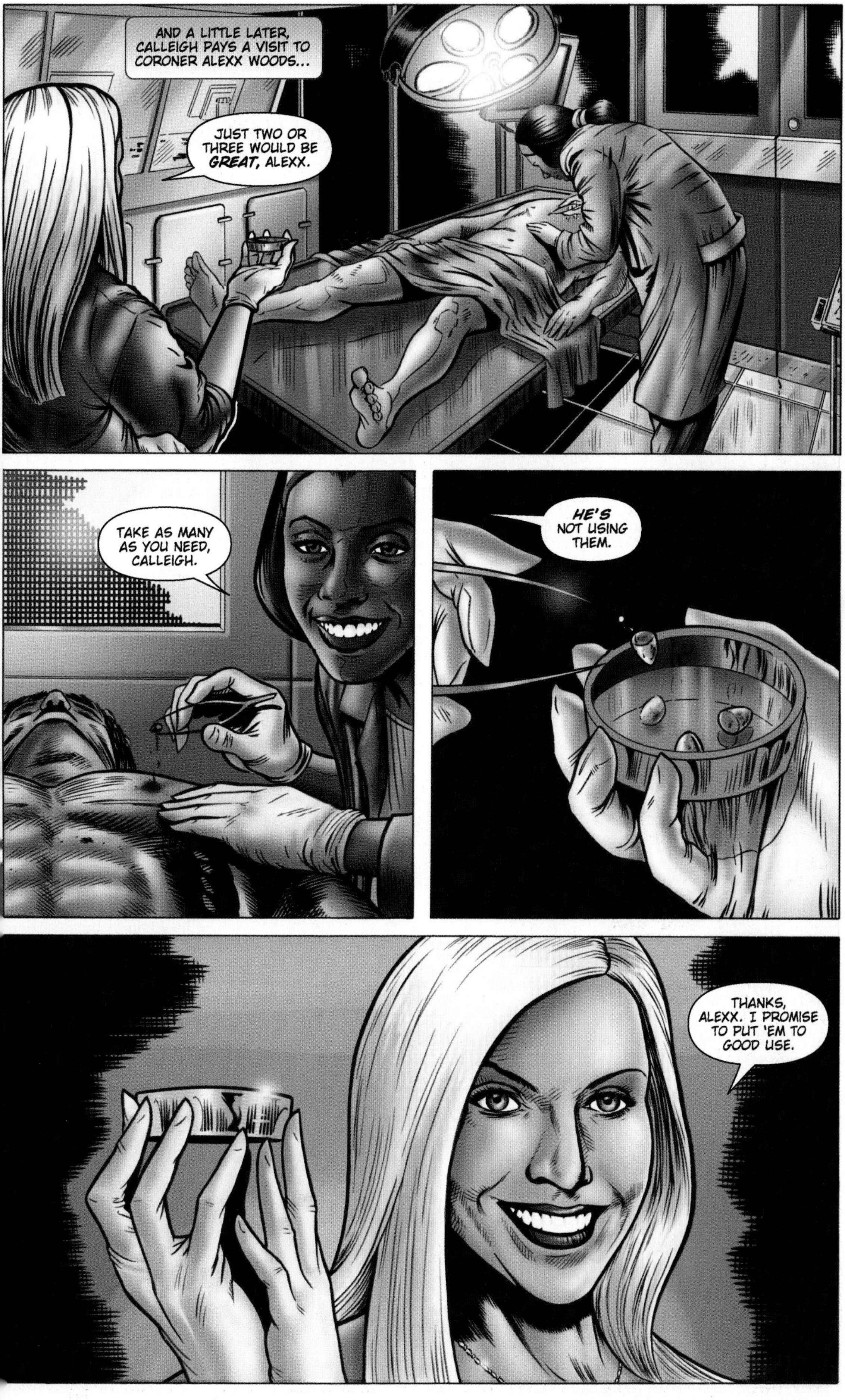
AND A LITTLE LATER, CALLEIGH PAYS A VISIT TO CORONER ALEXX WOODS...
JUST TWO OR THREE WOULD BE GREAT, ALEXX.
TAKE AS MANY AS YOU NEED, CALLEIGH.
HE'S NOT USING THEM.
THANKS, ALEXX. I PROMISE TO PUT 'EM TO GOOD USE.

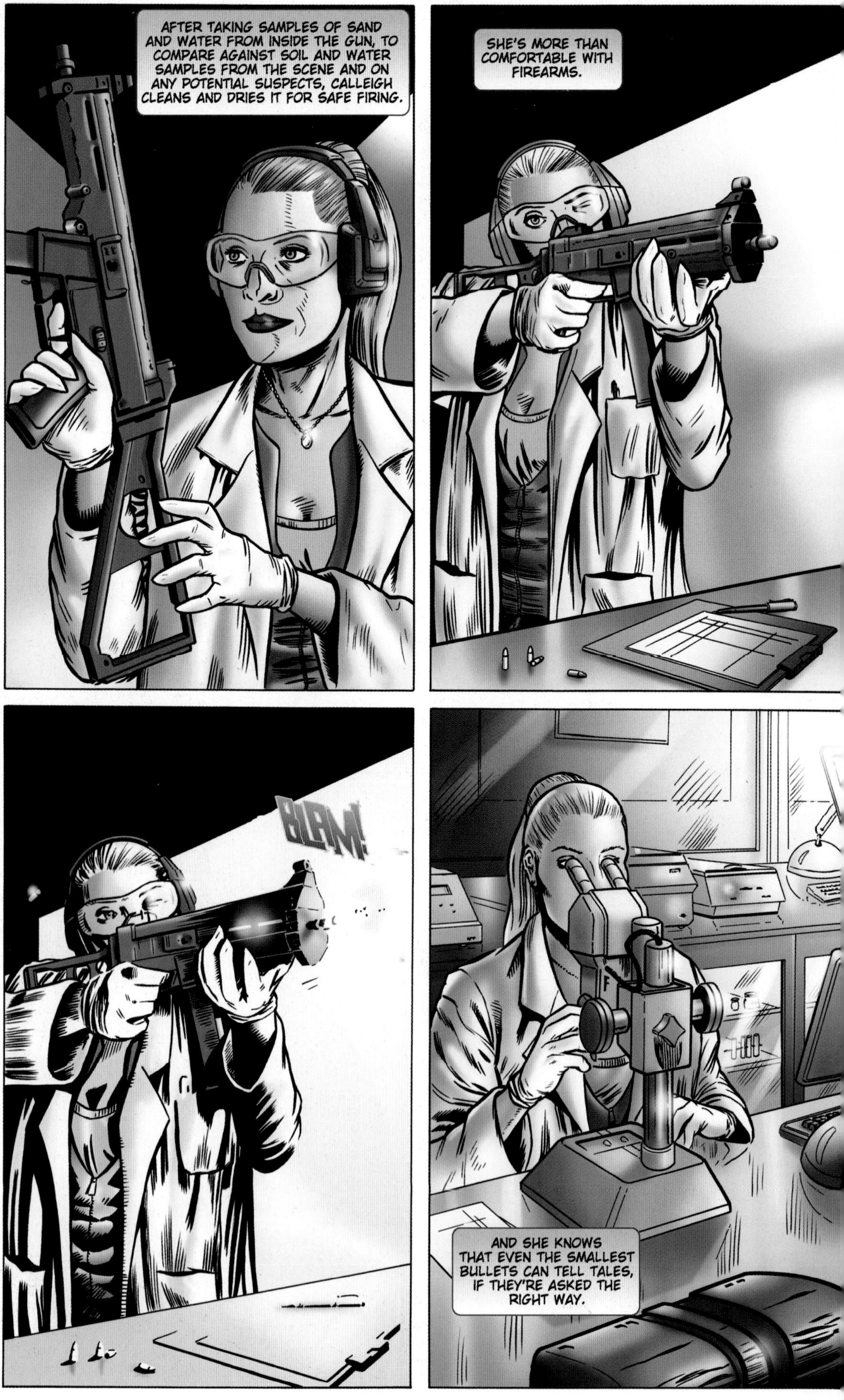
AFTER TAKING SAMPLES OF SAND AND WATER FROM INSIDE THE GUN, TO COMPARE AGAINST SOIL AND WATER SAMPLES FROM THE SCENE AND ON ANY POTENTIAL SUSPECTS, CALLEIGH CLEANS AND DRIES IT FOR SAFE FIRING.
SHE'S MORE THAN COMFORTABLE WITH FIREARMS.
BLAM!
AND SHE KNOWS THAT EVEN THE SMALLEST BULLETS CAN TELL TALES, IF THEY'RE ASKED THE RIGHT WAY.

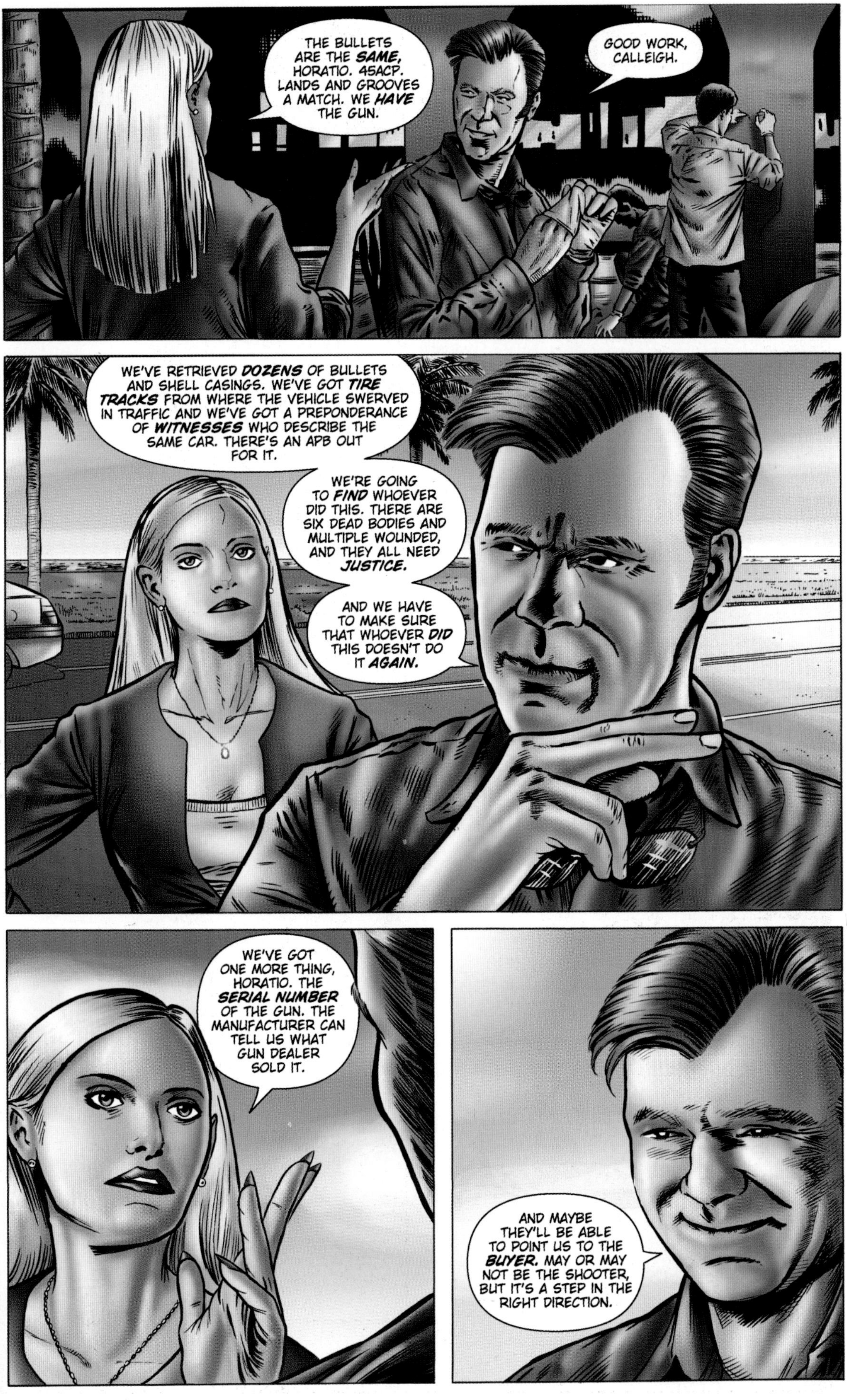
THE BULLETS ARE THE SAME, HORATIO. 45ACP. LANDS AND GROOVES A MATCH. WE HAVE THE GUN.
GOOD WORK, CALLEIGH.
WE'VE RETRIEVED DOZENS OF BULLETS AND SHELL CASINGS. WE'VE GOT TIRE TRACKS FROM WHERE THE VEHICLE SWERVED IN TRAFFIC AND WE'VE GOT A PREPONDERANCE OF WITNESSES WHO DESCRIBE THE SAME CAR. THERE'S AN APB OUT FOR IT.
WE'RE GOING TO FIND WHOEVER DID THIS. THERE ARE SIX DEAD BODIES AND MULTIPLE WOUNDED, AND THEY ALL NEED JUSTICE.
AND WE HAVE TO MAKE SURE THAT WHOEVER DID THIS DOESN'T DO IT AGAIN.
WE'VE GOT ONE MORE THING, HORATIO. THE SERIAL NUMBER OF THE GUN. THE MANUFACTURER CAN TELL US WHAT GUN DEALER SOLD IT.
AND MAYBE THEY'LL BE ABLE TO POINT US TO THE BUYER. MAY OR MAY NOT BE THE SHOOTER, BUT IT'S A STEP IN THE RIGHT DIRECTION.

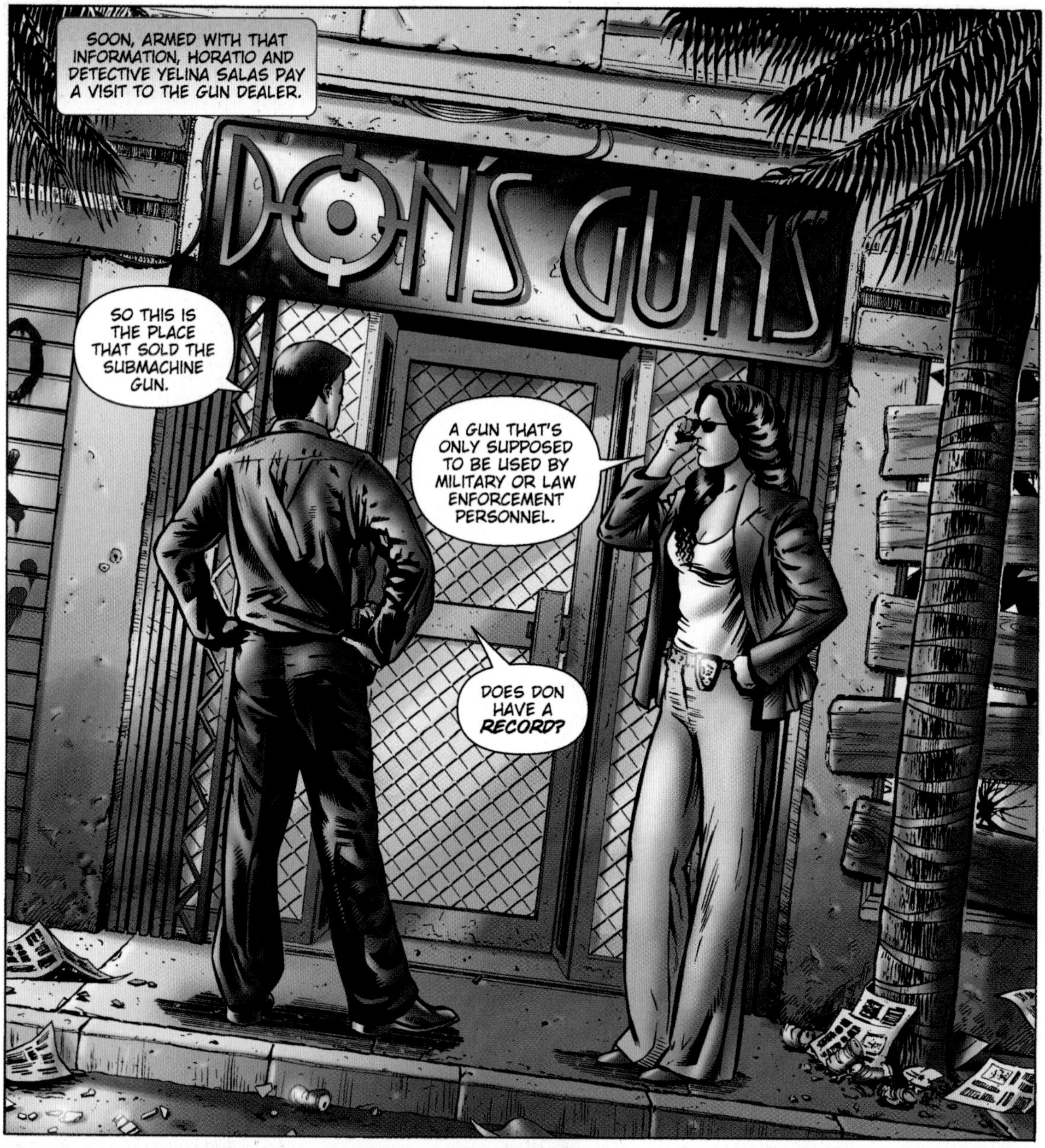
SOON, ARMED WITH THAT INFORMATION, HORATIO AND DETECTIVE YELINA SALAS PAY A VISIT TO THE GUN DEALER.
DON'S GUNS
SO THIS IS THE PLACE THAT SOLD THE SUBMACHINE GUN.
A GUN THAT'S ONLY SUPPOSED TO BE USED BY MILITARY OR LAW ENFORCEMENT PERSONNEL.
DOES DON HAVE A *RECORD?*

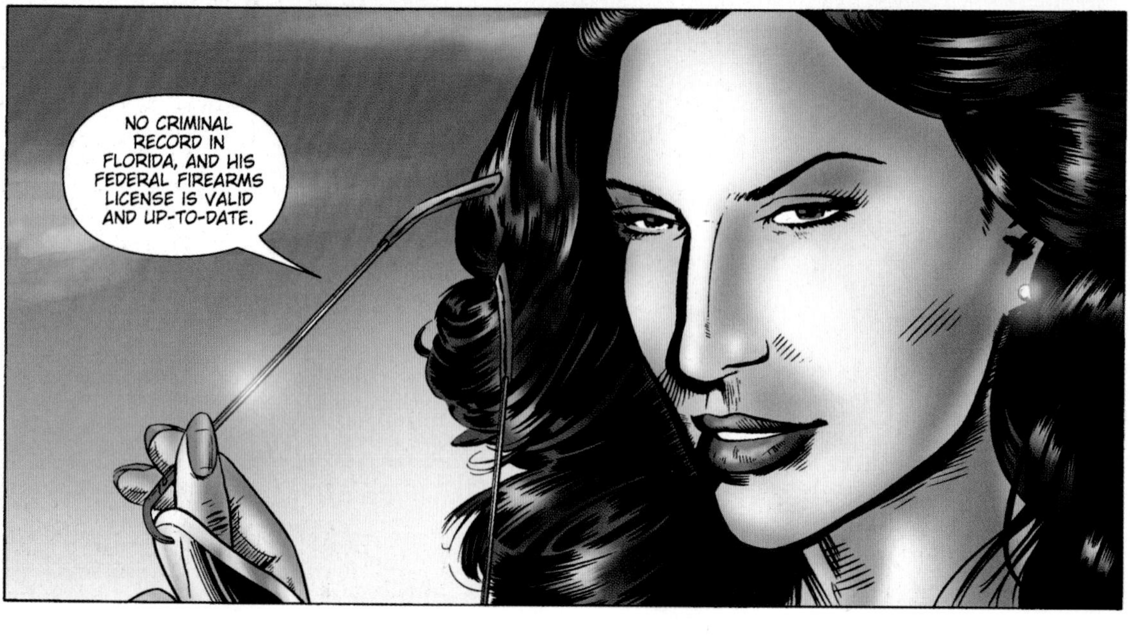
NO CRIMINAL RECORD IN FLORIDA, AND HIS FEDERAL FIREARMS LICENSE IS VALID AND UP-TO-DATE.

WE'RE LOOKING FOR DONALD FISCHER.

YOU *FOUND* HIM.

SOMETHIN' I CAN DO FOR YOU, MA'AM?

I'M DETECTIVE SALAS, MIAMI-DADE POLICE DEPARTMENT. THIS IS LIEUTENANT CAINE WITH THE CRIME LAB.

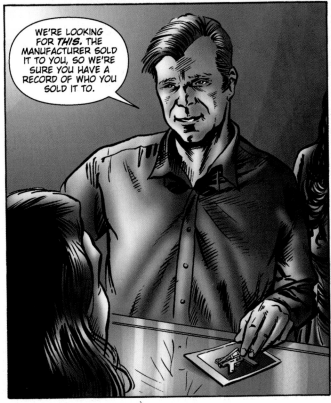

WE'RE LOOKING FOR *THIS.* THE MANUFACTURER SOLD IT TO YOU, SO WE'RE SURE YOU HAVE A RECORD OF WHO YOU SOLD IT TO.

WELL, THAT... THAT'S... I'D HAVE TO DO A LITTLE CHECKING ON THAT.

WE'LL WAIT.

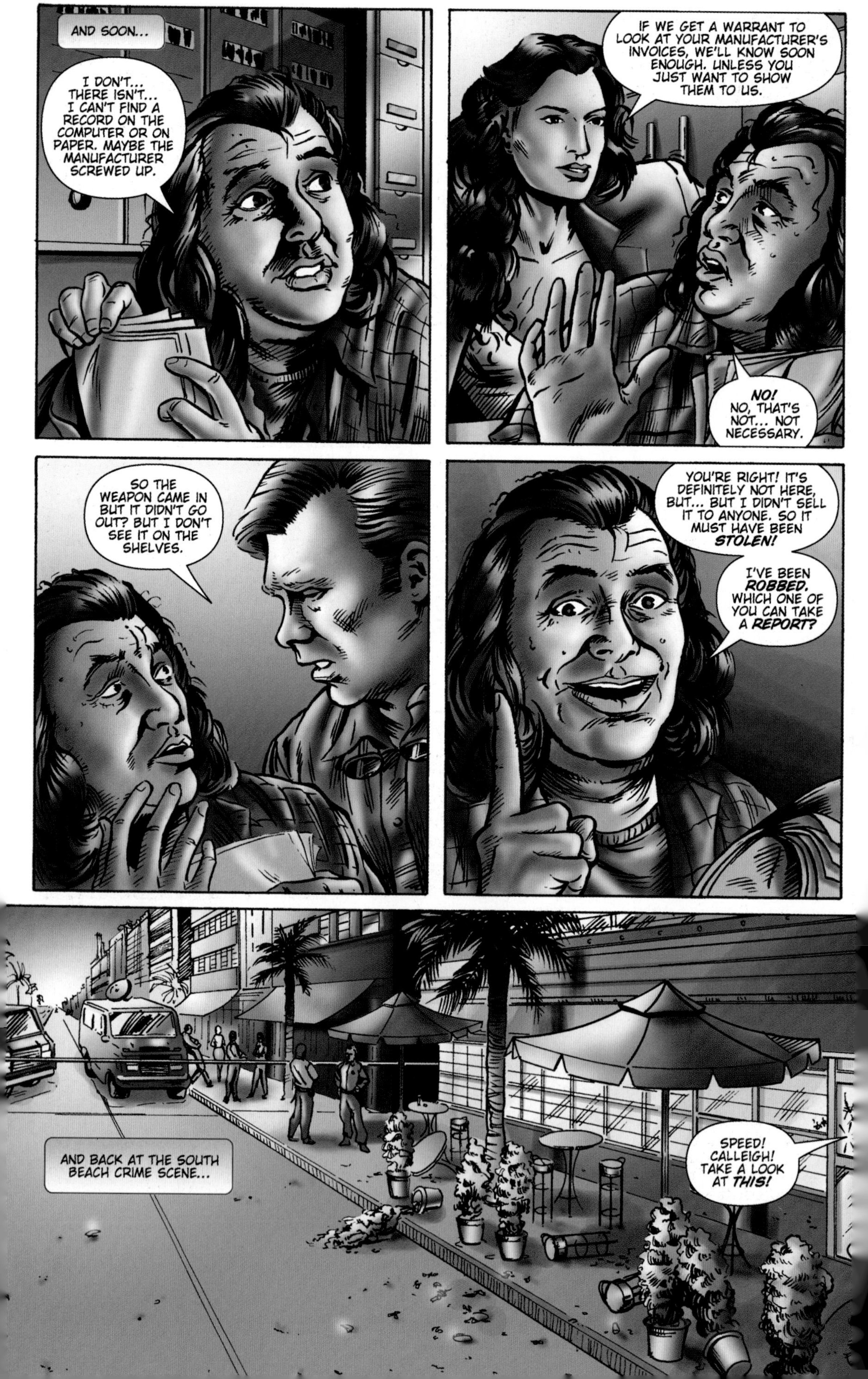
AND SOON...
I DON'T... THERE ISN'T... I CAN'T FIND A RECORD ON THE COMPUTER OR ON PAPER. MAYBE THE MANUFACTURER SCREWED UP.
IF WE GET A WARRANT TO LOOK AT YOUR MANUFACTURER'S INVOICES, WE'LL KNOW SOON ENOUGH. UNLESS YOU JUST WANT TO SHOW THEM TO US.
NO! NO, THAT'S NOT... NOT NECESSARY.
SO THE WEAPON CAME IN BUT IT DIDN'T GO OUT? BUT I DON'T SEE IT ON THE SHELVES.
YOU'RE RIGHT! IT'S DEFINITELY NOT HERE, BUT... BUT I DIDN'T SELL IT TO ANYONE. SO IT MUST HAVE BEEN STOLEN!
I'VE BEEN ROBBED. WHICH ONE OF YOU CAN TAKE A REPORT?
AND BACK AT THE SOUTH BEACH CRIME SCENE...
SPEED! CALLEIGH! TAKE A LOOK AT THIS!

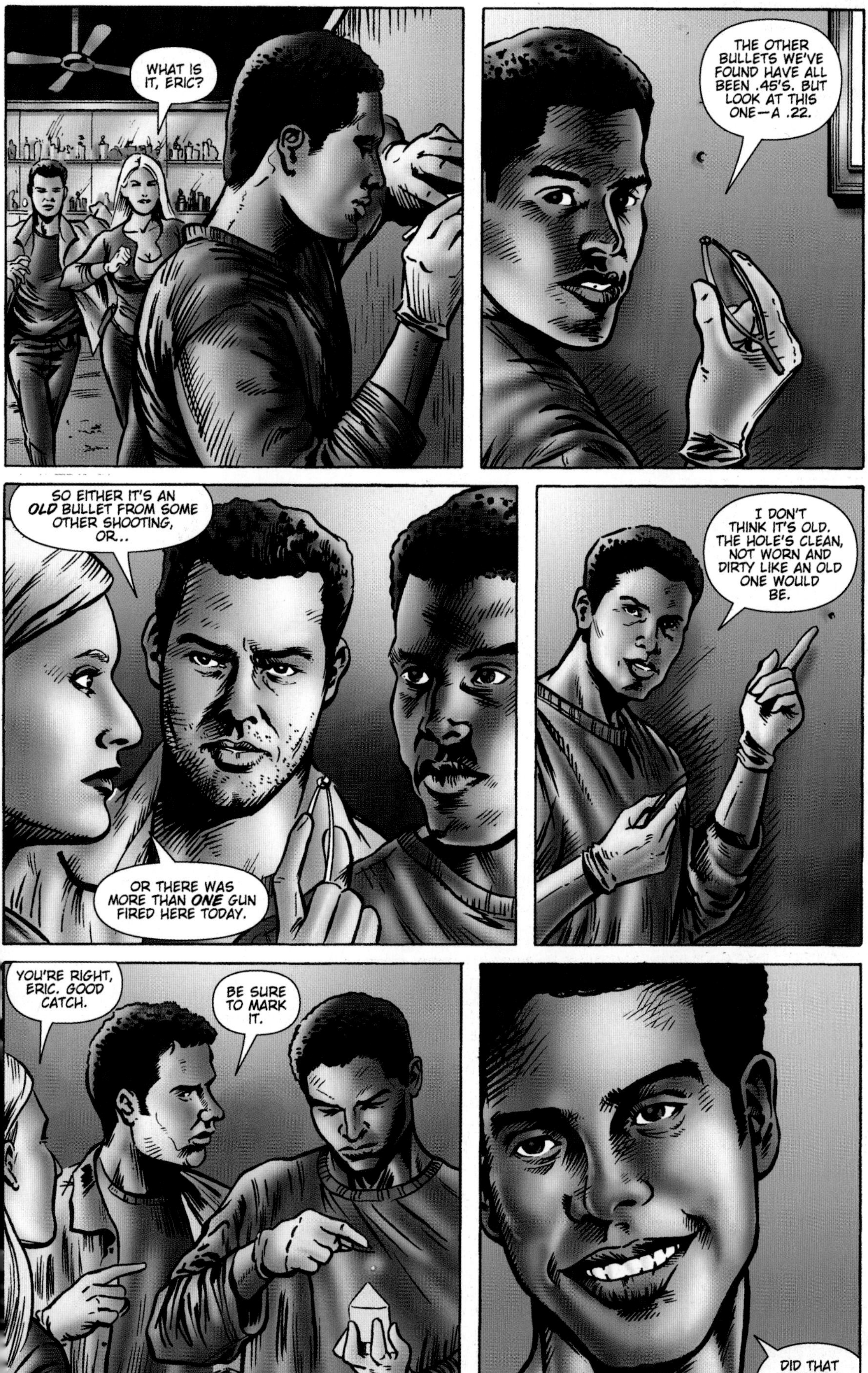
WHAT IS IT, ERIC?
THE OTHER BULLETS WE'VE FOUND HAVE ALL BEEN .45'S. BUT LOOK AT THIS ONE—A .22.
SO EITHER IT'S AN OLD BULLET FROM SOME OTHER SHOOTING, OR...
OR THERE WAS MORE THAN ONE GUN FIRED HERE TODAY.
I DON'T THINK IT'S OLD. THE HOLE'S CLEAN, NOT WORN AND DIRTY LIKE AN OLD ONE WOULD BE.
YOU'RE RIGHT, ERIC. GOOD CATCH.
BE SURE TO MARK IT.
DID THAT BEFORE I EVEN CALLED YOU GUYS.

"SHE'S STILL HEAVILY SEDATED, LT. CAINE."

WHAT'S HER PROGNOSIS, DOCTOR?

YOU HATE TO SEE SOMETHING LIKE THIS HAPPEN TO ANYONE, MUCH LESS A BEAUTIFUL YOUNG WOMAN.

EVEN MORE SO, ONE WHO MAKES HER LIVING WITH HER FACE.

HER LIFE ISN'T IN DANGER. BUT SHE'LL NEED A *LOT* OF RECONSTRUCTIVE SURGERY BEFORE HER FACE WILL EVEN BEGIN TO LOOK THE SAME.

I DOUBT THAT SHE'LL EVER GET HER LOOKS BACK COMPLETELY.

SHE'S NOT... A *SUSPECT* IN ANYTHING, IS SHE?

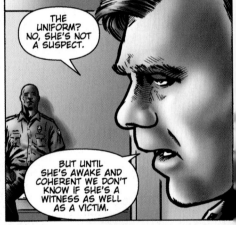

THE UNIFORM? NO, SHE'S NOT A SUSPECT.

BUT UNTIL SHE'S AWAKE AND COHERENT WE DON'T KNOW IF SHE'S A WITNESS AS WELL AS A VICTIM.

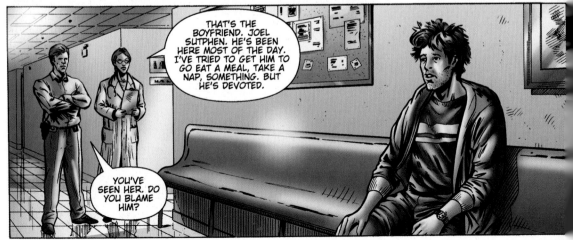

THAT'S THE BOYFRIEND. JOEL SUTPHEN. HE'S BEEN HERE MOST OF THE DAY. I'VE TRIED TO GET HIM TO GO EAT A MEAL, TAKE A NAP, SOMETHING. BUT HE'S DEVOTED.

YOU'VE SEEN HER. DO YOU BLAME HIM?

"NO, NOT A BIT."

DON'S GUNS? SURE, I KNOW THE PLACE.

BART HESKI

WHAT KIND OF REPUTATION DOES IT HAVE?

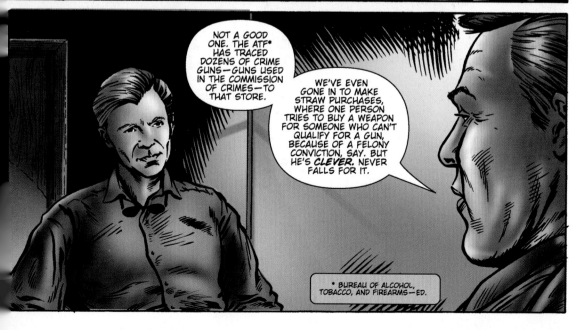

NOT A GOOD ONE. THE ATF* HAS TRACED DOZENS OF CRIME GUNS—GUNS USED IN THE COMMISSION OF CRIMES—TO THAT STORE.

WE'VE EVEN GONE IN TO MAKE STRAW PURCHASES, WHERE ONE PERSON TRIES TO BUY A WEAPON FOR SOMEONE WHO CAN'T QUALIFY FOR A GUN, BECAUSE OF A FELONY CONVICTION, SAY. BUT HE'S *CLEVER*. NEVER FALLS FOR IT.

* BUREAU OF ALCOHOL, TOBACCO, AND FIREARMS—ED.

SO MAYBE HE'S *CLEAN?*

I DON'T THINK SO. I JUST THINK HE'S *CAREFUL.*

SOMEHOW, THOUGH, HE'S SUPPLYING WEAPONS TO CRIMINALS.

IF YOU *KNOW* THAT, WHY HAVEN'T YOU BUSTED HIM?

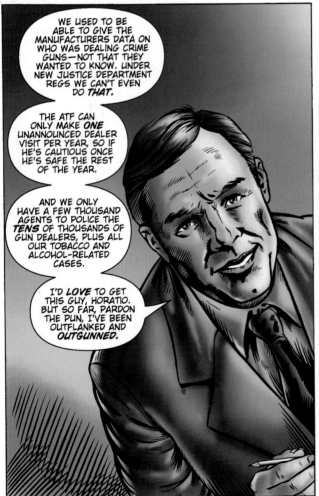

WE USED TO BE ABLE TO GIVE THE MANUFACTURERS DATA ON WHO WAS DEALING CRIME GUNS—NOT THAT THEY WANTED TO KNOW. UNDER NEW JUSTICE DEPARTMENT REGS WE CAN'T EVEN DO *THAT.*

THE ATF CAN ONLY MAKE *ONE* UNANNOUNCED DEALER VISIT PER YEAR, SO IF HE'S CAUTIOUS ONCE HE'S SAFE THE REST OF THE YEAR.

AND WE ONLY HAVE A FEW THOUSAND AGENTS TO POLICE THE *TENS* OF THOUSANDS OF GUN DEALERS, PLUS ALL OUR TOBACCO AND ALCOHOL-RELATED CASES.

I'D *LOVE* TO GET THIS GUY, HORATIO. BUT SO FAR, PARDON THE PUN, I'VE BEEN OUTFLANKED AND *OUTGUNNED.*

WELL, BART, MAYBE I CAN *HELP.*

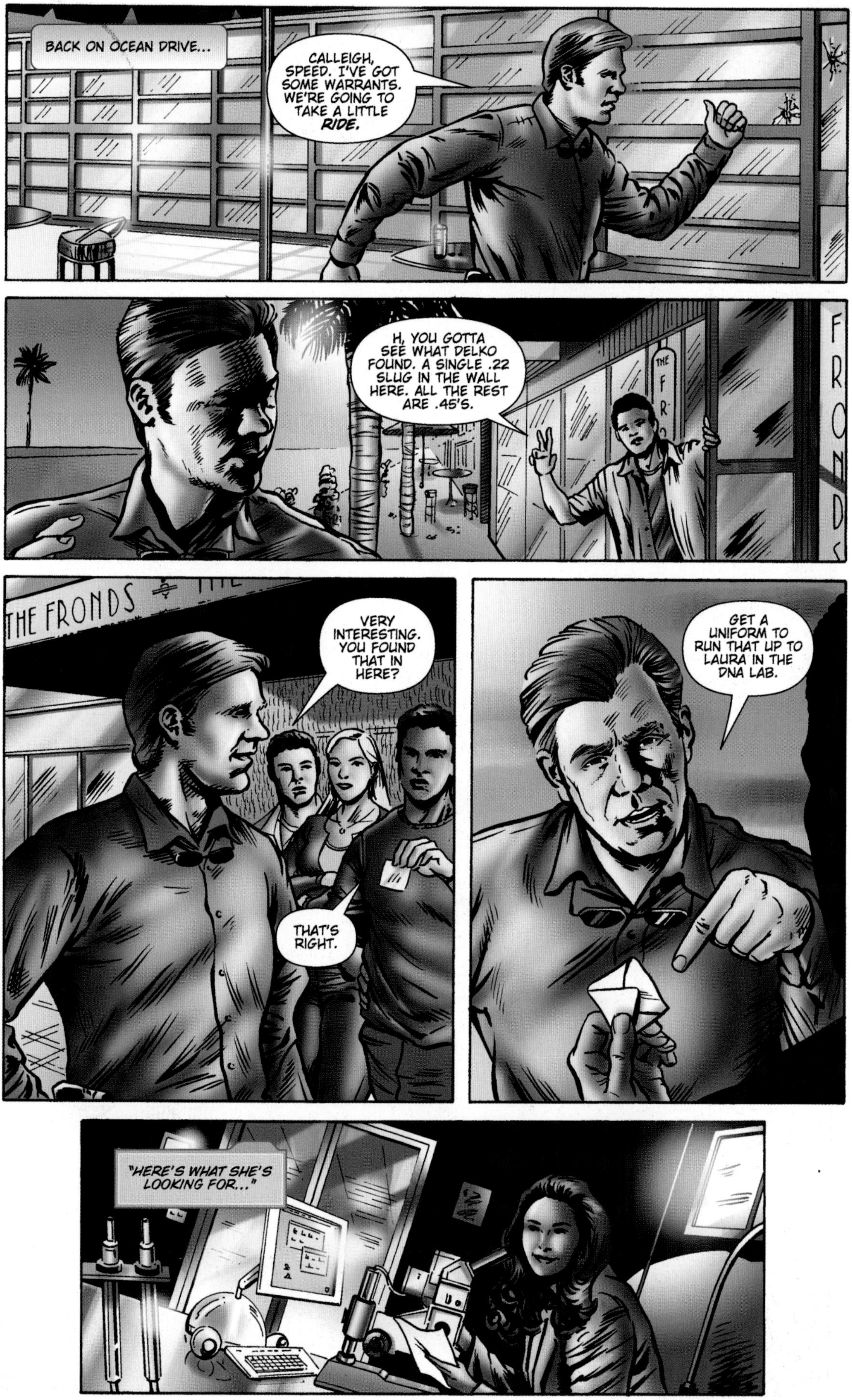
BACK ON OCEAN DRIVE...
CALLEIGH, SPEED. I'VE GOT SOME WARRANTS. WE'RE GOING TO TAKE A LITTLE RIDE.
H, YOU GOTTA SEE WHAT DELKO FOUND. A SINGLE .22 SLUG IN THE WALL HERE. ALL THE REST ARE .45'S.
THE FRONDS
VERY INTERESTING. YOU FOUND THAT IN HERE?
THAT'S RIGHT.
GET A UNIFORM TO RUN THAT UP TO LAURA IN THE DNA LAB.
"HERE'S WHAT SHE'S LOOKING FOR..."

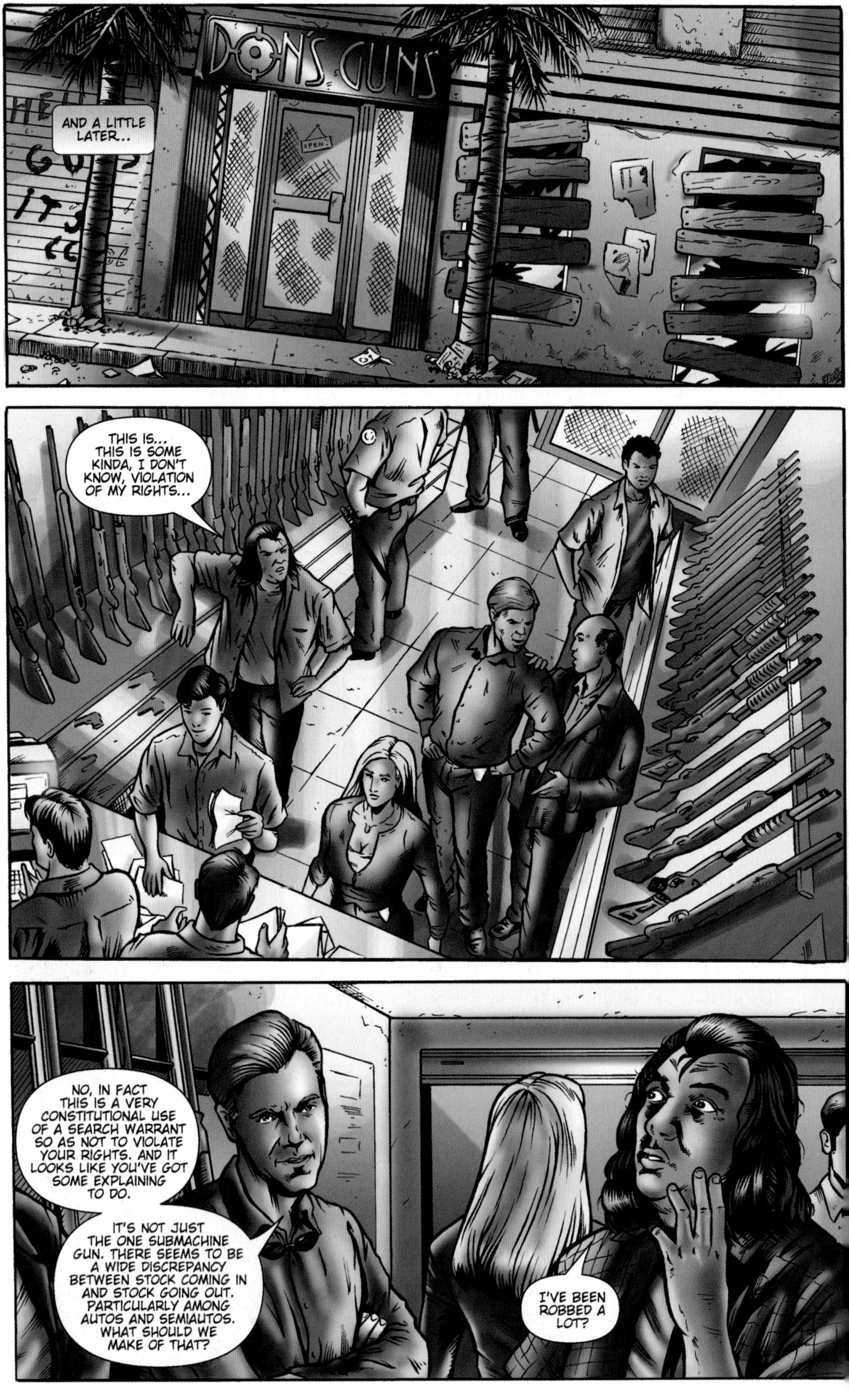
DON'S GUNS
AND A LITTLE LATER...
THIS IS... THIS IS SOME KINDA, I DON'T KNOW, VIOLATION OF MY RIGHTS...
NO, IN FACT THIS IS A VERY CONSTITUTIONAL USE OF A SEARCH WARRANT SO AS NOT TO VIOLATE YOUR RIGHTS. AND IT LOOKS LIKE YOU'VE GOT SOME EXPLAINING TO DO.
IT'S NOT JUST THE ONE SUBMACHINE GUN. THERE SEEMS TO BE A WIDE DISCREPANCY BETWEEN STOCK COMING IN AND STOCK GOING OUT. PARTICULARLY AMONG AUTOS AND SEMIAUTOS. WHAT SHOULD WE MAKE OF THAT?
I'VE BEEN ROBBED A LOT?

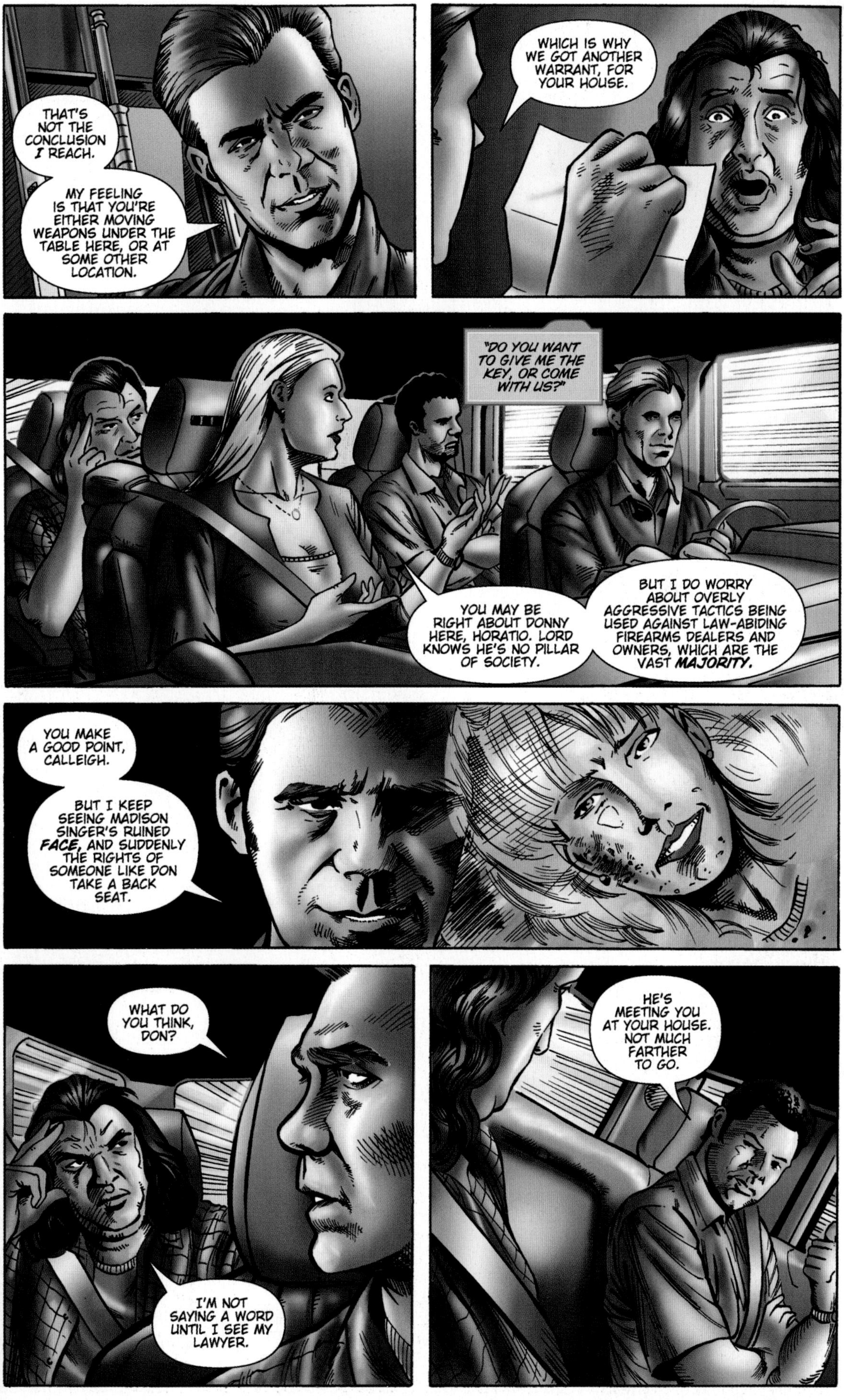
THAT'S NOT THE CONCLUSION *I* REACH.
MY FEELING IS THAT YOU'RE EITHER MOVING WEAPONS UNDER THE TABLE HERE, OR AT SOME OTHER LOCATION.
WHICH IS WHY WE GOT ANOTHER WARRANT, FOR YOUR HOUSE.
"DO YOU WANT TO GIVE ME THE KEY, OR COME WITH US?"
YOU MAY BE RIGHT ABOUT DONNY HERE, HORATIO. LORD KNOWS HE'S NO PILLAR OF SOCIETY.
BUT I DO WORRY ABOUT OVERLY AGGRESSIVE TACTICS BEING USED AGAINST LAW-ABIDING FIREARMS DEALERS AND OWNERS, WHICH ARE THE VAST *MAJORITY.*
YOU MAKE A GOOD POINT, CALLEIGH.
BUT I KEEP SEEING MADISON SINGER'S RUINED *FACE,* AND SUDDENLY THE RIGHTS OF SOMEONE LIKE DON TAKE A BACK SEAT.
WHAT DO YOU THINK, DON?
I'M NOT SAYING A WORD UNTIL I SEE MY LAWYER.
HE'S MEETING YOU AT YOUR HOUSE. NOT MUCH FARTHER TO GO.

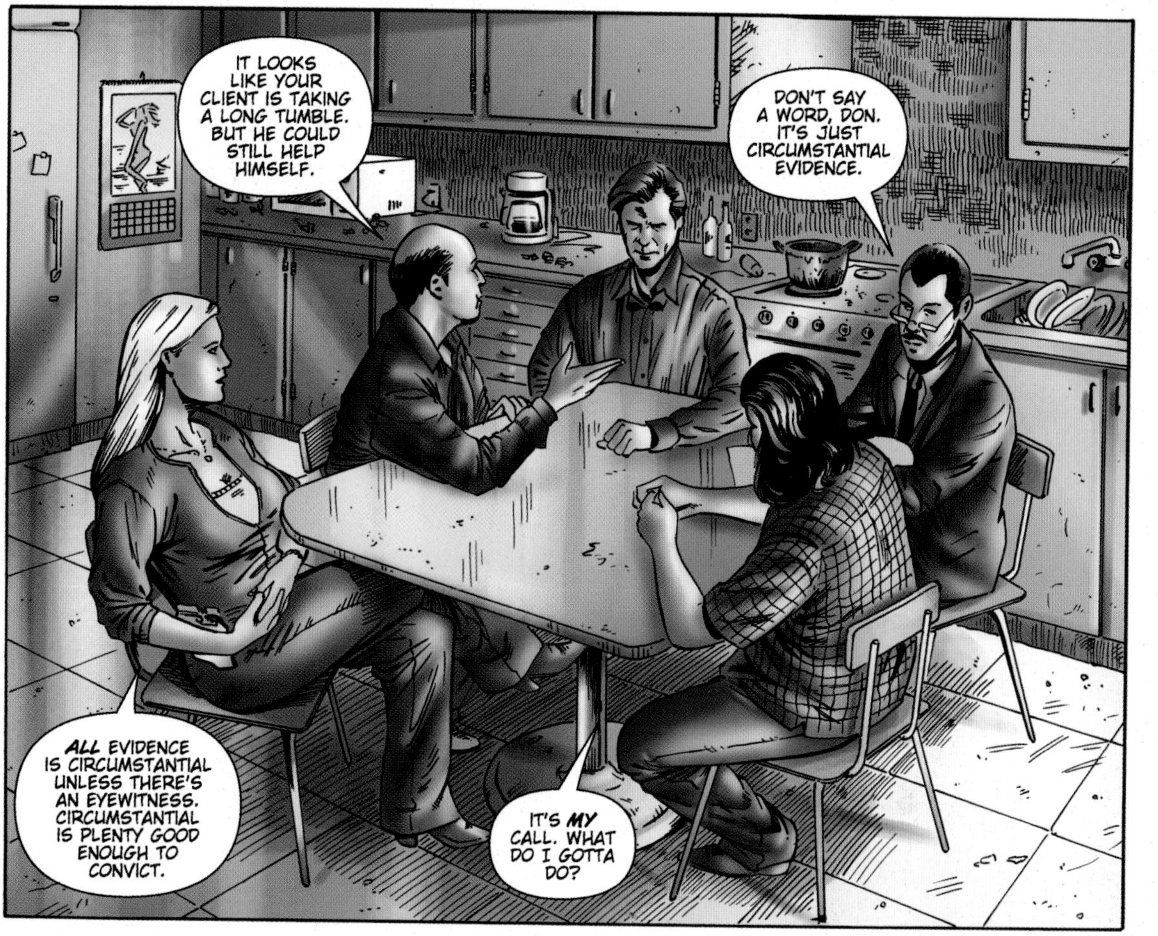
IT LOOKS LIKE YOUR CLIENT IS TAKING A LONG TUMBLE. BUT HE COULD STILL HELP HIMSELF.
DON'T SAY A WORD, DON. IT'S JUST CIRCUMSTANTIAL EVIDENCE.
ALL EVIDENCE IS CIRCUMSTANTIAL UNLESS THERE'S AN EYEWITNESS. CIRCUMSTANTIAL IS PLENTY GOOD ENOUGH TO CONVICT.
IT'S MY CALL. WHAT DO I GOTTA DO?

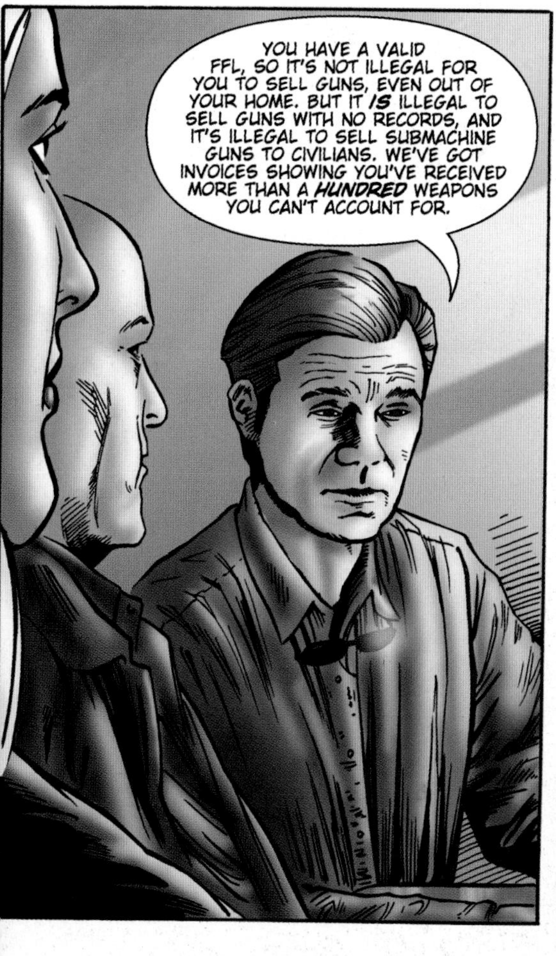
YOU HAVE A VALID FFL, SO IT'S NOT ILLEGAL FOR YOU TO SELL GUNS, EVEN OUT OF YOUR HOME. BUT IT IS ILLEGAL TO SELL GUNS WITH NO RECORDS, AND IT'S ILLEGAL TO SELL SUBMACHINE GUNS TO CIVILIANS. WE'VE GOT INVOICES SHOWING YOU'VE RECEIVED MORE THAN A HUNDRED WEAPONS YOU CAN'T ACCOUNT FOR.

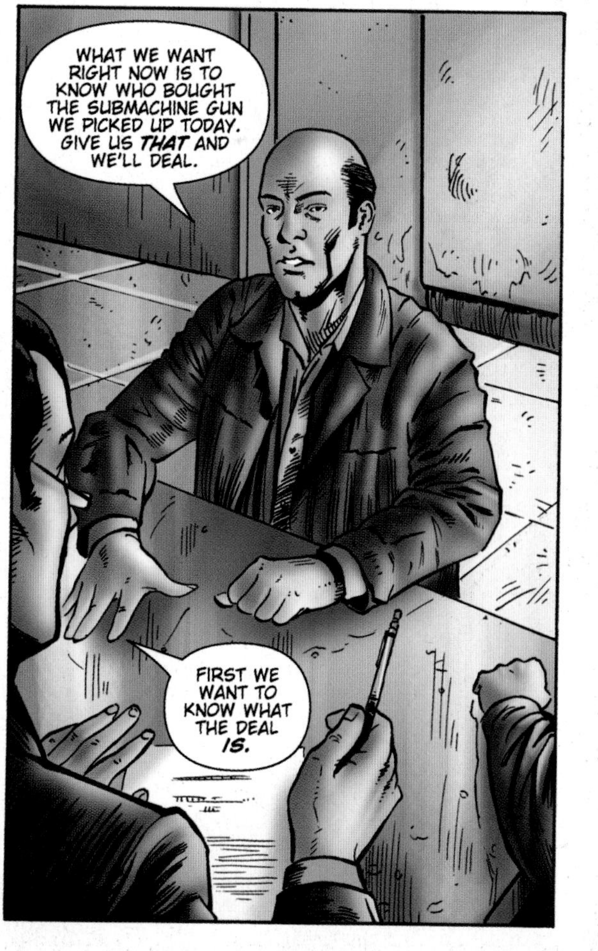
WHAT WE WANT RIGHT NOW IS TO KNOW WHO BOUGHT THE SUBMACHINE GUN WE PICKED UP TODAY. GIVE US THAT AND WE'LL DEAL.
FIRST WE WANT TO KNOW WHAT THE DEAL IS.

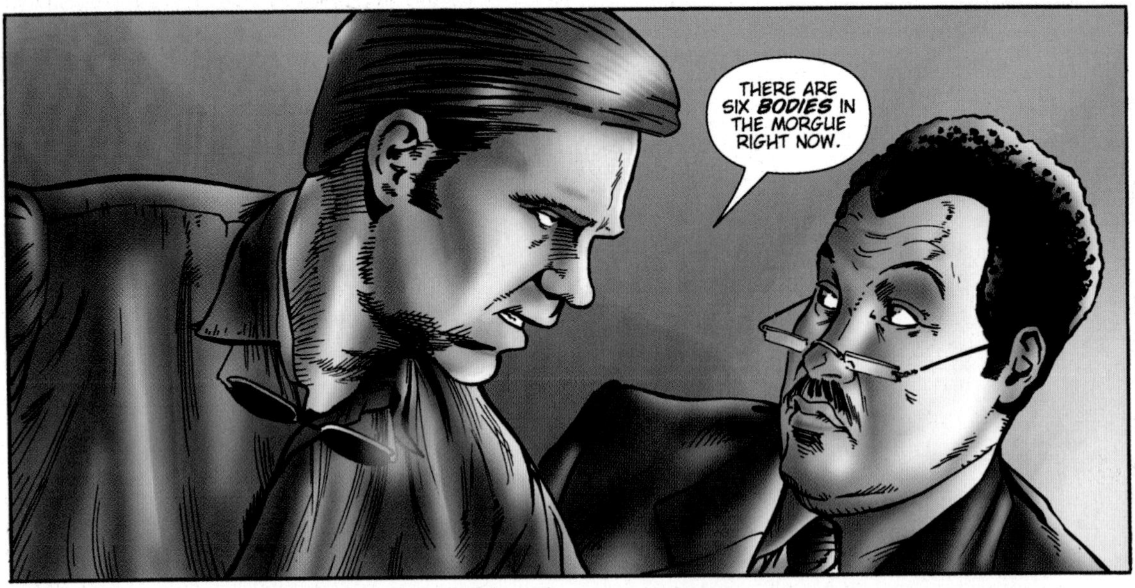
THERE ARE SIX BODIES IN THE MORGUE RIGHT NOW.

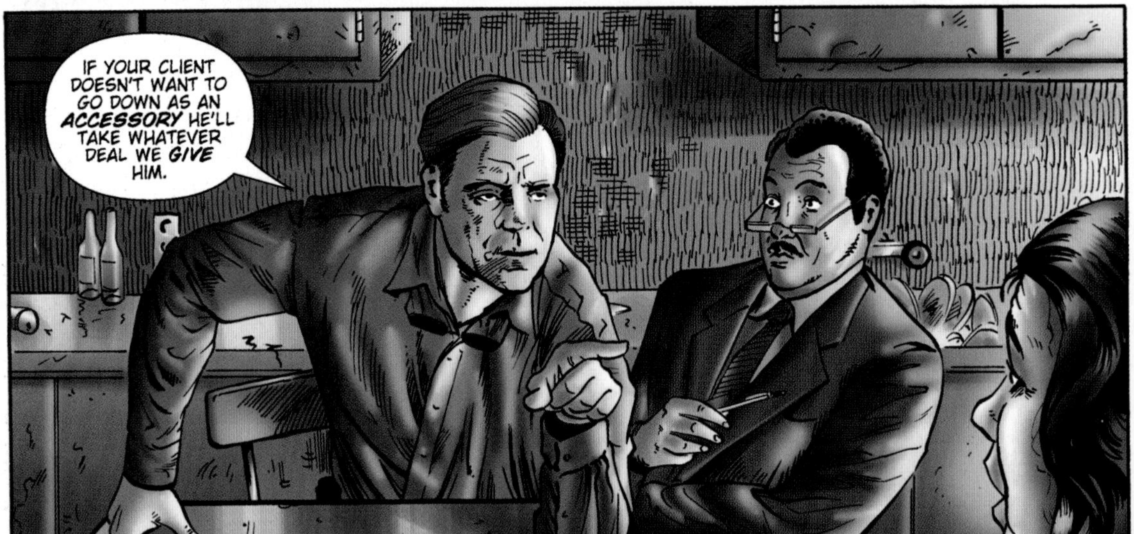
IF YOUR CLIENT DOESN'T WANT TO GO DOWN AS AN ACCESSORY HE'LL TAKE WHATEVER DEAL WE GIVE HIM.

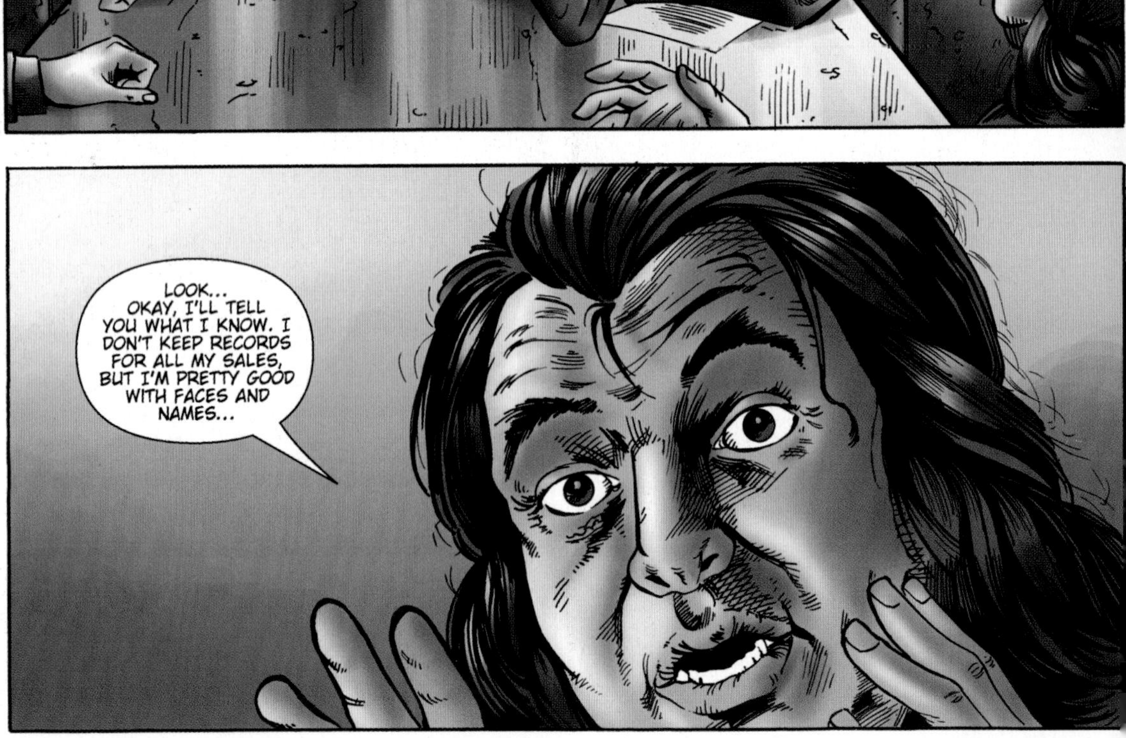
LOOK... OKAY, I'LL TELL YOU WHAT I KNOW. I DON'T KEEP RECORDS FOR ALL MY SALES, BUT I'M PRETTY GOOD WITH FACES AND NAMES...

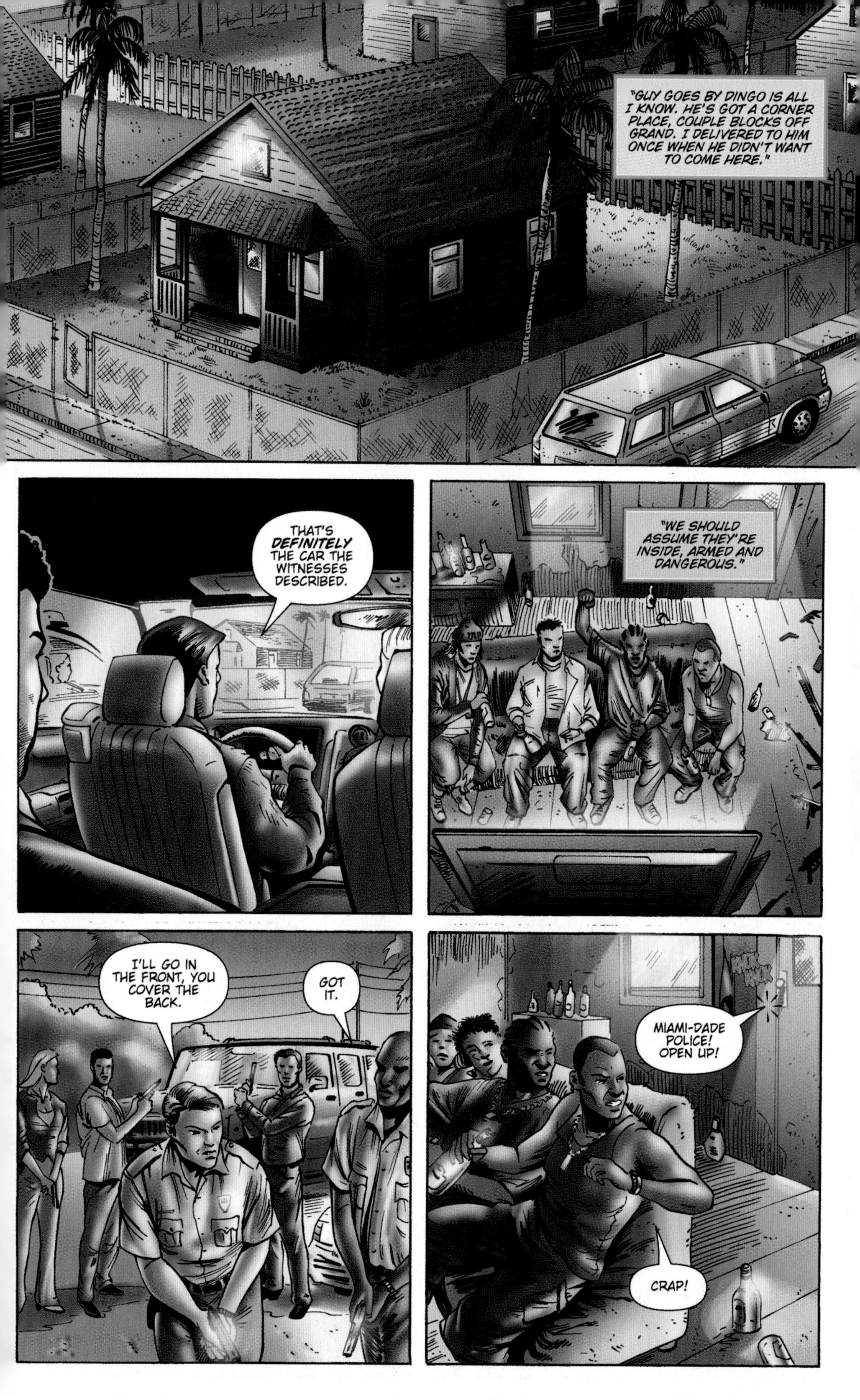
"GUY GOES BY DINGO IS ALL I KNOW. HE'S GOT A CORNER PLACE, COUPLE BLOCKS OFF GRAND. I DELIVERED TO HIM ONCE WHEN HE DIDN'T WANT TO COME HERE."
THAT'S *DEFINITELY* THE CAR THE WITNESSES DESCRIBED.
"WE SHOULD ASSUME THEY'RE INSIDE, ARMED AND DANGEROUS."
I'LL GO IN THE FRONT, YOU COVER THE BACK.
GOT IT.
KNOK KNOK
MIAMI-DADE POLICE! OPEN UP!
CRAP!

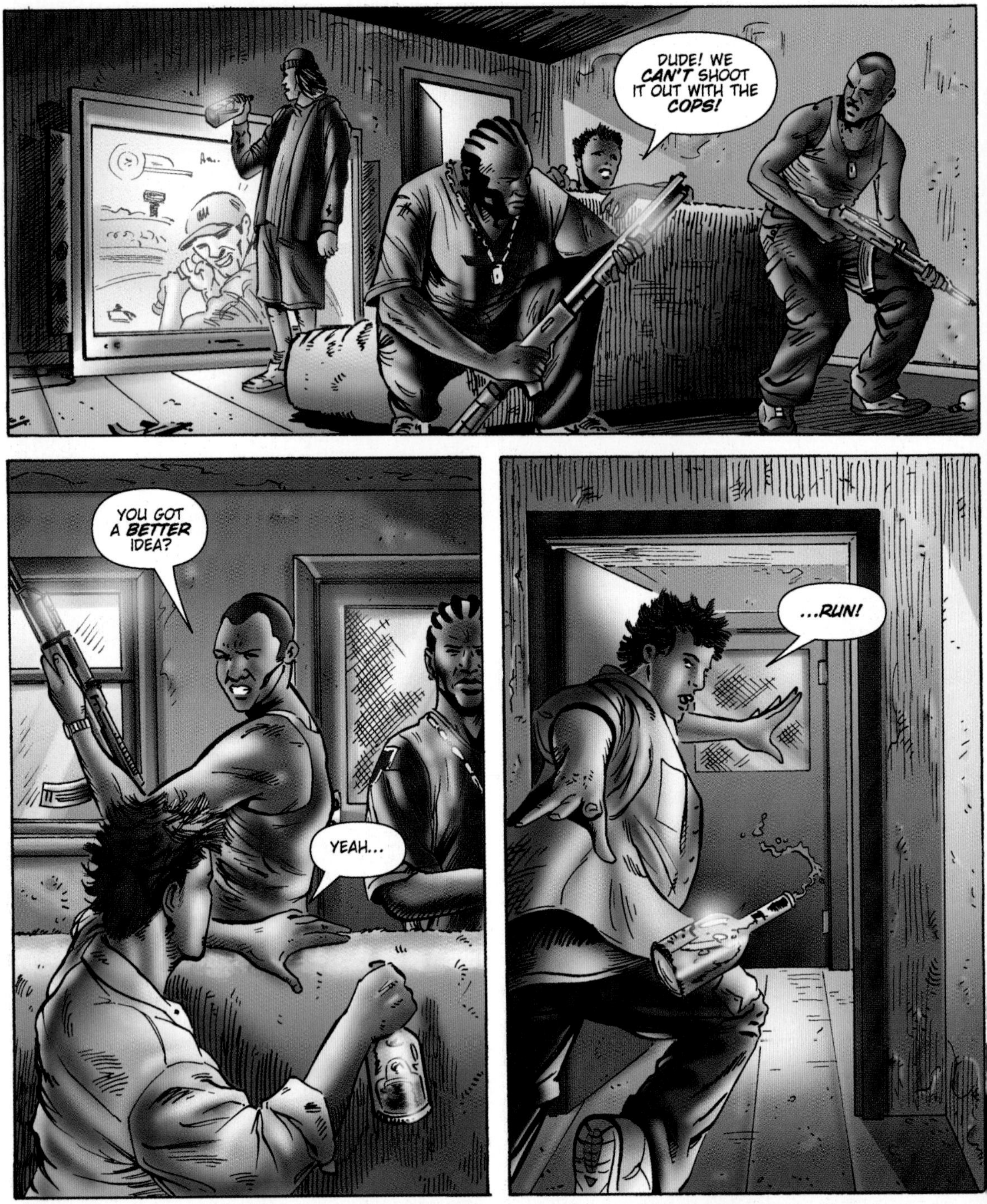
DUDE! WE CAN'T SHOOT IT OUT WITH THE COPS!
YOU GOT A BETTER IDEA?
YEAH...
...RUN!

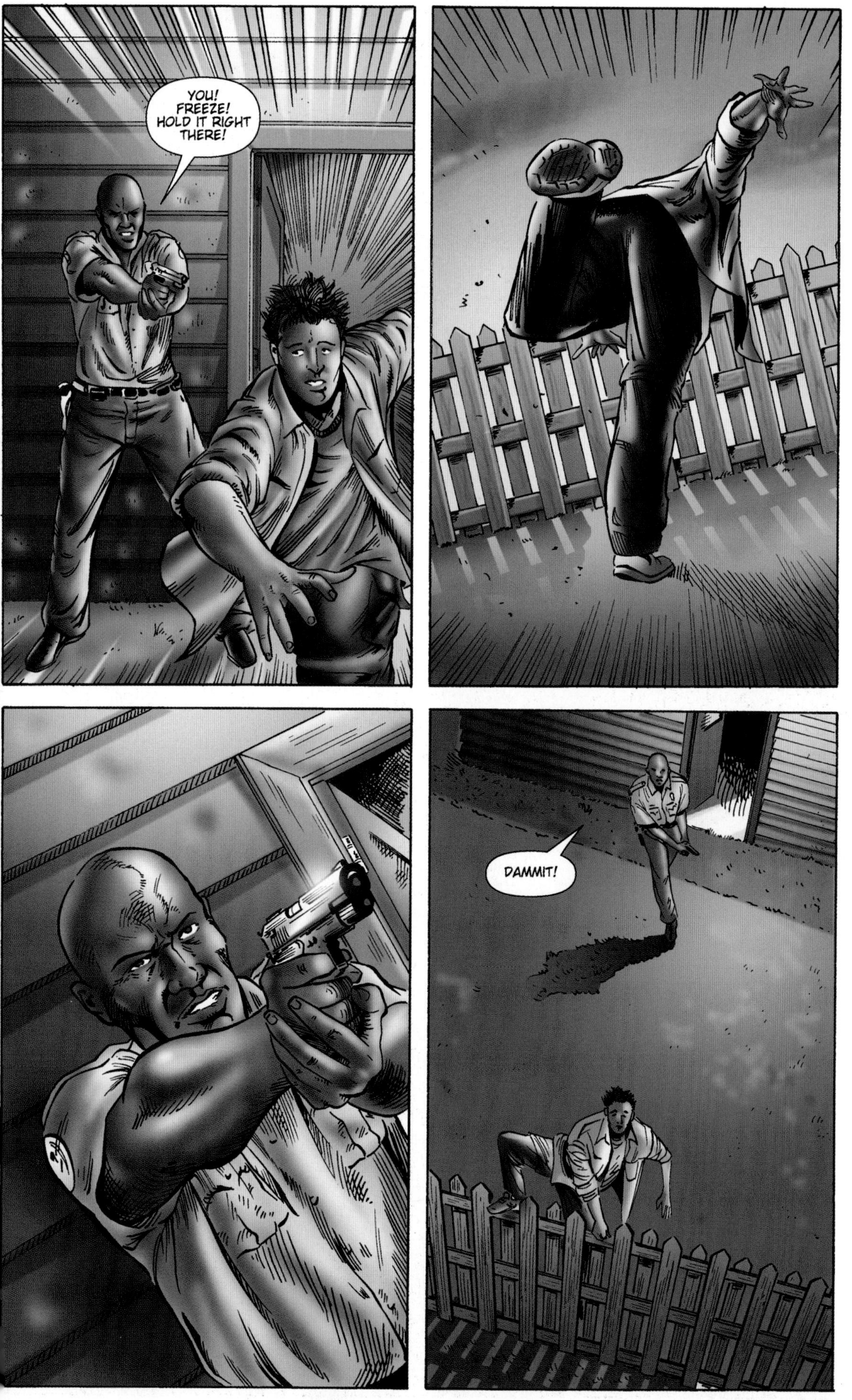
YOU! FREEZE! HOLD IT RIGHT THERE!
DAMMIT!

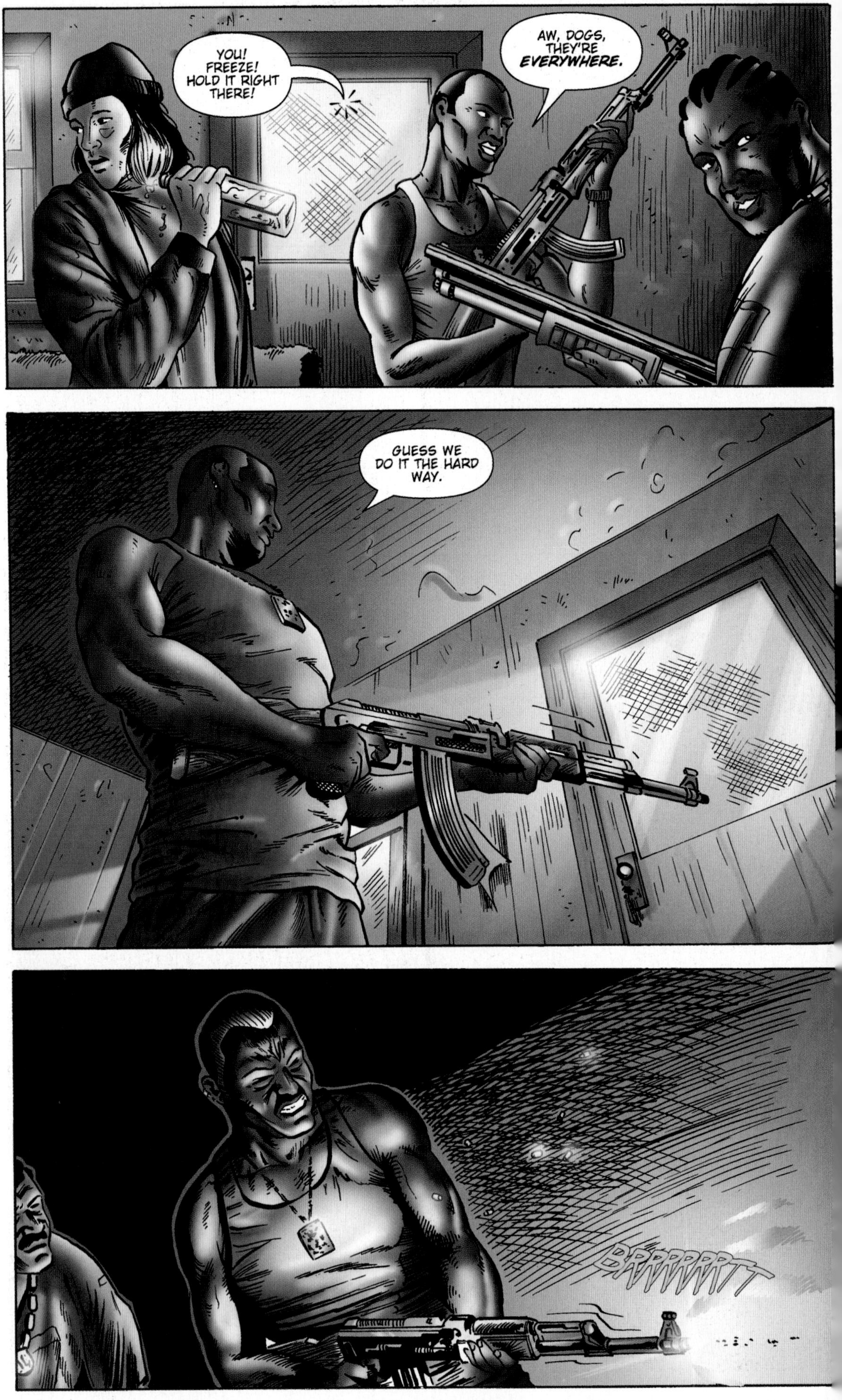
YOU! FREEZE! HOLD IT RIGHT THERE!
AW, DOGS, THEY'RE *EVERYWHERE.*
GUESS WE DO IT THE HARD WAY.
BRRRRRRRTT

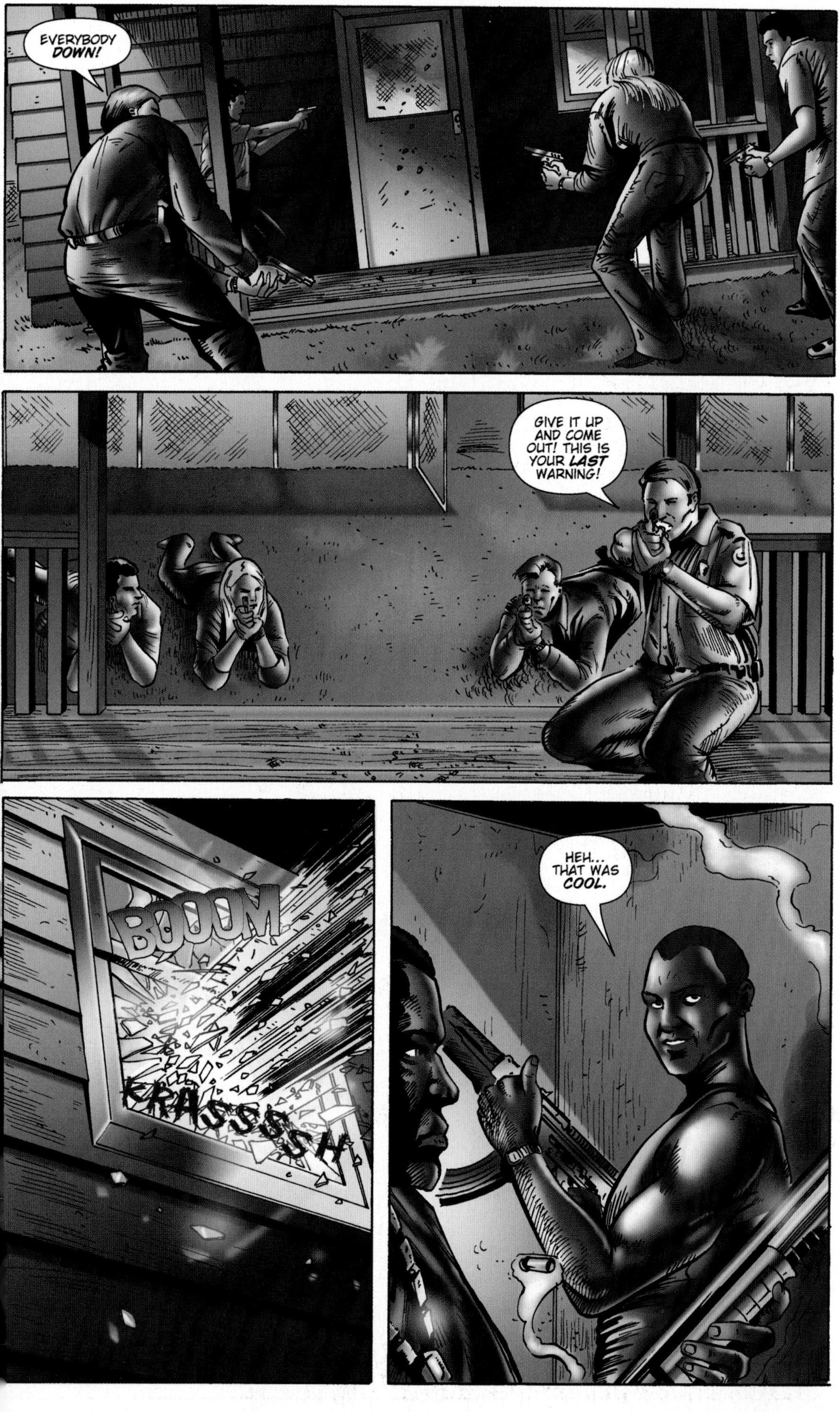
EVERYBODY DOWN!
GIVE IT UP AND COME OUT! THIS IS YOUR LAST WARNING!
BOOOM!
KRASSSSH
HEH... THAT WAS COOL.

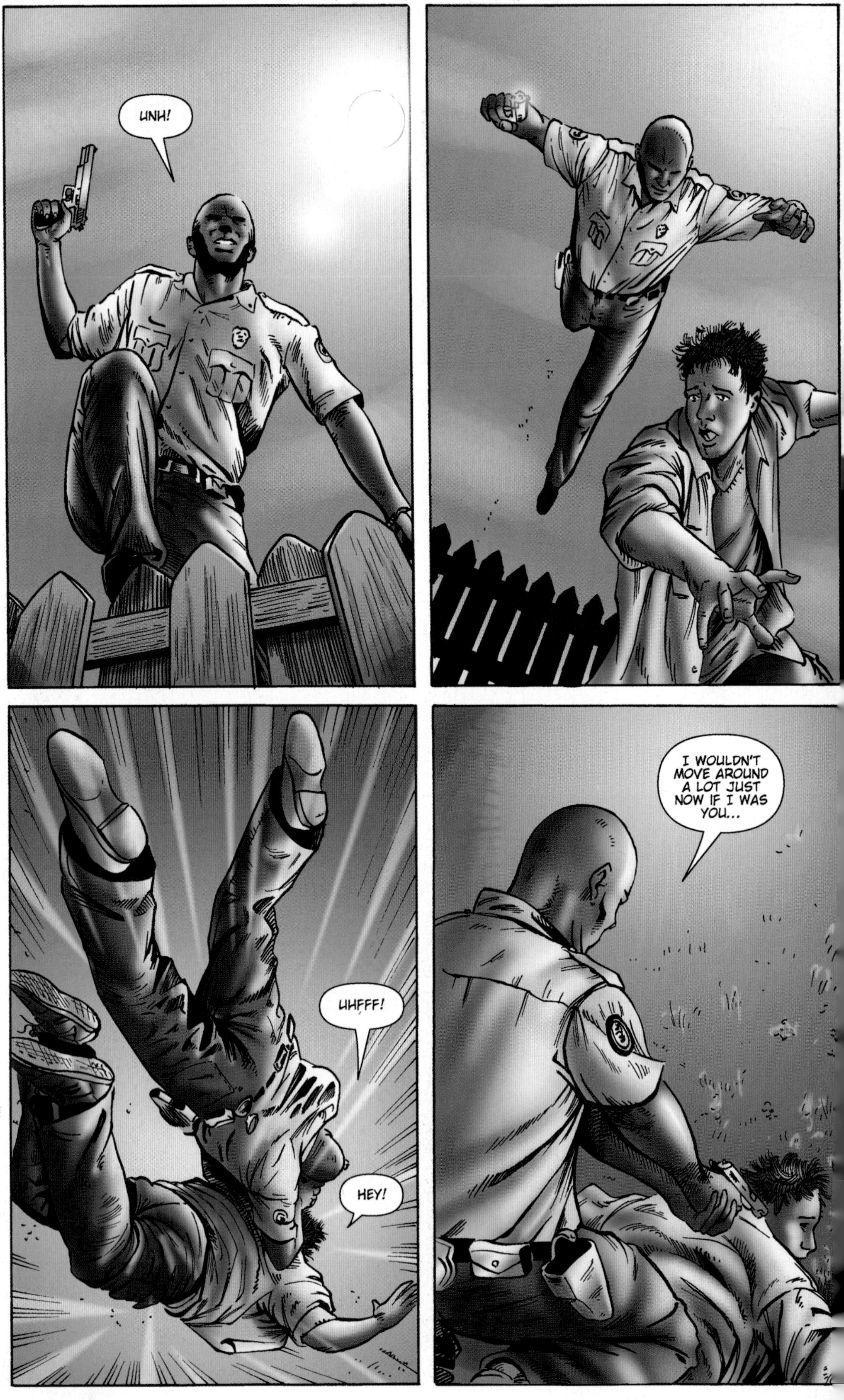
UNH!
UHFFF!
HEY!
I WOULDN'T MOVE AROUND A LOT JUST NOW IF I WAS YOU...

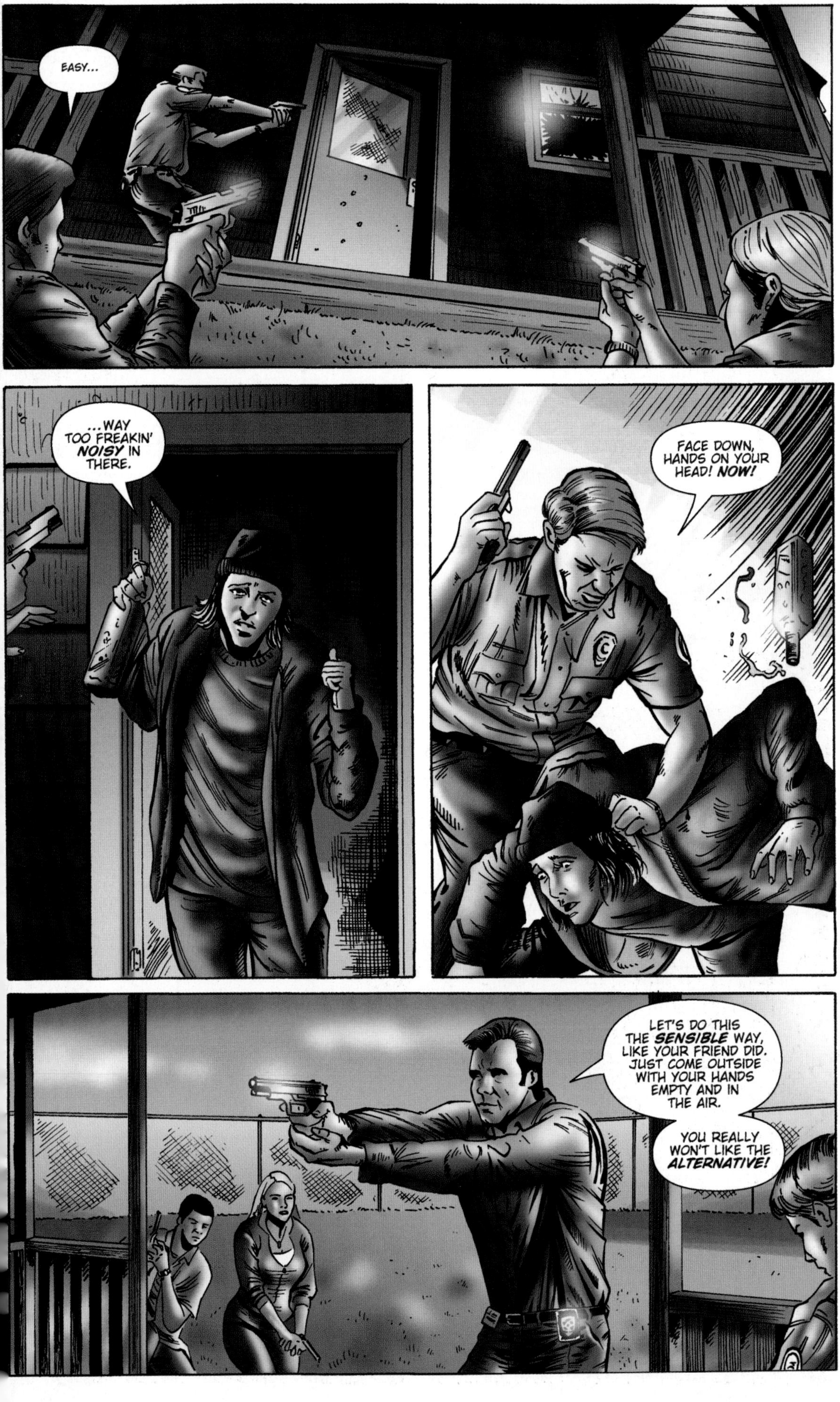
EASY...
...WAY TOO FREAKIN' *NOISY* IN THERE.
FACE DOWN, HANDS ON YOUR HEAD! *NOW!*
LET'S DO THIS THE *SENSIBLE* WAY, LIKE YOUR FRIEND DID. JUST COME OUTSIDE WITH YOUR HANDS EMPTY AND IN THE AIR.
YOU REALLY WON'T LIKE THE *ALTERNATIVE!*

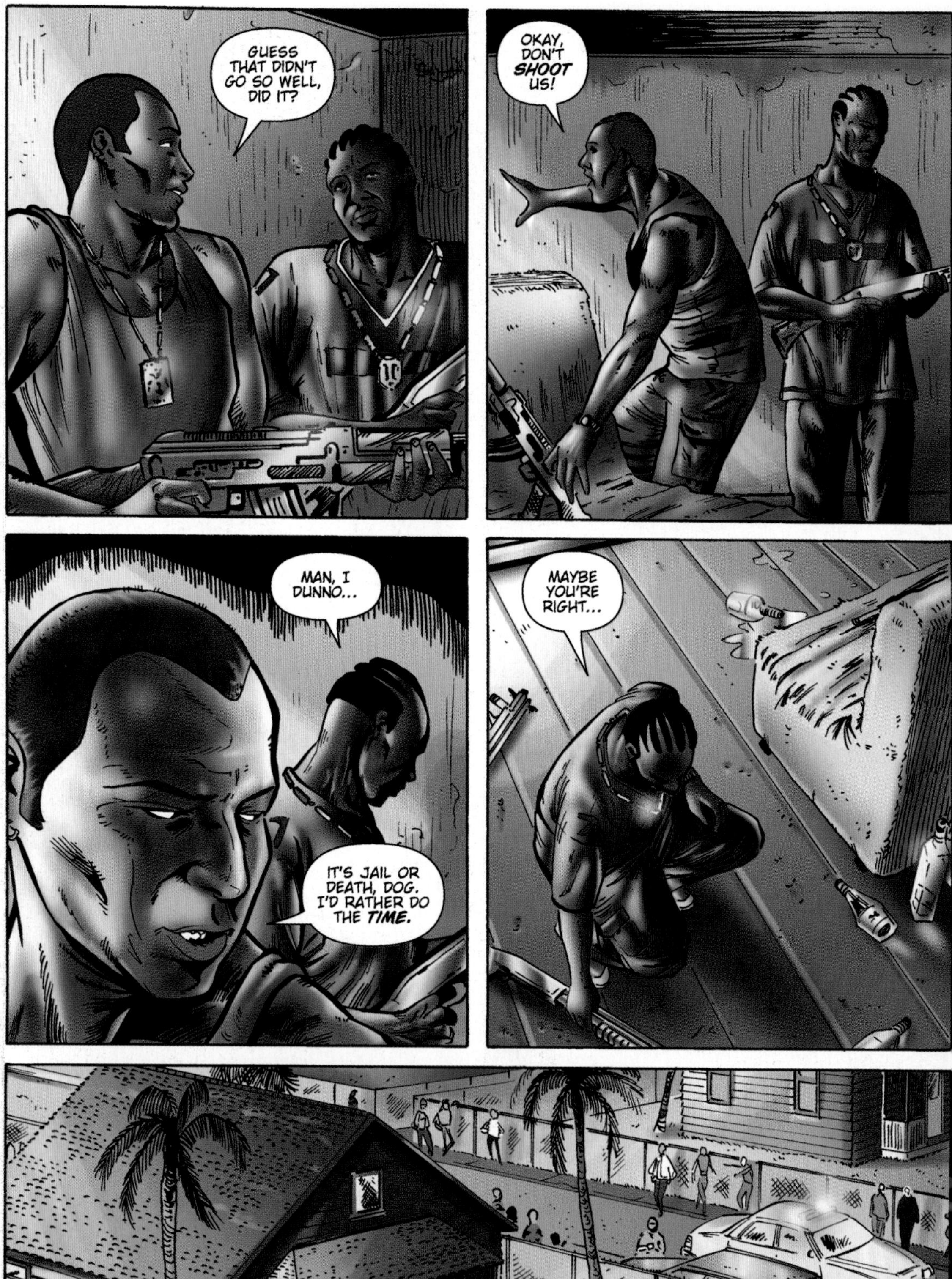
GUESS THAT DIDN'T GO SO WELL, DID IT?
OKAY, DON'T SHOOT US!
MAN, I DUNNO...
IT'S JAIL OR DEATH, DOG. I'D RATHER DO THE TIME.
MAYBE YOU'RE RIGHT...

...SIX VICTIMS, LARRY. AND THEN YOUR PALS SHOT AT SOME COPS. THEY'RE TAKING A HARD FALL, BUT I'M NOT SURE YOU WANT TO GO DOWN WITH THEM.

YEAH, BUT *I* DIDN'T...

...SHOOT ANYONE AT ALL.

CALLEIGH'S STILL AT THE SCENE, TRYING TO TIE THE WEAPONS WE FOUND TO DON, BY PHYSICAL EVIDENCE AS WELL AS SERIAL NUMBERS. AND SPEED'S GETTING IMPRESSIONS FROM THE CAR TIRES TO COMPARE WITH THE TREADMARKS ON OCEAN DRIVE.

THAT'S *GOOD*. TELL ME WHO PULLED THE TRIGGER, AND WHY, AND WE'LL *WRAP* THIS UP.

IT WAS DINGO DID THE *SHOOTING*. CHUCK WAS DRIVING. BODIE AND ME, WE WAS JUST IN THE BACK SEAT.

WHY'D THEY DO IT, LARRY?

FOR THE MONEY.

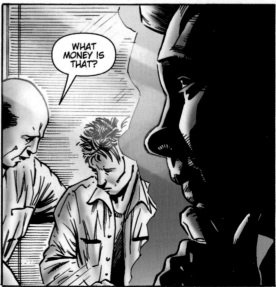

WHAT MONEY IS THAT?

THIS SHOULD BE GOOD.

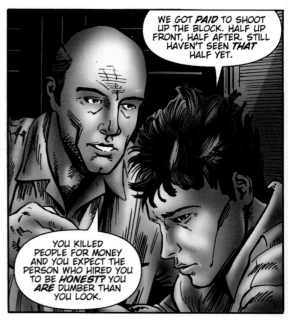

WE GOT *PAID* TO SHOOT UP THE BLOCK. HALF UP FRONT, HALF AFTER. STILL HAVEN'T SEEN *THAT* HALF YET.

YOU KILLED PEOPLE FOR MONEY AND YOU EXPECT THE PERSON WHO HIRED YOU TO BE *HONEST?* YOU *ARE* DUMBER THAN YOU LOOK.

WE DIDN'T *MEAN* TO KILL ANYONE. WE WAS JUST STIRRING UP SOME TROUBLE, Y'KNOW? *SCARING* PEOPLE.

WHO WAS IT?

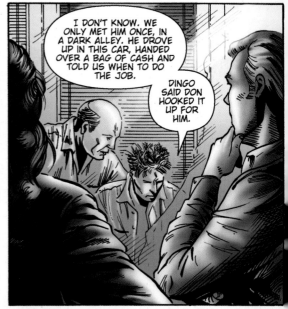

I DON'T KNOW. WE ONLY MET HIM ONCE, IN A DARK ALLEY. HE DROVE UP IN THIS CAR, HANDED OVER A BAG OF CASH AND TOLD US WHEN TO DO THE JOB.

DINGO SAID DON HOOKED IT UP FOR HIM.

DON FISCHER, THE *GUN SHOP* OWNER?

THAT'S RIGHT. DINGO'S BEEN A CUSTOMER OF HIS FOR YEARS.

IT LOOKS LIKE WHATEVER DEAL DON CUT JUST WENT OUT THE *WINDOW.*

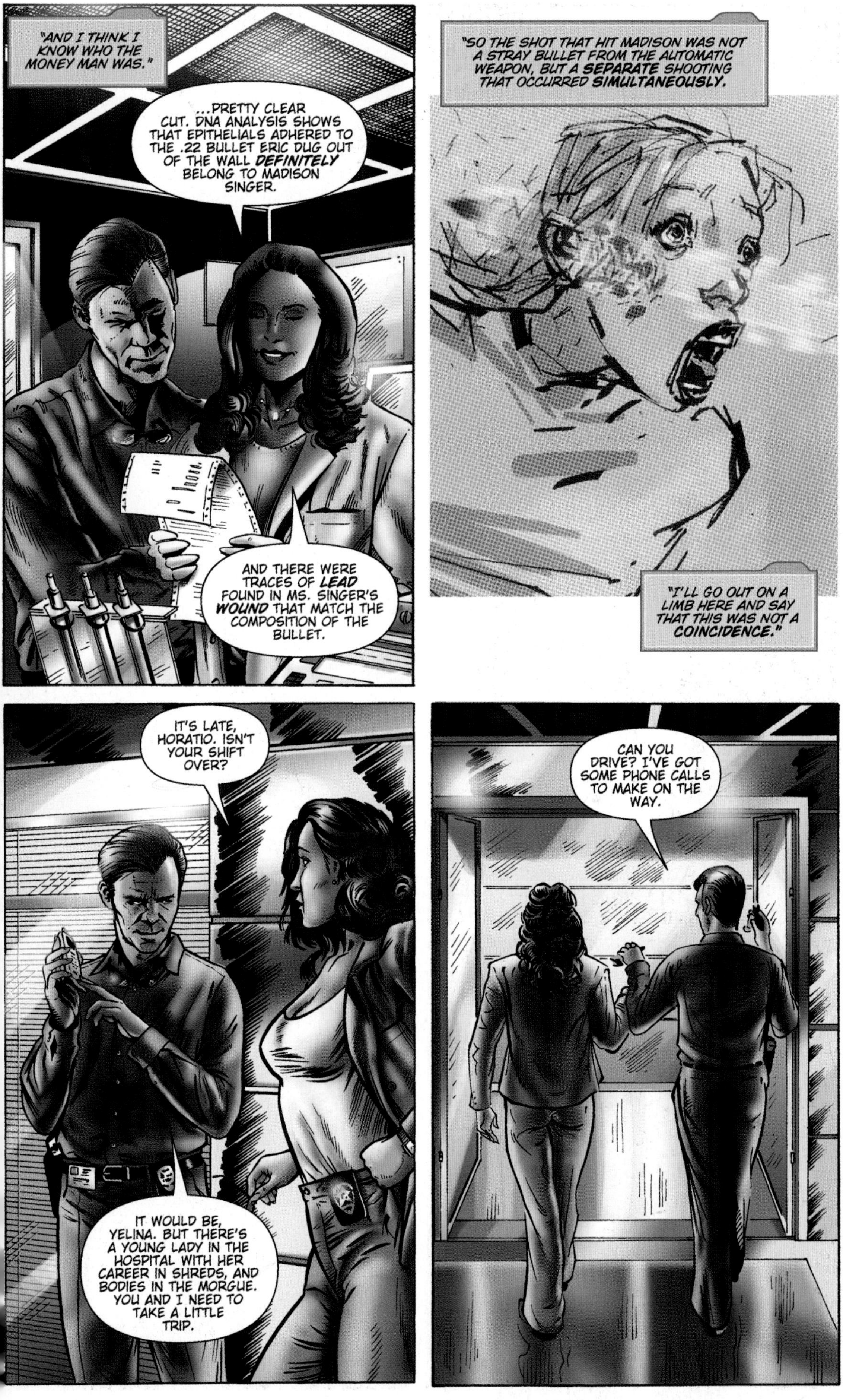
"AND I THINK I KNOW WHO THE MONEY MAN WAS."
...PRETTY CLEAR CUT. DNA ANALYSIS SHOWS THAT EPITHELIALS ADHERED TO THE .22 BULLET ERIC DUG OUT OF THE WALL DEFINITELY BELONG TO MADISON SINGER.
AND THERE WERE TRACES OF LEAD FOUND IN MS. SINGER'S WOUND THAT MATCH THE COMPOSITION OF THE BULLET.
"SO THE SHOT THAT HIT MADISON WAS NOT A STRAY BULLET FROM THE AUTOMATIC WEAPON, BUT A SEPARATE SHOOTING THAT OCCURRED SIMULTANEOUSLY.
"I'LL GO OUT ON A LIMB HERE AND SAY THAT THIS WAS NOT A COINCIDENCE."
IT'S LATE, HORATIO. ISN'T YOUR SHIFT OVER?
IT WOULD BE, YELINA. BUT THERE'S A YOUNG LADY IN THE HOSPITAL WITH HER CAREER IN SHREDS, AND BODIES IN THE MORGUE. YOU AND I NEED TO TAKE A LITTLE TRIP.
CAN YOU DRIVE? I'VE GOT SOME PHONE CALLS TO MAKE ON THE WAY.

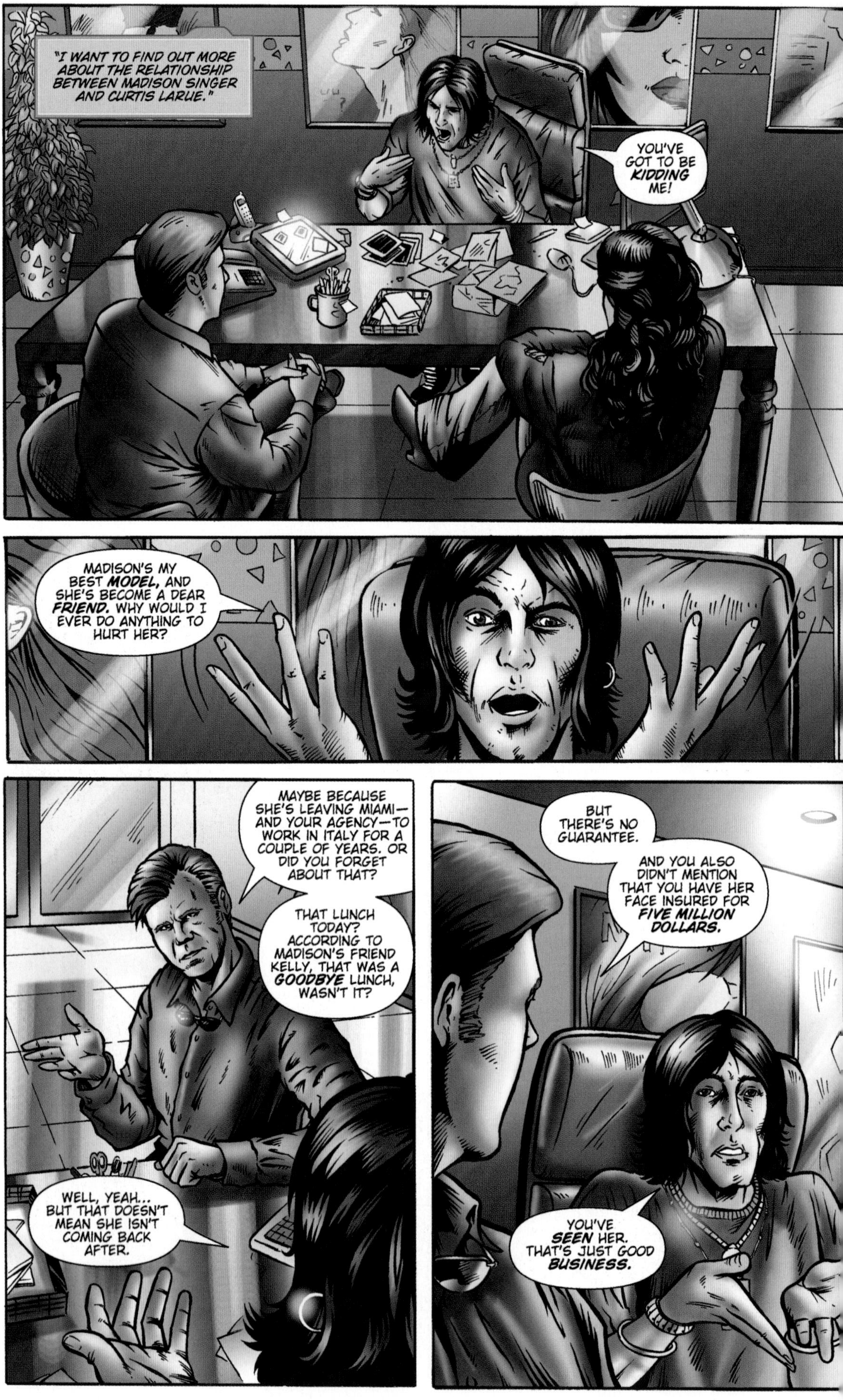
"I WANT TO FIND OUT MORE ABOUT THE RELATIONSHIP BETWEEN MADISON SINGER AND CURTIS LARUE."
YOU'VE GOT TO BE KIDDING ME!
MADISON'S MY BEST MODEL, AND SHE'S BECOME A DEAR FRIEND. WHY WOULD I EVER DO ANYTHING TO HURT HER?
MAYBE BECAUSE SHE'S LEAVING MIAMI— AND YOUR AGENCY—TO WORK IN ITALY FOR A COUPLE OF YEARS. OR DID YOU FORGET ABOUT THAT?
THAT LUNCH TODAY? ACCORDING TO MADISON'S FRIEND KELLY, THAT WAS A GOODBYE LUNCH, WASN'T IT?
WELL, YEAH... BUT THAT DOESN'T MEAN SHE ISN'T COMING BACK AFTER.
BUT THERE'S NO GUARANTEE.
AND YOU ALSO DIDN'T MENTION THAT YOU HAVE HER FACE INSURED FOR FIVE MILLION DOLLARS.
YOU'VE SEEN HER. THAT'S JUST GOOD BUSINESS.

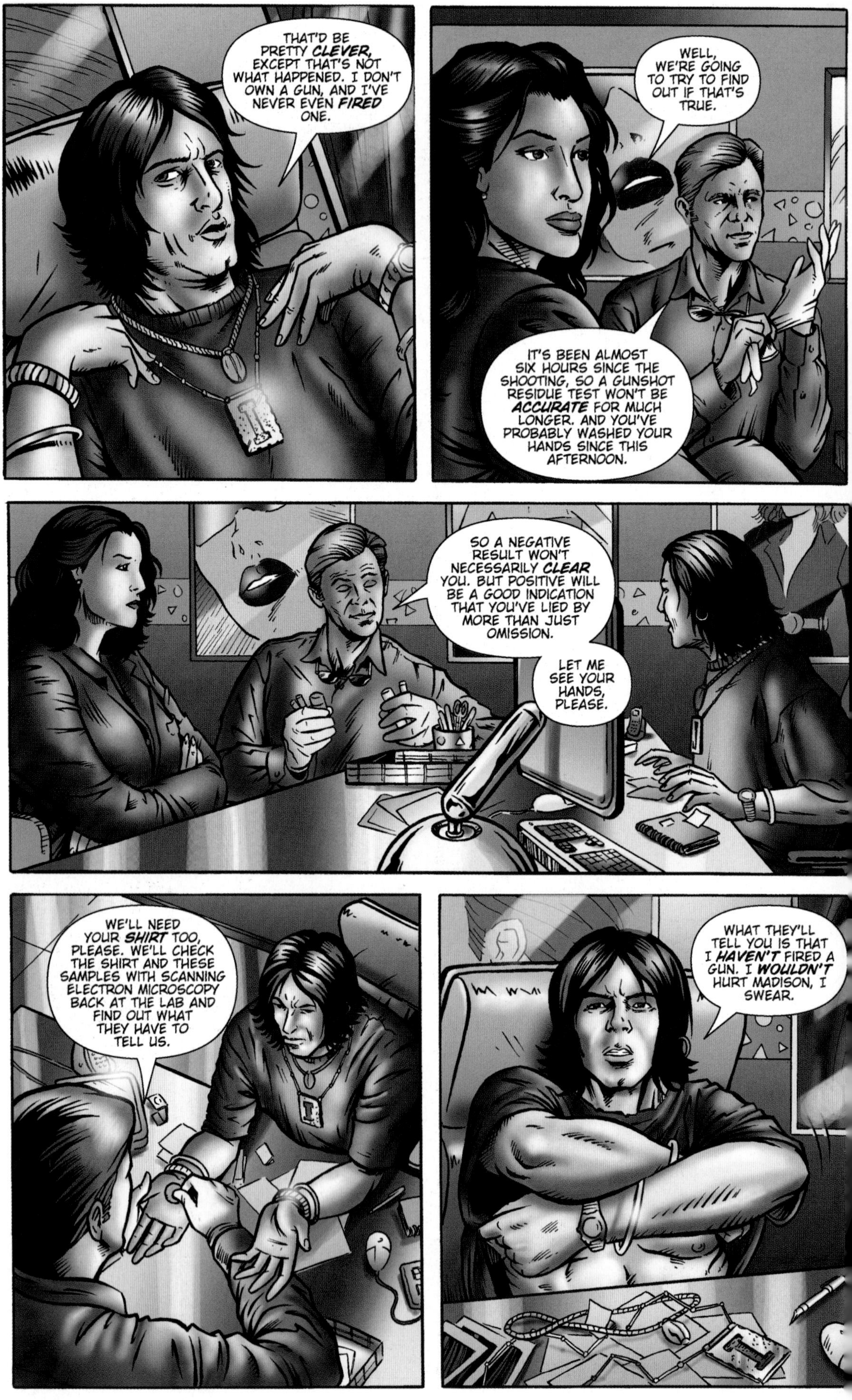
THAT'D BE PRETTY CLEVER, EXCEPT THAT'S NOT WHAT HAPPENED. I DON'T OWN A GUN, AND I'VE NEVER EVEN FIRED ONE.
WELL, WE'RE GOING TO TRY TO FIND OUT IF THAT'S TRUE.
IT'S BEEN ALMOST SIX HOURS SINCE THE SHOOTING, SO A GUNSHOT RESIDUE TEST WON'T BE ACCURATE FOR MUCH LONGER. AND YOU'VE PROBABLY WASHED YOUR HANDS SINCE THIS AFTERNOON.
SO A NEGATIVE RESULT WON'T NECESSARILY CLEAR YOU. BUT POSITIVE WILL BE A GOOD INDICATION THAT YOU'VE LIED BY MORE THAN JUST OMISSION.
LET ME SEE YOUR HANDS, PLEASE.
WE'LL NEED YOUR SHIRT TOO, PLEASE. WE'LL CHECK THE SHIRT AND THESE SAMPLES WITH SCANNING ELECTRON MICROSCOPY BACK AT THE LAB AND FIND OUT WHAT THEY HAVE TO TELL US.
WHAT THEY'LL TELL YOU IS THAT I HAVEN'T FIRED A GUN. I WOULDN'T HURT MADISON, I SWEAR.

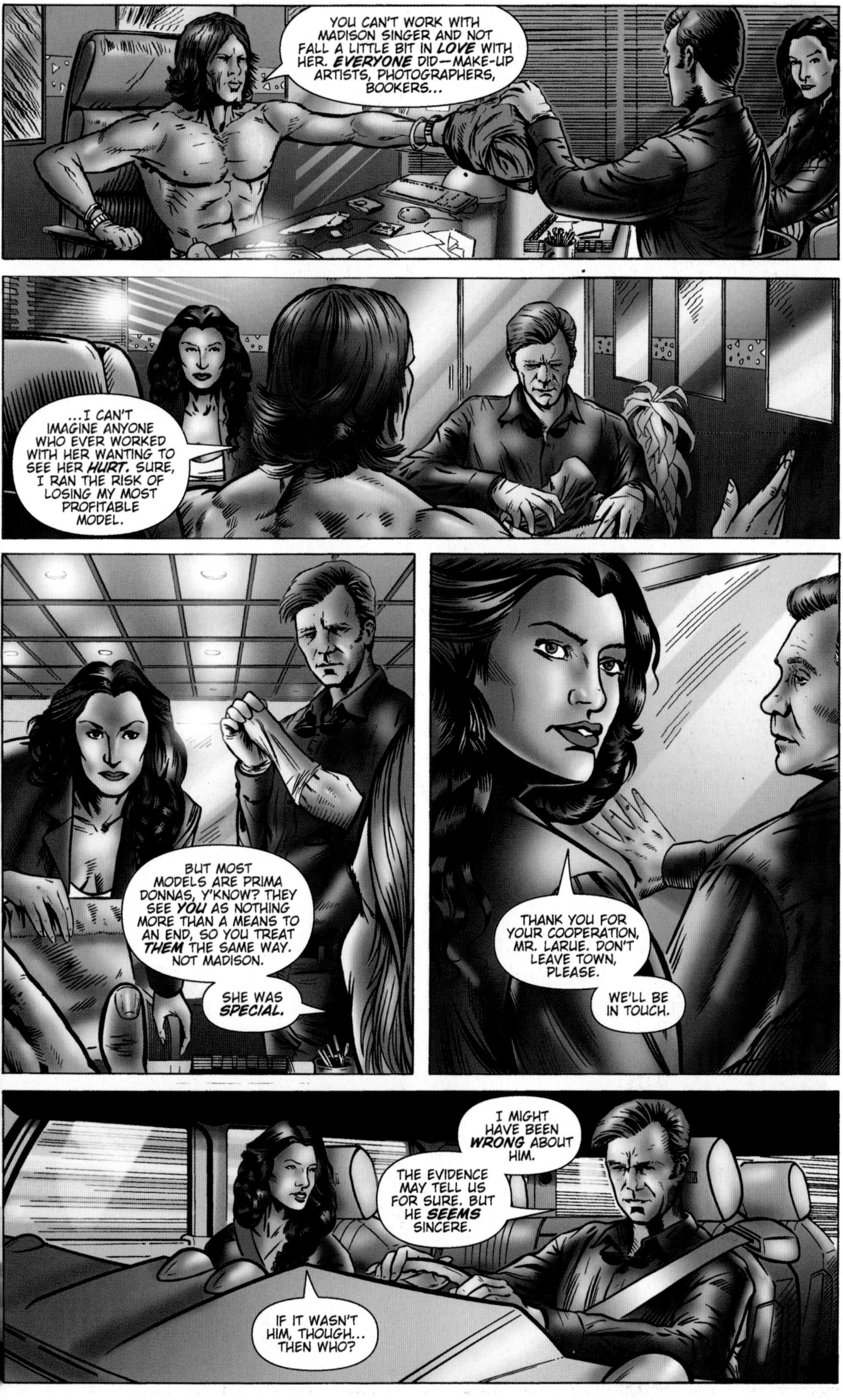
YOU CAN'T WORK WITH MADISON SINGER AND NOT FALL A LITTLE BIT IN LOVE WITH HER. EVERYONE DID—MAKE-UP ARTISTS, PHOTOGRAPHERS, BOOKERS...
...I CAN'T IMAGINE ANYONE WHO EVER WORKED WITH HER WANTING TO SEE HER HURT. SURE, I RAN THE RISK OF LOSING MY MOST PROFITABLE MODEL.
BUT MOST MODELS ARE PRIMA DONNAS, Y'KNOW? THEY SEE YOU AS NOTHING MORE THAN A MEANS TO AN END, SO YOU TREAT THEM THE SAME WAY. NOT MADISON.
SHE WAS SPECIAL.
THANK YOU FOR YOUR COOPERATION, MR. LARUE. DON'T LEAVE TOWN, PLEASE.
WE'LL BE IN TOUCH.
I MIGHT HAVE BEEN WRONG ABOUT HIM.
THE EVIDENCE MAY TELL US FOR SURE. BUT HE SEEMS SINCERE.
IF IT WASN'T HIM, THOUGH... THEN WHO?

"I HAVE A BAD FEELING ABOUT THAT."

TIME FOR A REFILL. I'LL BE BACK IN A MOMENT, MS. SINGER.

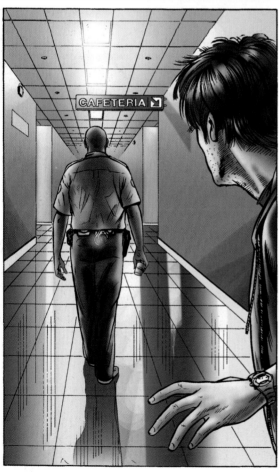

CAFETERIA

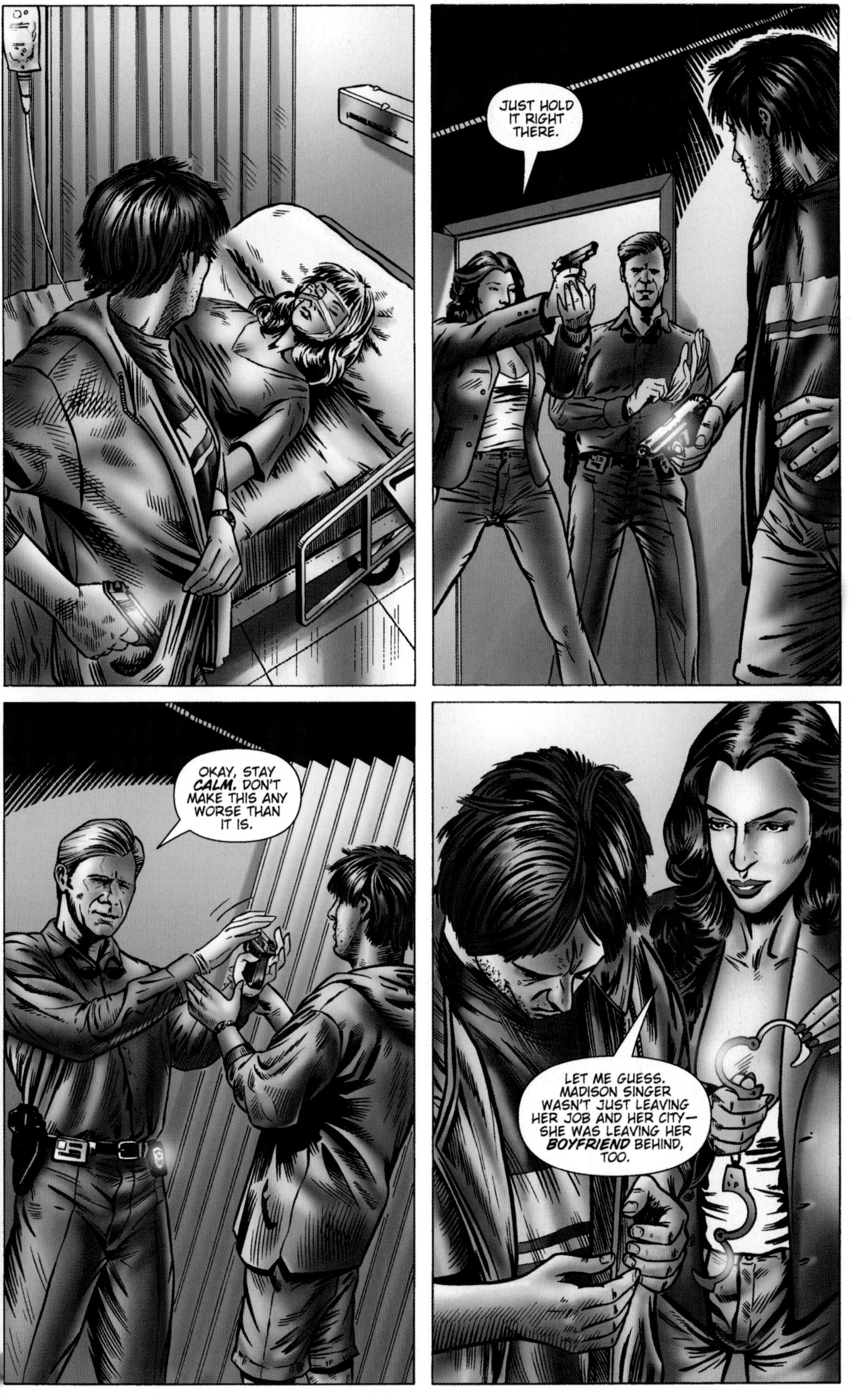
JUST HOLD IT RIGHT THERE.
OKAY, STAY CALM. DON'T MAKE THIS ANY WORSE THAN IT IS.
LET ME GUESS. MADISON SINGER WASN'T JUST LEAVING HER JOB AND HER CITY— SHE WAS LEAVING HER BOYFRIEND BEHIND, TOO.

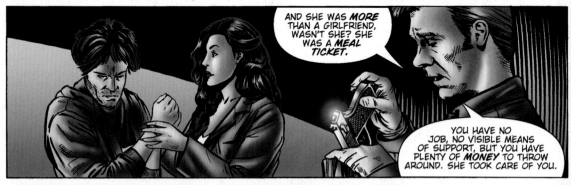

AND SHE WAS *MORE* THAN A GIRLFRIEND, WASN'T SHE? SHE WAS A *MEAL TICKET.*

YOU HAVE NO JOB, NO VISIBLE MEANS OF SUPPORT, BUT YOU HAVE PLENTY OF *MONEY* TO THROW AROUND. SHE TOOK CARE OF YOU.

ALL THAT WAS ENDING, THOUGH, WASN'T IT? AND YOU JUST COULDN'T *STAND* THAT. IF YOU COULDN'T HAVE MADISON, NO ONE ELSE WOULD EITHER, RIGHT?

YOU'RE JUST *GUESSING.* YOU CAN'T PROVE ANY OF THAT.

ALL THE PROOF WE NEED IS IN HERE.

HEY, I HAVE A SECOND AMENDMENT RIGHT TO OWN A GUN. THAT DOESN'T MEAN *ANYTHING.*

MR. SUTPHEN, IF I WERE YOU I'D WORRY A LOT *LESS* ABOUT THE SECOND AMENDMENT...

...AND A LOT *MORE* ABOUT THE *FIFTH.*

THE END.

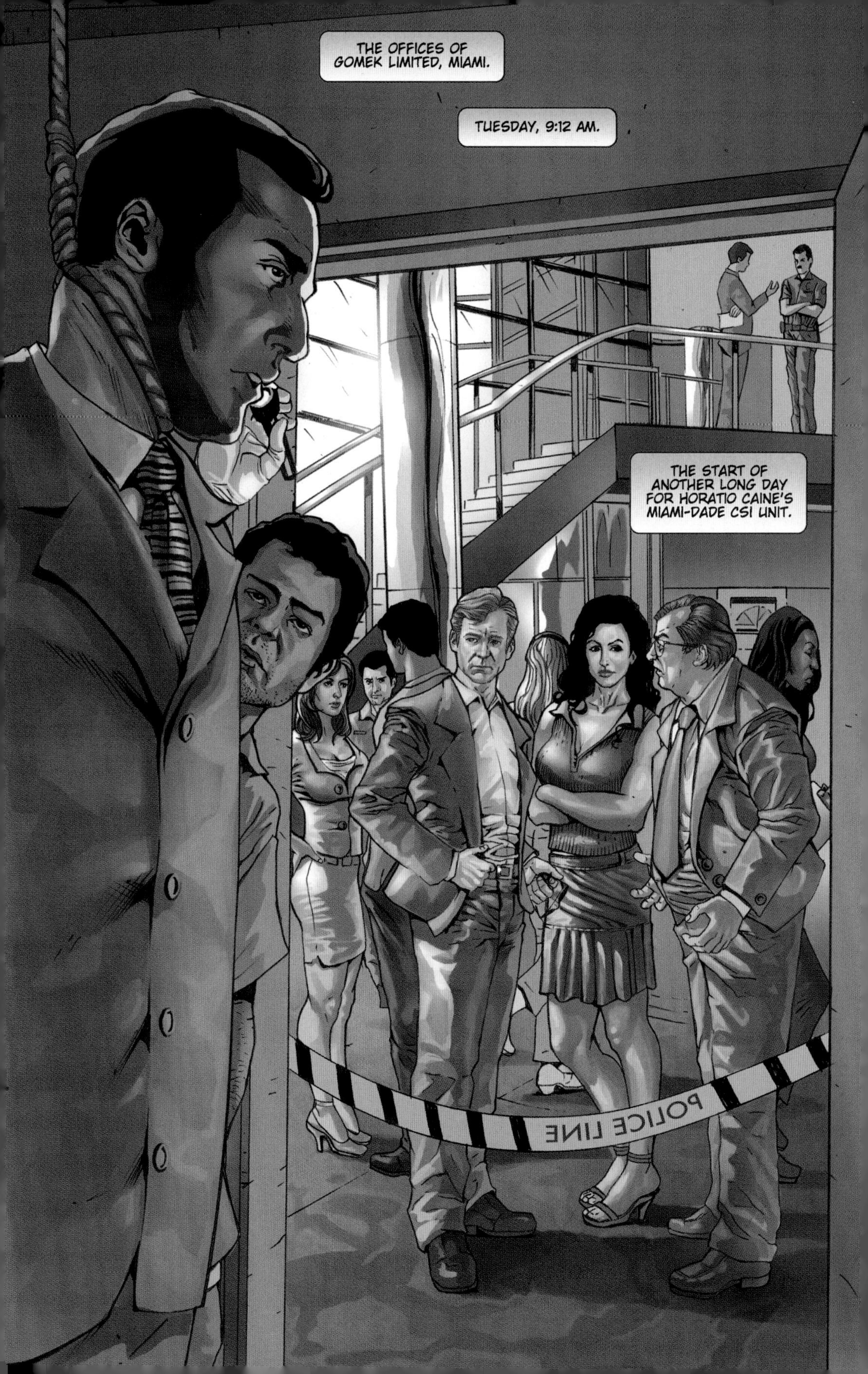
THE OFFICES OF GOMEK LIMITED, MIAMI.
TUESDAY, 9:12 AM.
THE START OF ANOTHER LONG DAY FOR HORATIO CAINE'S MIAMI-DADE CSI UNIT.
POLICE LINE

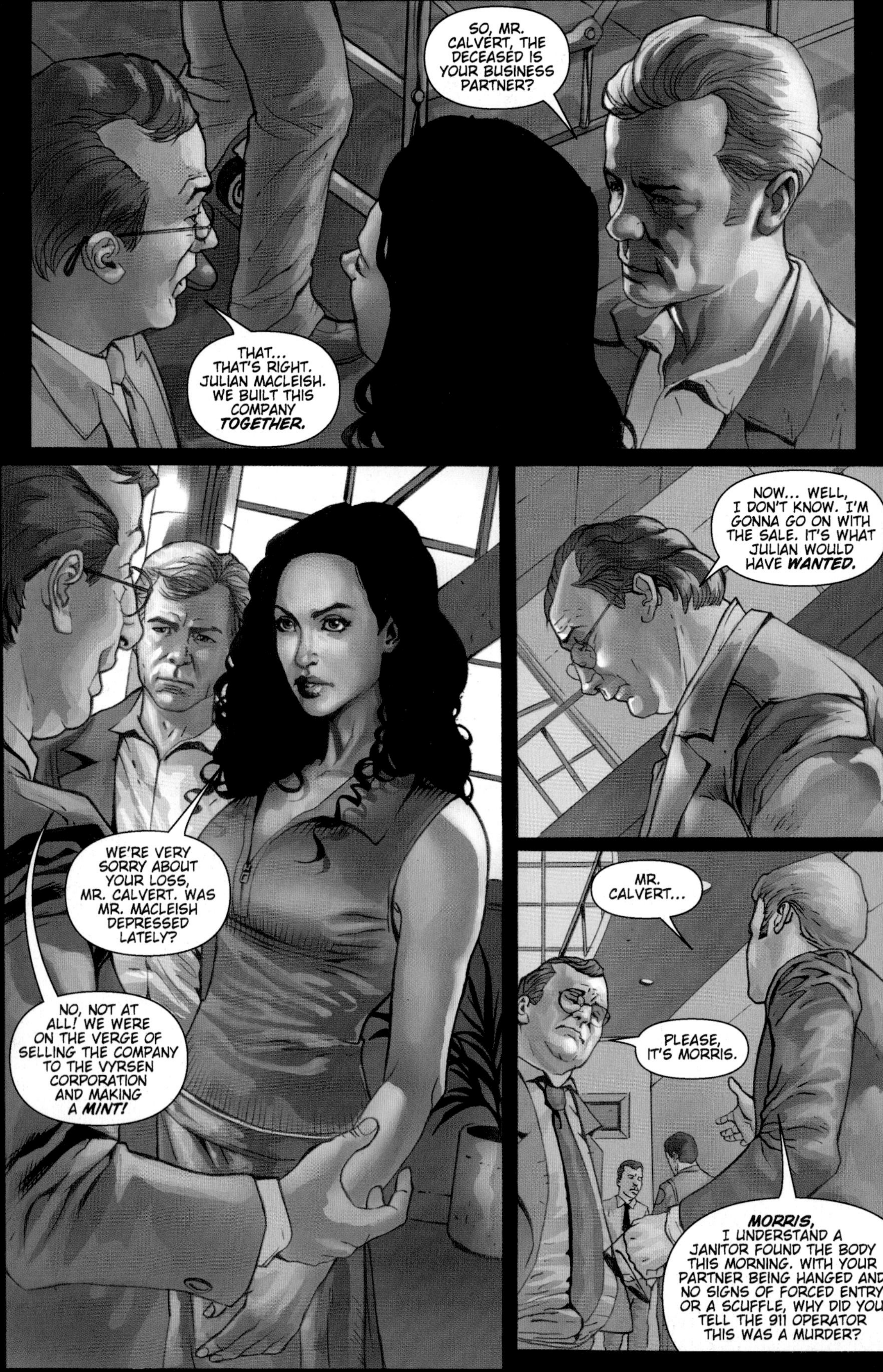
SO, MR. CALVERT, THE DECEASED IS YOUR BUSINESS PARTNER?
THAT... THAT'S RIGHT. JULIAN MACLEISH. WE BUILT THIS COMPANY ***TOGETHER.***
WE'RE VERY SORRY ABOUT YOUR LOSS, MR. CALVERT. WAS MR. MACLEISH DEPRESSED LATELY?
NO, NOT AT ALL! WE WERE ON THE VERGE OF SELLING THE COMPANY TO THE VYRSEN CORPORATION AND MAKING A ***MINT!***
NOW... WELL, I DON'T KNOW. I'M GONNA GO ON WITH THE SALE. IT'S WHAT JULIAN WOULD HAVE ***WANTED.***
MR. CALVERT...
PLEASE, IT'S MORRIS.
MORRIS, I UNDERSTAND A JANITOR FOUND THE BODY THIS MORNING. WITH YOUR PARTNER BEING HANGED AND NO SIGNS OF FORCED ENTRY OR A SCUFFLE, WHY DID YOU TELL THE 911 OPERATOR THIS WAS A MURDER?

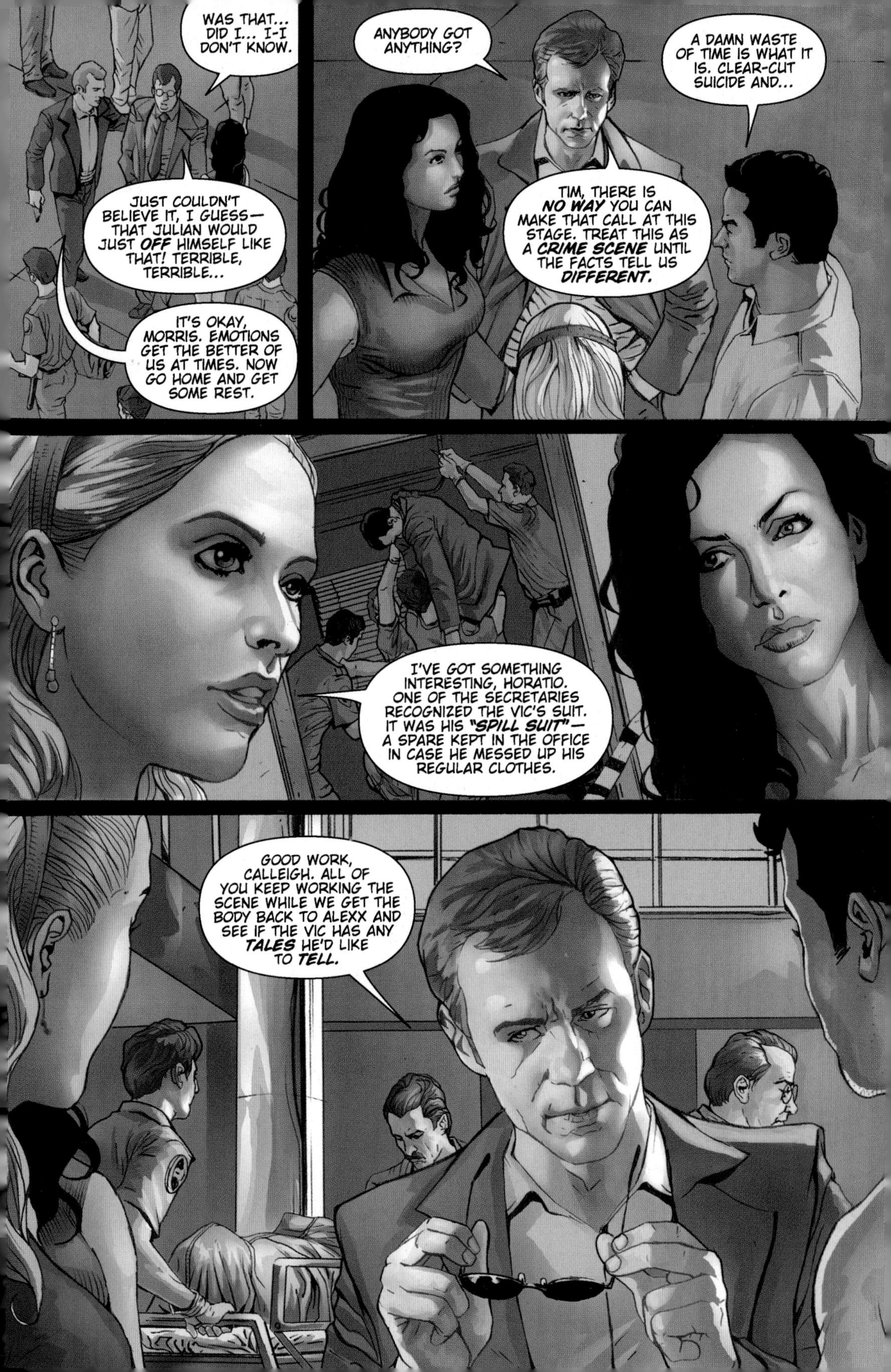

WAS THAT... DID I... I-I DON'T KNOW.
JUST COULDN'T BELIEVE IT, I GUESS— THAT JULIAN WOULD JUST OFF HIMSELF LIKE THAT! TERRIBLE, TERRIBLE...
IT'S OKAY, MORRIS. EMOTIONS GET THE BETTER OF US AT TIMES. NOW GO HOME AND GET SOME REST.
ANYBODY GOT ANYTHING?
A DAMN WASTE OF TIME IS WHAT IT IS. CLEAR-CUT SUICIDE AND...
TIM, THERE IS NO WAY YOU CAN MAKE THAT CALL AT THIS STAGE. TREAT THIS AS A CRIME SCENE UNTIL THE FACTS TELL US DIFFERENT.
I'VE GOT SOMETHING INTERESTING, HORATIO. ONE OF THE SECRETARIES RECOGNIZED THE VIC'S SUIT. IT WAS HIS "SPILL SUIT"— A SPARE KEPT IN THE OFFICE IN CASE HE MESSED UP HIS REGULAR CLOTHES.
GOOD WORK, CALLEIGH. ALL OF YOU KEEP WORKING THE SCENE WHILE WE GET THE BODY BACK TO ALEXX AND SEE IF THE VIC HAS ANY TALES HE'D LIKE TO TELL.

...SO I PLACE THE TIME OF DEATH SOMETIME ON MONDAY EVENING. BUT THAT'S NOT THE MOST *INTERESTING* THING I'VE FOUND.

THE HYOID BONE'S BROKEN. THAT *ALMOST NEVER* HAPPENS WITH A HANGING...

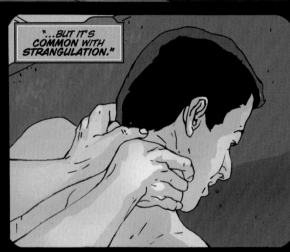

"...BUT IT'S *COMMON* WITH *STRANGULATION.*"

TRUE, BUT IT'S STILL *POSSIBLE.* WE CAN'T JUMP TO CONCLUSIONS WITHOUT MORE *FACTS.* GOT ANYTHING ELSE?

OH, YES, HORATIO...

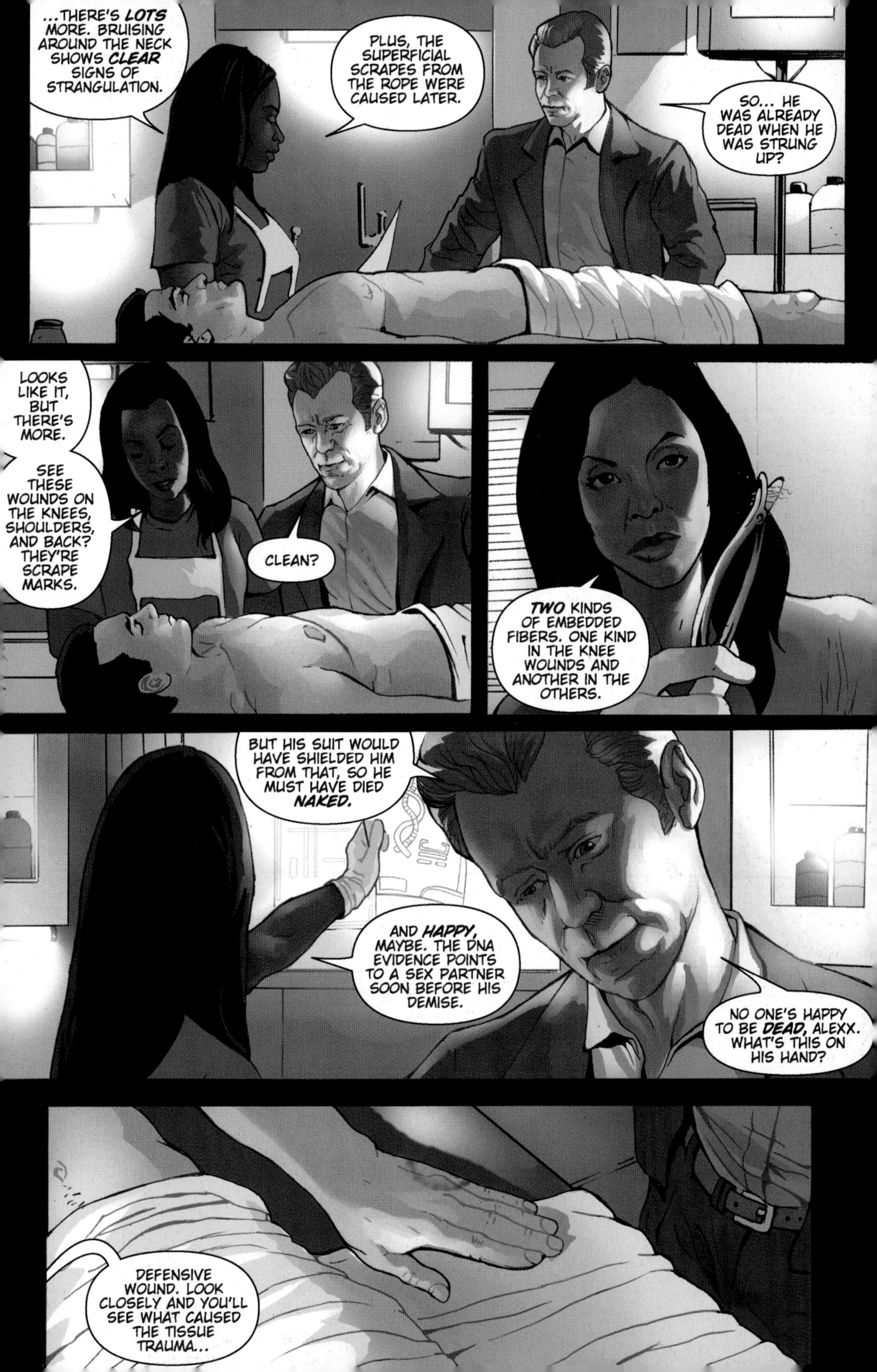

...THERE'S LOTS MORE. BRUISING AROUND THE NECK SHOWS CLEAR SIGNS OF STRANGULATION.
PLUS, THE SUPERFICIAL SCRAPES FROM THE ROPE WERE CAUSED LATER.
SO... HE WAS ALREADY DEAD WHEN HE WAS STRUNG UP?
LOOKS LIKE IT, BUT THERE'S MORE.
SEE THESE WOUNDS ON THE KNEES, SHOULDERS, AND BACK? THEY'RE SCRAPE MARKS.
CLEAN?
TWO KINDS OF EMBEDDED FIBERS. ONE KIND IN THE KNEE WOUNDS AND ANOTHER IN THE OTHERS.
BUT HIS SUIT WOULD HAVE SHIELDED HIM FROM THAT, SO HE MUST HAVE DIED NAKED.
AND HAPPY, MAYBE. THE DNA EVIDENCE POINTS TO A SEX PARTNER SOON BEFORE HIS DEMISE.
NO ONE'S HAPPY TO BE DEAD, ALEXX. WHAT'S THIS ON HIS HAND?
DEFENSIVE WOUND. LOOK CLOSELY AND YOU'LL SEE WHAT CAUSED THE TISSUE TRAUMA...

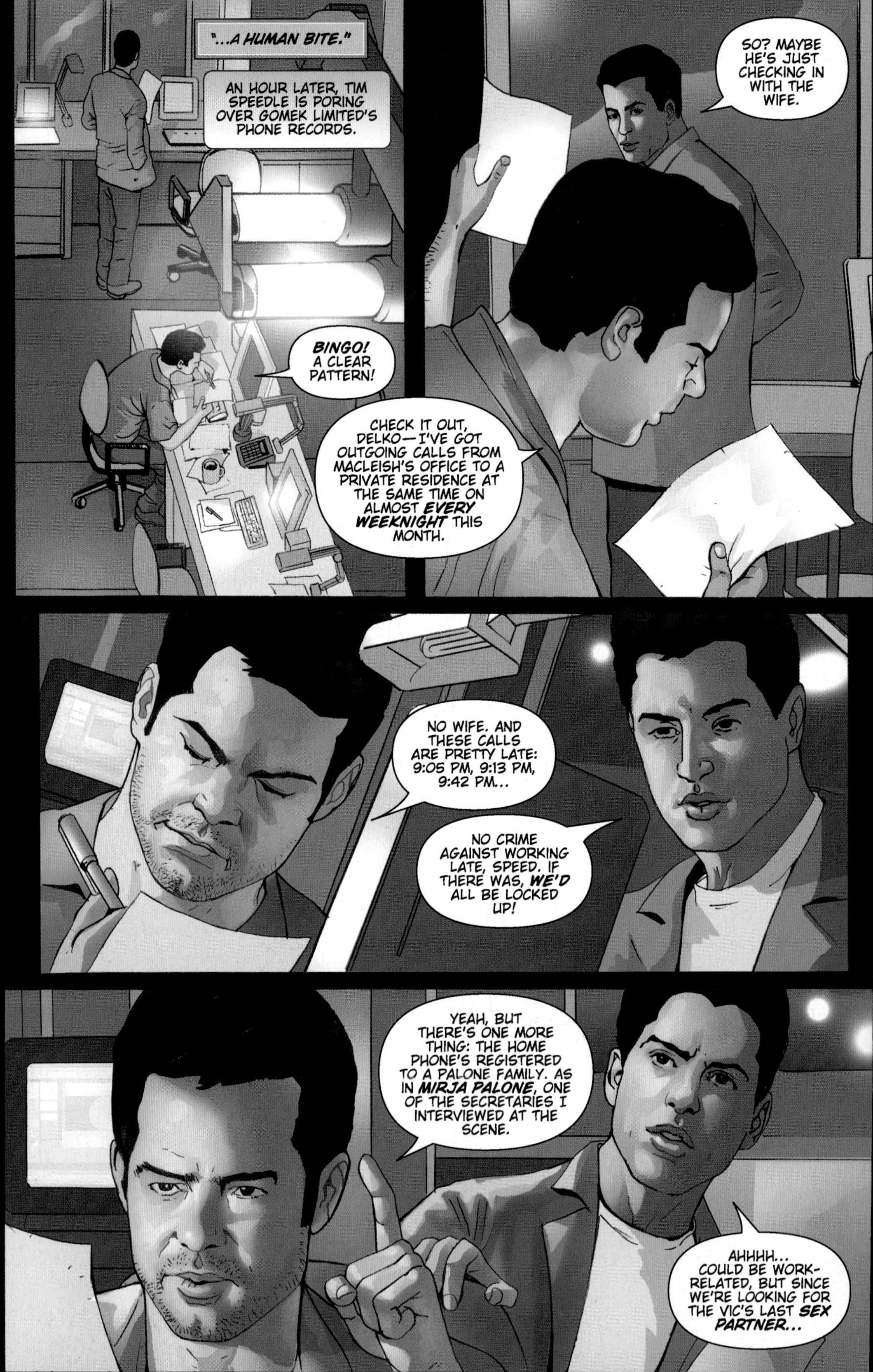
"...A HUMAN BITE."
AN HOUR LATER, TIM SPEEDLE IS PORING OVER GOMEK LIMITED'S PHONE RECORDS.
BINGO! A CLEAR PATTERN!
CHECK IT OUT, DELKO—I'VE GOT OUTGOING CALLS FROM MACLEISH'S OFFICE TO A PRIVATE RESIDENCE AT THE SAME TIME ON ALMOST EVERY WEEKNIGHT THIS MONTH.
SO? MAYBE HE'S JUST CHECKING IN WITH THE WIFE.
NO WIFE. AND THESE CALLS ARE PRETTY LATE: 9:05 PM, 9:13 PM, 9:42 PM...
NO CRIME AGAINST WORKING LATE, SPEED. IF THERE WAS, WE'D ALL BE LOCKED UP!
YEAH, BUT THERE'S ONE MORE THING: THE HOME PHONE'S REGISTERED TO A PALONE FAMILY. AS IN MIRJA PALONE, ONE OF THE SECRETARIES I INTERVIEWED AT THE SCENE.
AHHHH... COULD BE WORK-RELATED, BUT SINCE WE'RE LOOKING FOR THE VIC'S LAST SEX PARTNER...

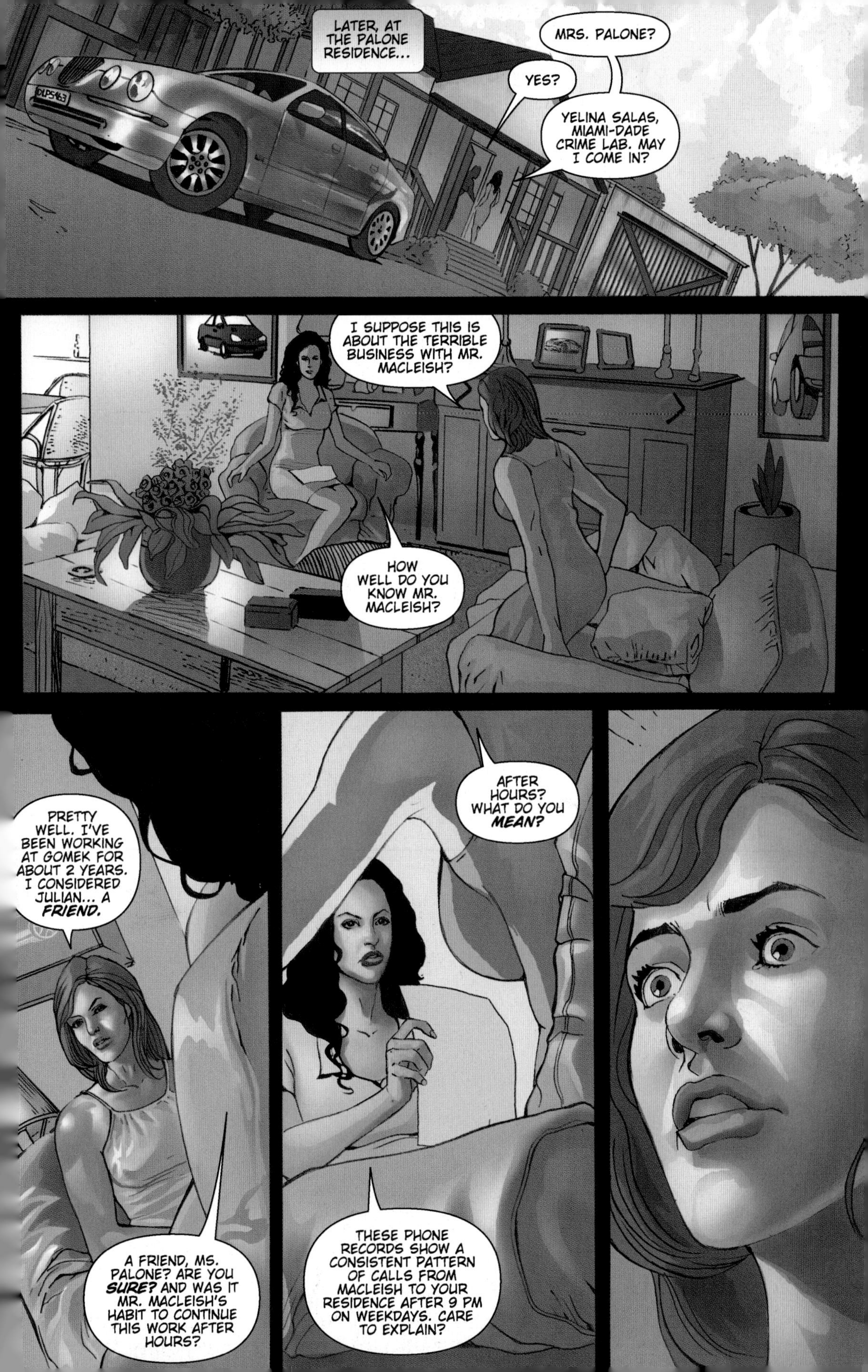
LATER, AT THE PALONE RESIDENCE...
MRS. PALONE?
YES?
YELINA SALAS, MIAMI-DADE CRIME LAB. MAY I COME IN?
I SUPPOSE THIS IS ABOUT THE TERRIBLE BUSINESS WITH MR. MACLEISH?
HOW WELL DO YOU KNOW MR. MACLEISH?
PRETTY WELL. I'VE BEEN WORKING AT GOMEK FOR ABOUT 2 YEARS. I CONSIDERED JULIAN... A FRIEND.
A FRIEND, MS. PALONE? ARE YOU SURE? AND WAS IT MR. MACLEISH'S HABIT TO CONTINUE THIS WORK AFTER HOURS?
AFTER HOURS? WHAT DO YOU MEAN?
THESE PHONE RECORDS SHOW A CONSISTENT PATTERN OF CALLS FROM MACLEISH TO YOUR RESIDENCE AFTER 9 PM ON WEEKDAYS. CARE TO EXPLAIN?

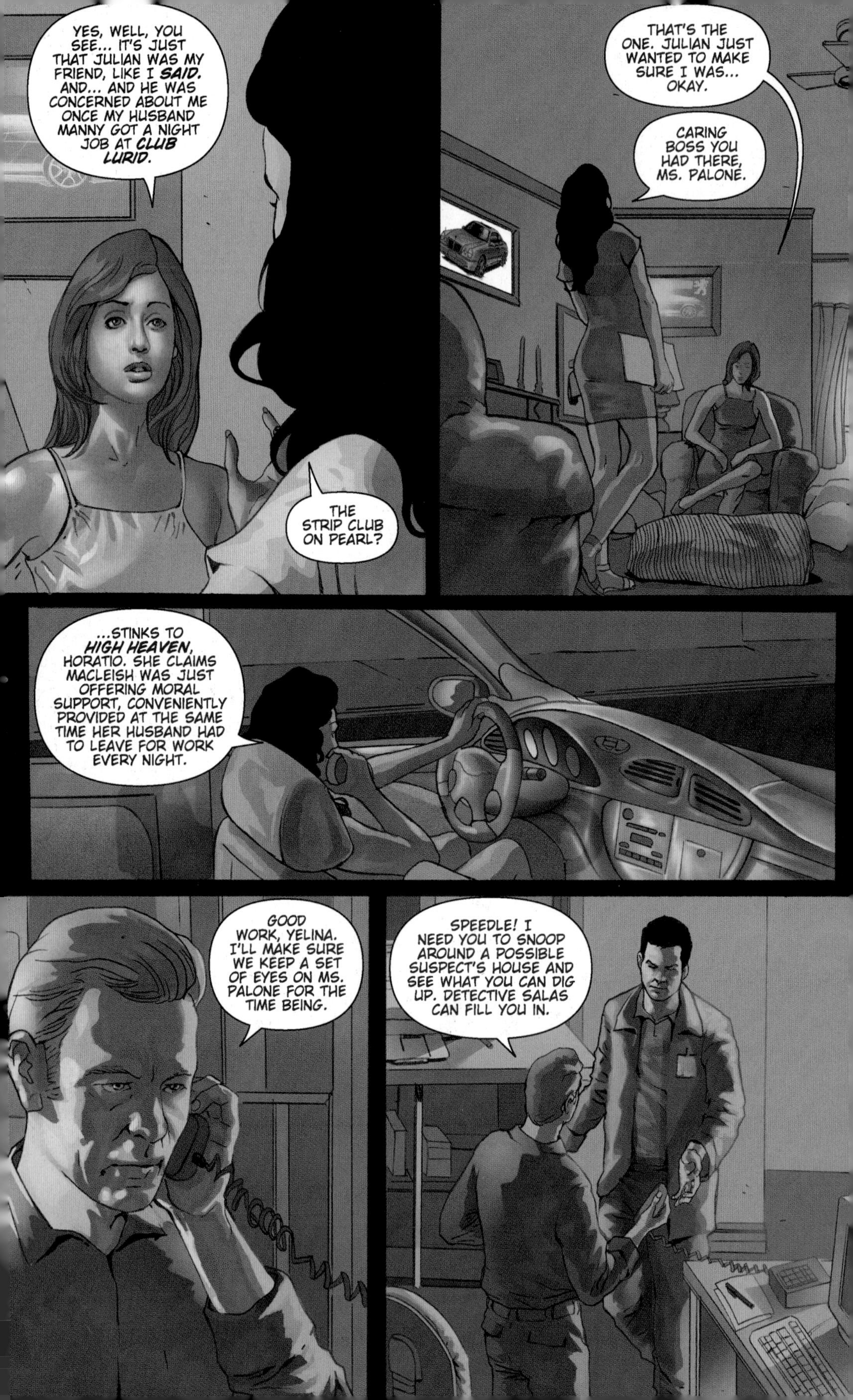
YES, WELL, YOU SEE... IT'S JUST THAT JULIAN WAS MY FRIEND, LIKE I *SAID.* AND... AND HE WAS CONCERNED ABOUT ME ONCE MY HUSBAND MANNY GOT A NIGHT JOB AT *CLUB LURID*.
THE STRIP CLUB ON PEARL?
THAT'S THE ONE. JULIAN JUST WANTED TO MAKE SURE I WAS... OKAY.
CARING BOSS YOU HAD THERE, MS. PALONE.
...STINKS TO *HIGH HEAVEN*, HORATIO. SHE CLAIMS MACLEISH WAS JUST OFFERING MORAL SUPPORT, CONVENIENTLY PROVIDED AT THE SAME TIME HER HUSBAND HAD TO LEAVE FOR WORK EVERY NIGHT.
GOOD WORK, YELINA. I'LL MAKE SURE WE KEEP A SET OF EYES ON MS. PALONE FOR THE TIME BEING.
SPEEDLE! I NEED YOU TO SNOOP AROUND A POSSIBLE SUSPECT'S HOUSE AND SEE WHAT YOU CAN DIG UP. DETECTIVE SALAS CAN FILL YOU IN.

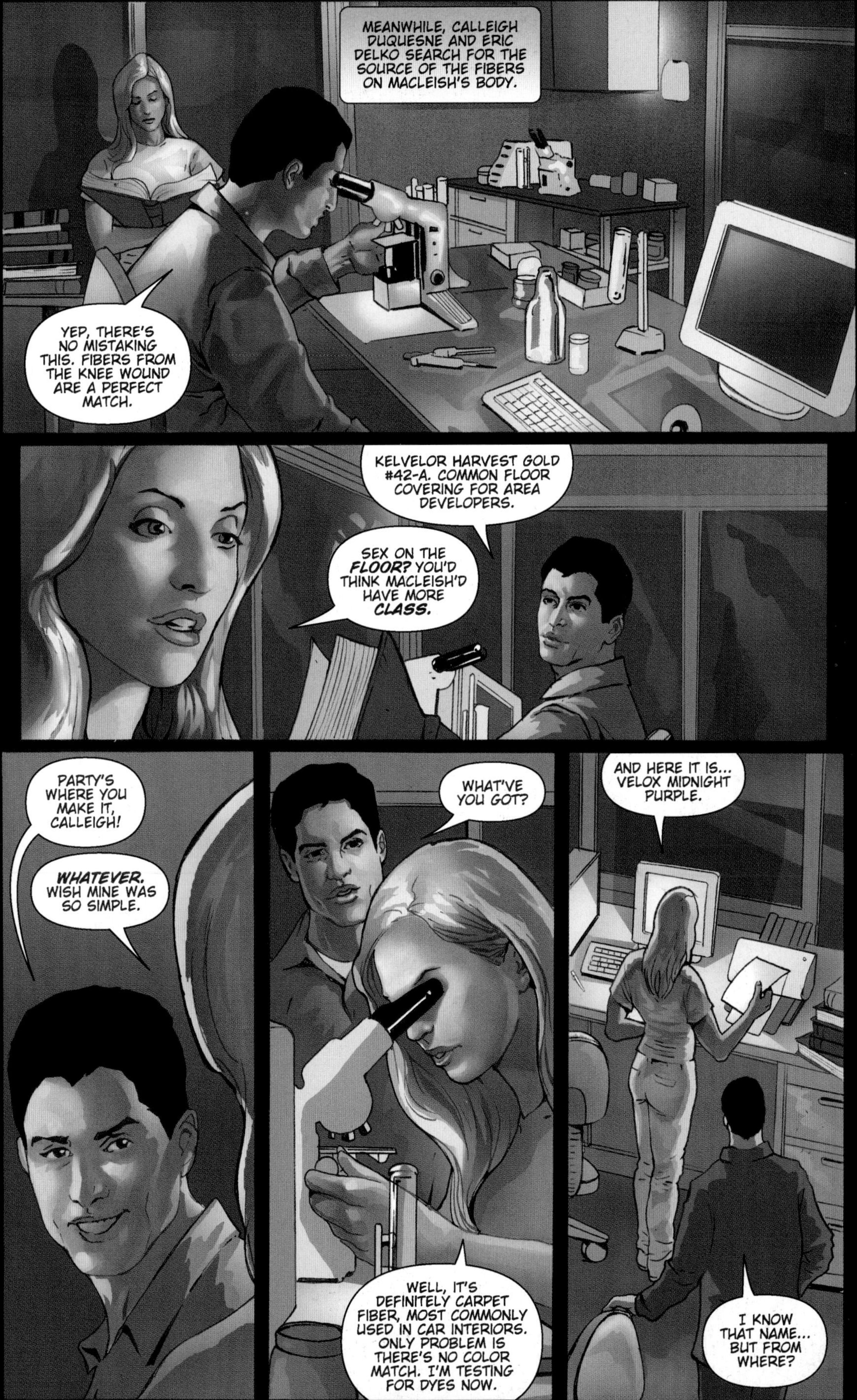
MEANWHILE, CALLEIGH DUQUESNE AND ERIC DELKO SEARCH FOR THE SOURCE OF THE FIBERS ON MACLEISH'S BODY.
YEP, THERE'S NO MISTAKING THIS. FIBERS FROM THE KNEE WOUND ARE A PERFECT MATCH.
KELVELOR HARVEST GOLD #42-A. COMMON FLOOR COVERING FOR AREA DEVELOPERS.
SEX ON THE **FLOOR?** YOU'D THINK MACLEISH'D HAVE MORE **CLASS.**
PARTY'S WHERE YOU MAKE IT, CALLEIGH!
WHATEVER. WISH MINE WAS SO SIMPLE.
WHAT'VE YOU GOT?
WELL, IT'S DEFINITELY CARPET FIBER, MOST COMMONLY USED IN CAR INTERIORS. ONLY PROBLEM IS THERE'S NO COLOR MATCH. I'M TESTING FOR DYES NOW.
AND HERE IT IS... VELOX MIDNIGHT PURPLE.
I KNOW THAT NAME... BUT FROM WHERE?

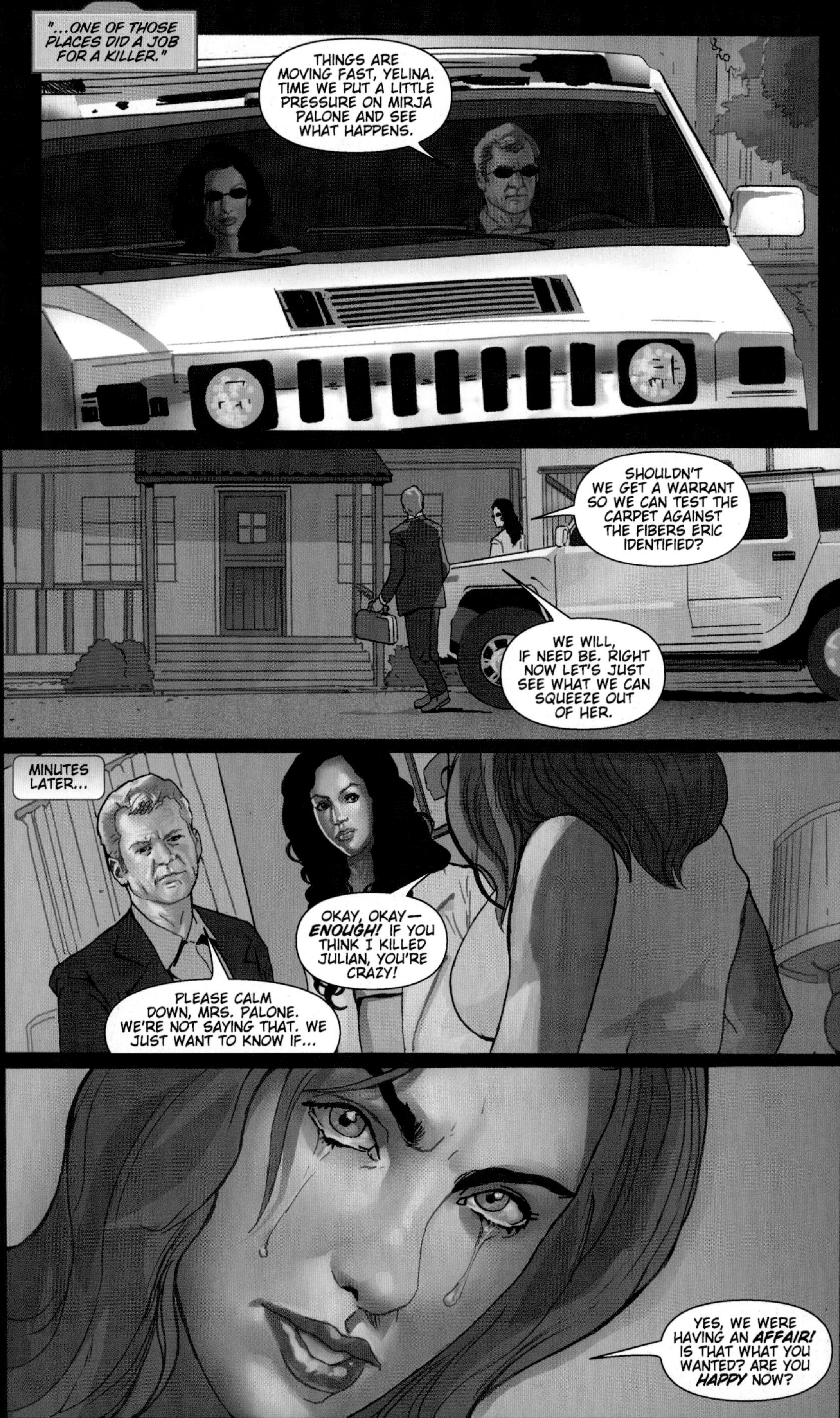
"...ONE OF THOSE PLACES DID A JOB FOR A KILLER."
THINGS ARE MOVING FAST, YELINA. TIME WE PUT A LITTLE PRESSURE ON MIRJA PALONE AND SEE WHAT HAPPENS.
SHOULDN'T WE GET A WARRANT SO WE CAN TEST THE CARPET AGAINST THE FIBERS ERIC IDENTIFIED?
WE WILL, IF NEED BE. RIGHT NOW LET'S JUST SEE WHAT WE CAN SQUEEZE OUT OF HER.
MINUTES LATER...
OKAY, OKAY— ENOUGH! IF YOU THINK I KILLED JULIAN, YOU'RE CRAZY!
PLEASE CALM DOWN, MRS. PALONE. WE'RE NOT SAYING THAT. WE JUST WANT TO KNOW IF...
YES, WE WERE HAVING AN AFFAIR! IS THAT WHAT YOU WANTED? ARE YOU HAPPY NOW?

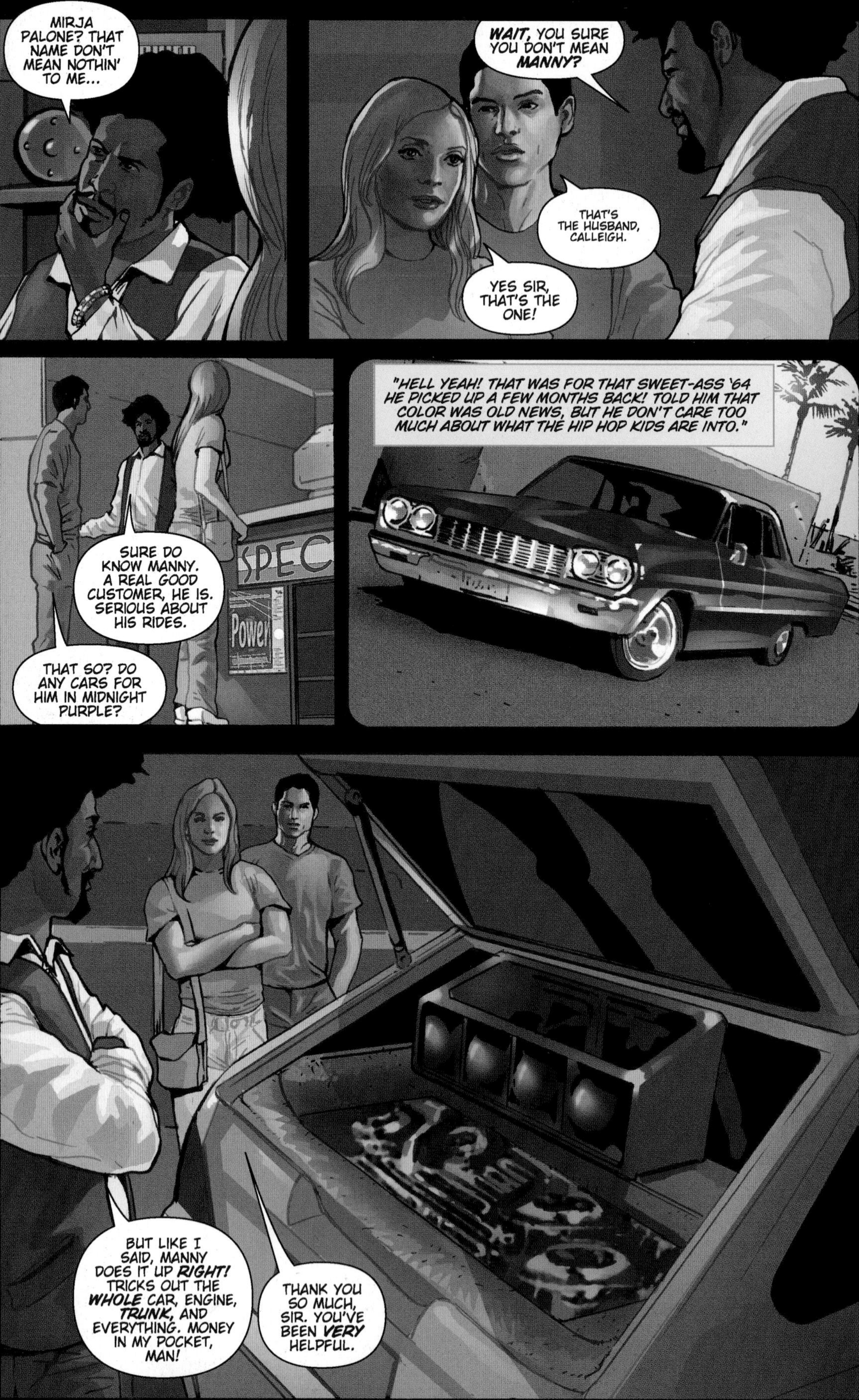
MIRJA PALONE? THAT NAME DON'T MEAN NOTHIN' TO ME...
WAIT, YOU SURE YOU DON'T MEAN MANNY?
THAT'S THE HUSBAND, CALLEIGH.
YES SIR, THAT'S THE ONE!
SURE DO KNOW MANNY. A REAL GOOD CUSTOMER, HE IS. SERIOUS ABOUT HIS RIDES.
THAT SO? DO ANY CARS FOR HIM IN MIDNIGHT PURPLE?
SPEC
Power
"HELL YEAH! THAT WAS FOR THAT SWEET-ASS '64 HE PICKED UP A FEW MONTHS BACK! TOLD HIM THAT COLOR WAS OLD NEWS, BUT HE DON'T CARE TOO MUCH ABOUT WHAT THE HIP HOP KIDS ARE INTO."
BUT LIKE I SAID, MANNY DOES IT UP RIGHT! TRICKS OUT THE WHOLE CAR, ENGINE, TRUNK, AND EVERYTHING. MONEY IN MY POCKET, MAN!
THANK YOU SO MUCH, SIR. YOU'VE BEEN VERY HELPFUL.

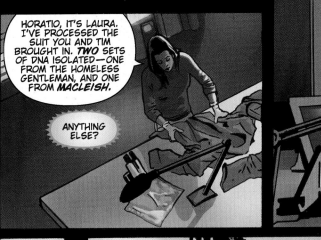

HORATIO, IT'S LAURA. I'VE PROCESSED THE SUIT YOU AND TIM BROUGHT IN. *TWO* SETS OF DNA ISOLATED—ONE FROM THE HOMELESS GENTLEMAN, AND ONE FROM *MACLEISH.*

ANYTHING ELSE?

TESTED THE SUIT FOR BLOOD IN THE AREAS THAT MACLEISH'S BODY WAS WOUNDED: *NEGATIVE.*

WHAT ABOUT *SEMEN?*

ALSO A NEGATIVE. THIS SUIT WAS TAKEN OFF *BEFORE* ANY SEX OR INJURIES OCCURRED.

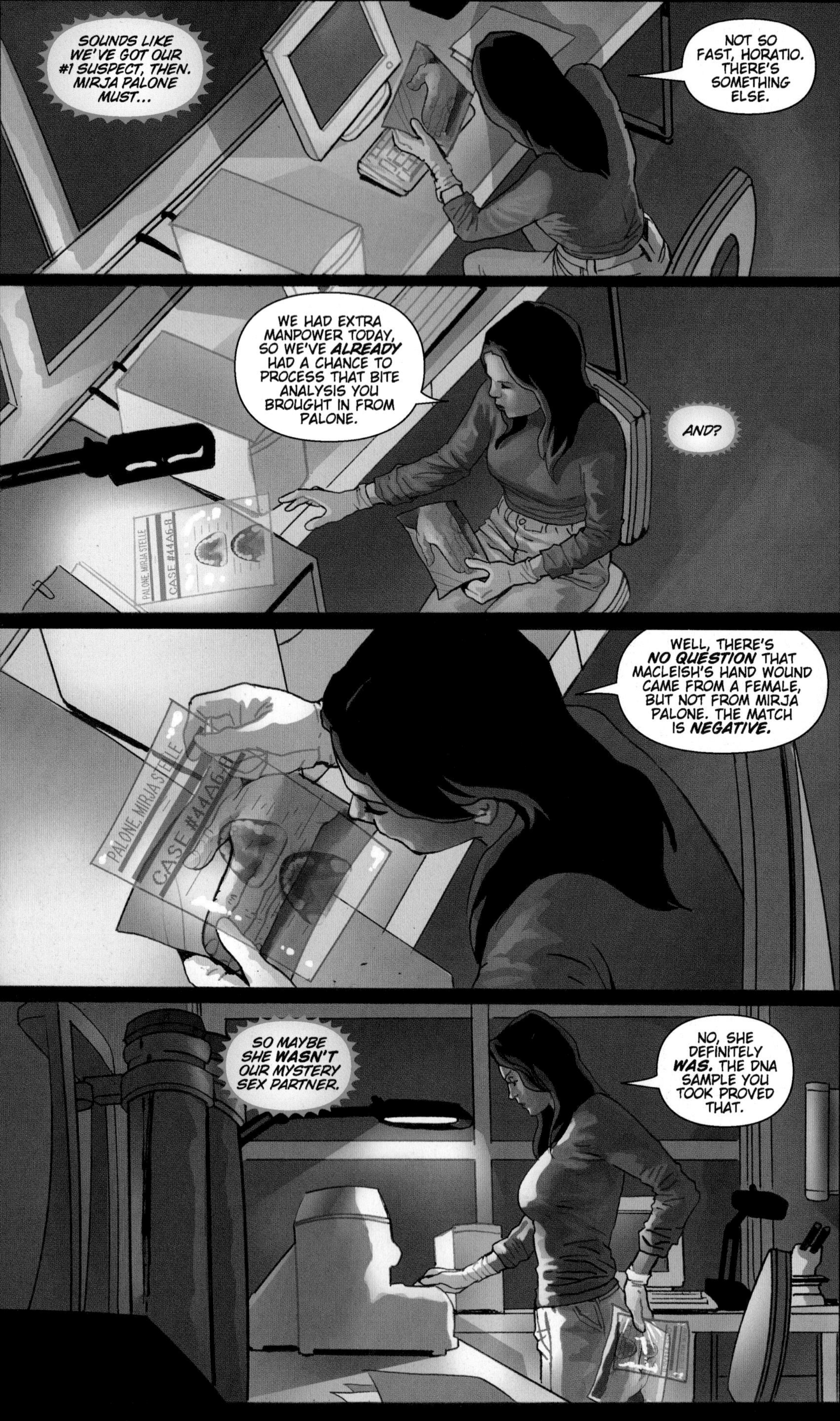
SOUNDS LIKE WE'VE GOT OUR #1 SUSPECT, THEN. MIRJA PALONE MUST...
NOT SO FAST, HORATIO. THERE'S SOMETHING ELSE.
WE HAD EXTRA MANPOWER TODAY, SO WE'VE ALREADY HAD A CHANCE TO PROCESS THAT BITE ANALYSIS YOU BROUGHT IN FROM PALONE.
AND?
PALONE, MIRJA STELLE
CASE #44A6-8
WELL, THERE'S NO QUESTION THAT MACLEISH'S HAND WOUND CAME FROM A FEMALE, BUT NOT FROM MIRJA PALONE. THE MATCH IS NEGATIVE.
PALONE, MIRJA STELLE
CASE #44A6-8
SO MAYBE SHE WASN'T OUR MYSTERY SEX PARTNER.
NO, SHE DEFINITELY WAS. THE DNA SAMPLE YOU TOOK PROVED THAT.

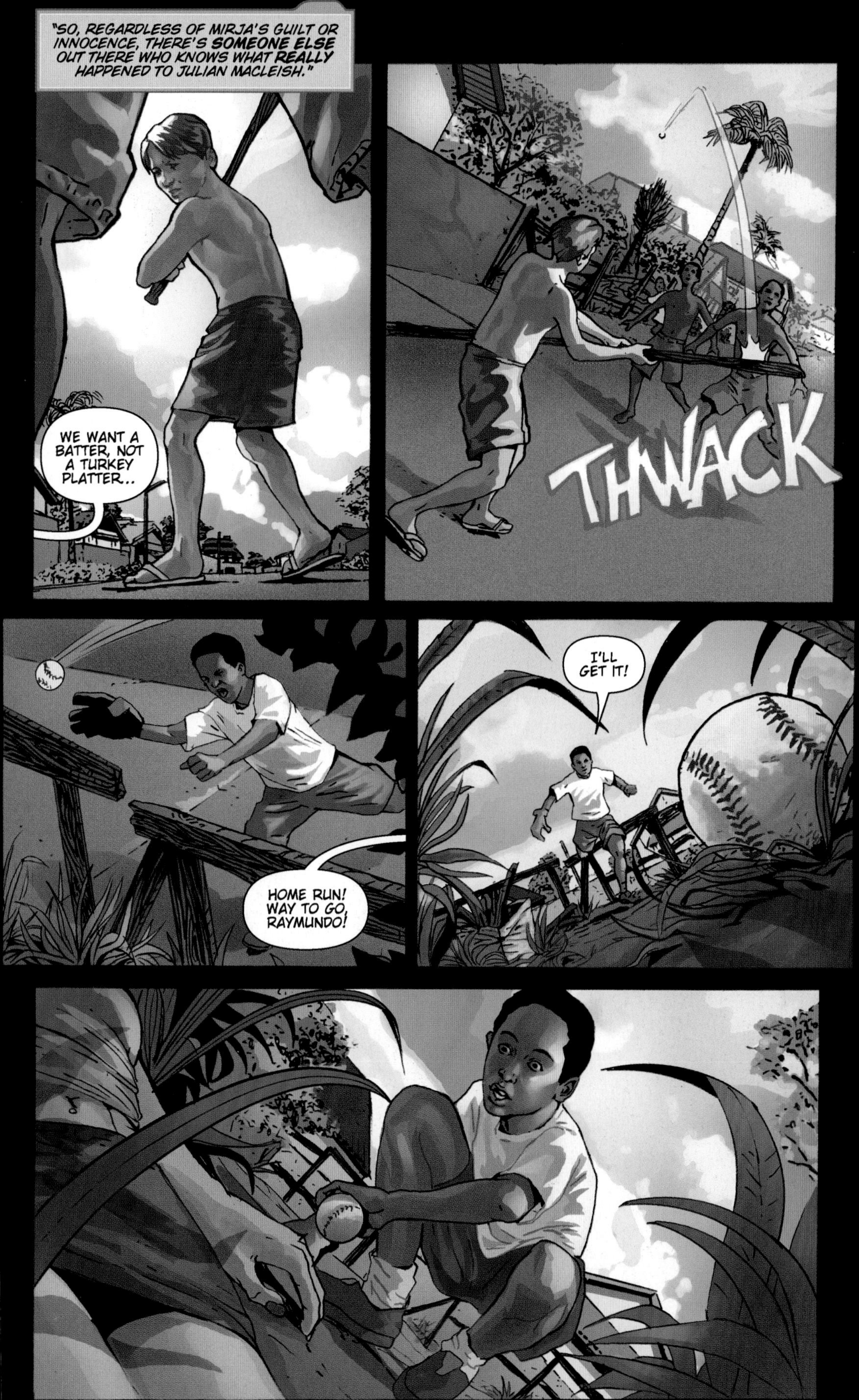
"SO, REGARDLESS OF MIRJA'S GUILT OR INNOCENCE, THERE'S SOMEONE ELSE OUT THERE WHO KNOWS WHAT REALLY HAPPENED TO JULIAN MACLEISH."
WE WANT A BATTER, NOT A TURKEY PLATTER..
THWACK
HOME RUN! WAY TO GO, RAYMUNDO!
I'LL GET IT!

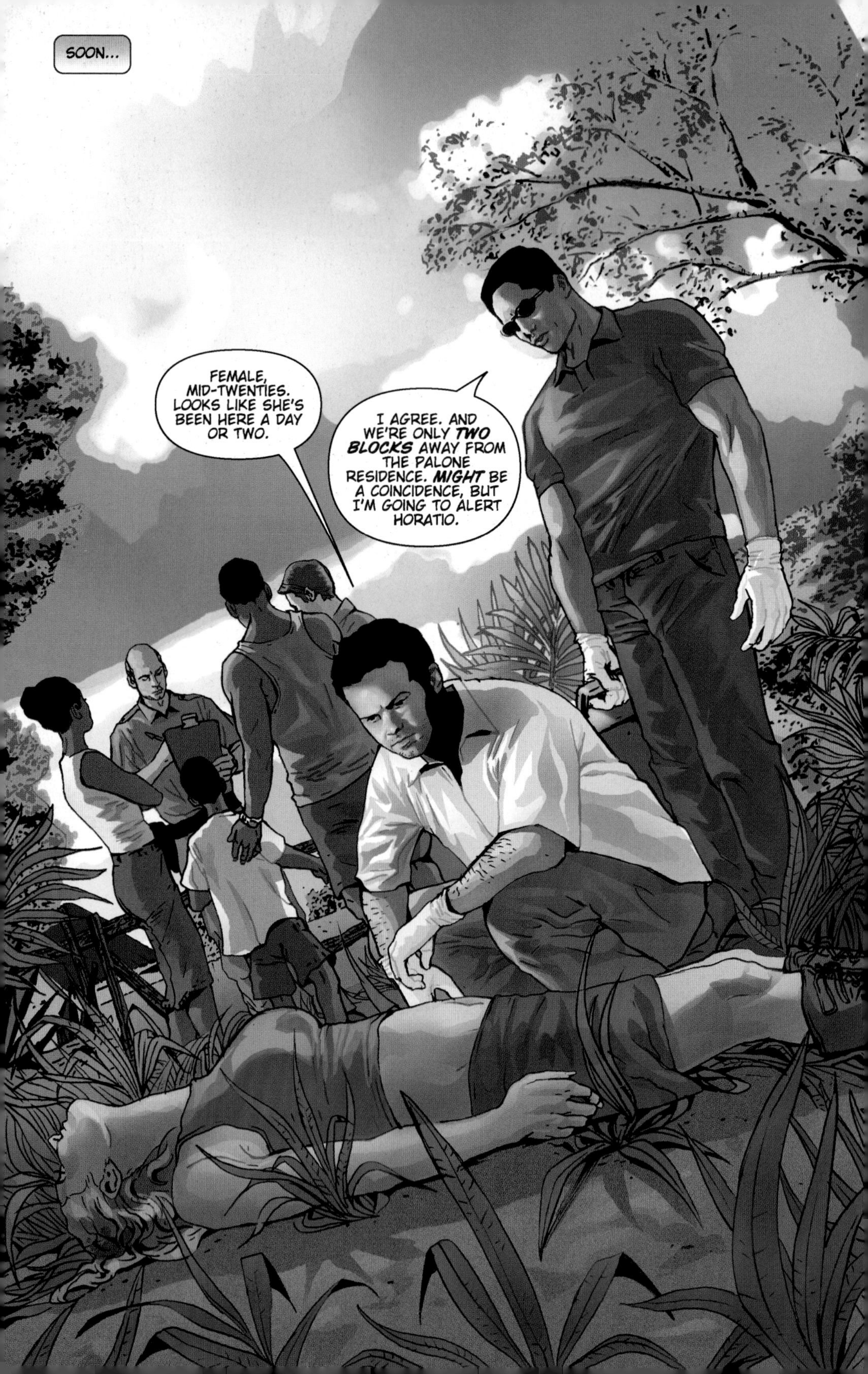
SOON...
FEMALE, MID-TWENTIES. LOOKS LIKE SHE'S BEEN HERE A DAY OR TWO.
I AGREE. AND WE'RE ONLY TWO BLOCKS AWAY FROM THE PALONE RESIDENCE. MIGHT BE A COINCIDENCE, BUT I'M GOING TO ALERT HORATIO.

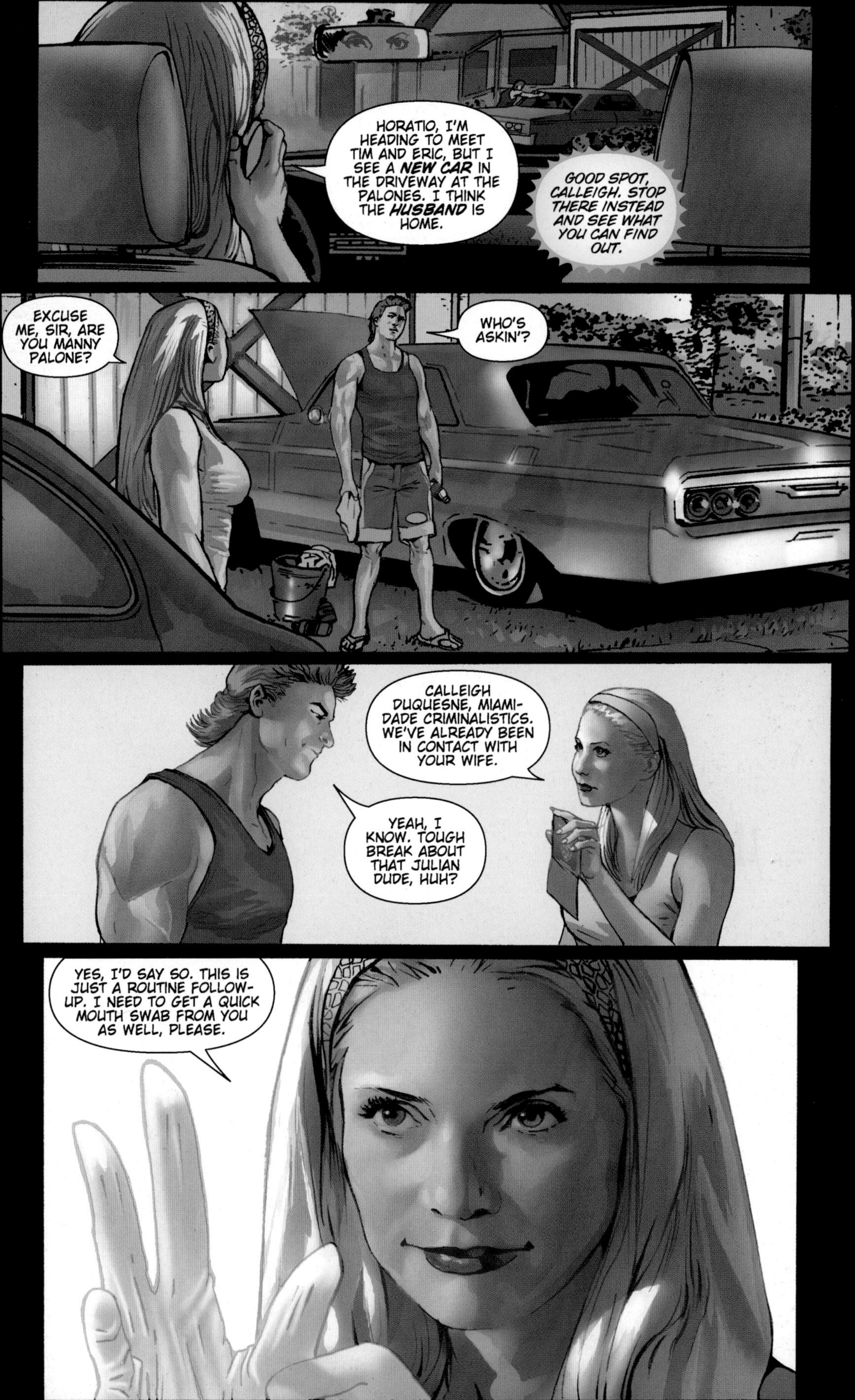
HORATIO, I'M HEADING TO MEET TIM AND ERIC, BUT I SEE A NEW CAR IN THE DRIVEWAY AT THE PALONES. I THINK THE HUSBAND IS HOME.
GOOD SPOT, CALLEIGH. STOP THERE INSTEAD AND SEE WHAT YOU CAN FIND OUT.
EXCUSE ME, SIR, ARE YOU MANNY PALONE?
WHO'S ASKIN'?
CALLEIGH DUQUESNE, MIAMI-DADE CRIMINALISTICS. WE'VE ALREADY BEEN IN CONTACT WITH YOUR WIFE.
YEAH, I KNOW. TOUGH BREAK ABOUT THAT JULIAN DUDE, HUH?
YES, I'D SAY SO. THIS IS JUST A ROUTINE FOLLOW-UP. I NEED TO GET A QUICK MOUTH SWAB FROM YOU AS WELL, PLEASE.

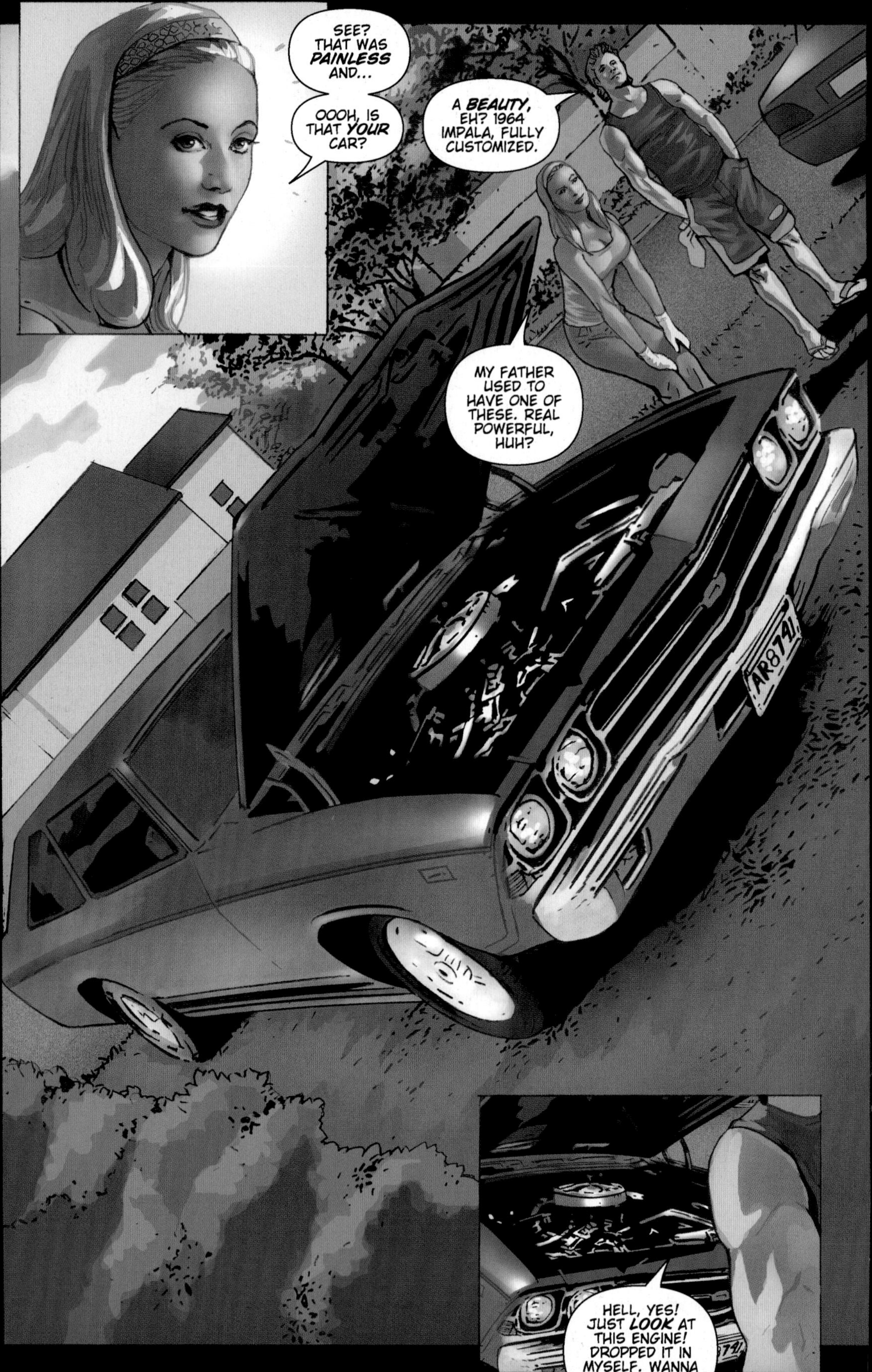
SEE? THAT WAS PAINLESS AND...
OOOH, IS THAT YOUR CAR?
A BEAUTY, EH? 1964 IMPALA, FULLY CUSTOMIZED.
MY FATHER USED TO HAVE ONE OF THESE. REAL POWERFUL, HUH?
AR874
HELL, YES! JUST LOOK AT THIS ENGINE! DROPPED IT IN MYSELF. WANNA FEEL THE POWER?

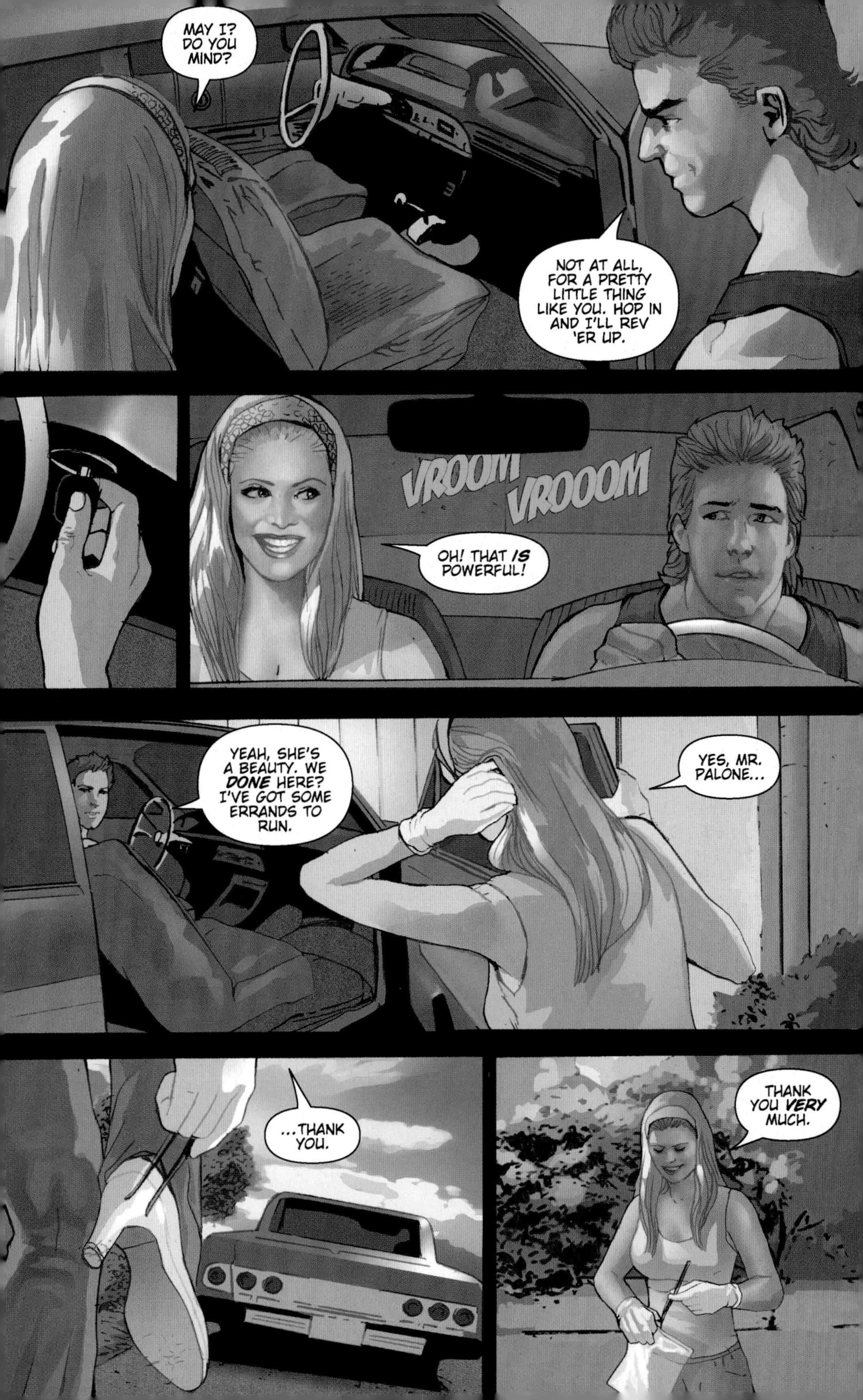
MAY I? DO YOU MIND?
NOT AT ALL, FOR A PRETTY LITTLE THING LIKE YOU. HOP IN AND I'LL REV 'ER UP.
VROOM
VROOOM
OH! THAT IS POWERFUL!
YEAH, SHE'S A BEAUTY. WE DONE HERE? I'VE GOT SOME ERRANDS TO RUN.
YES, MR. PALONE...
...THANK YOU.
THANK YOU VERY MUCH.

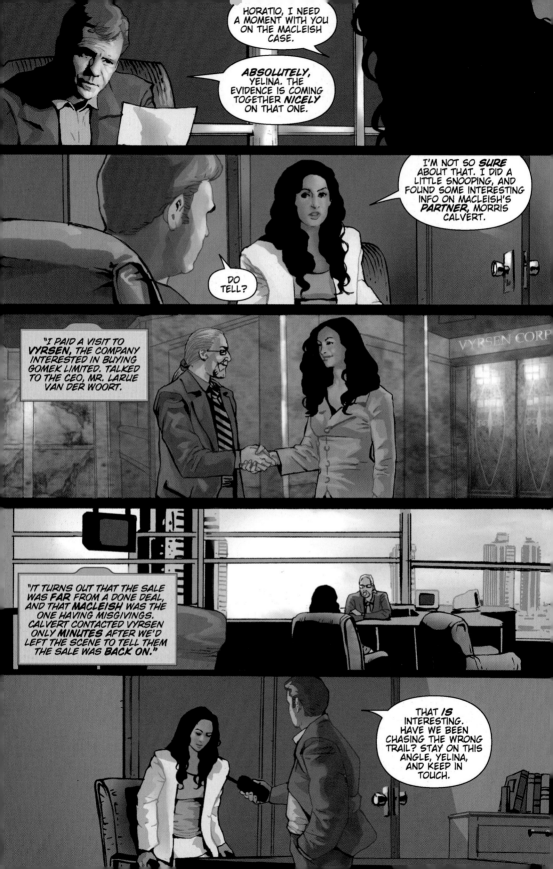

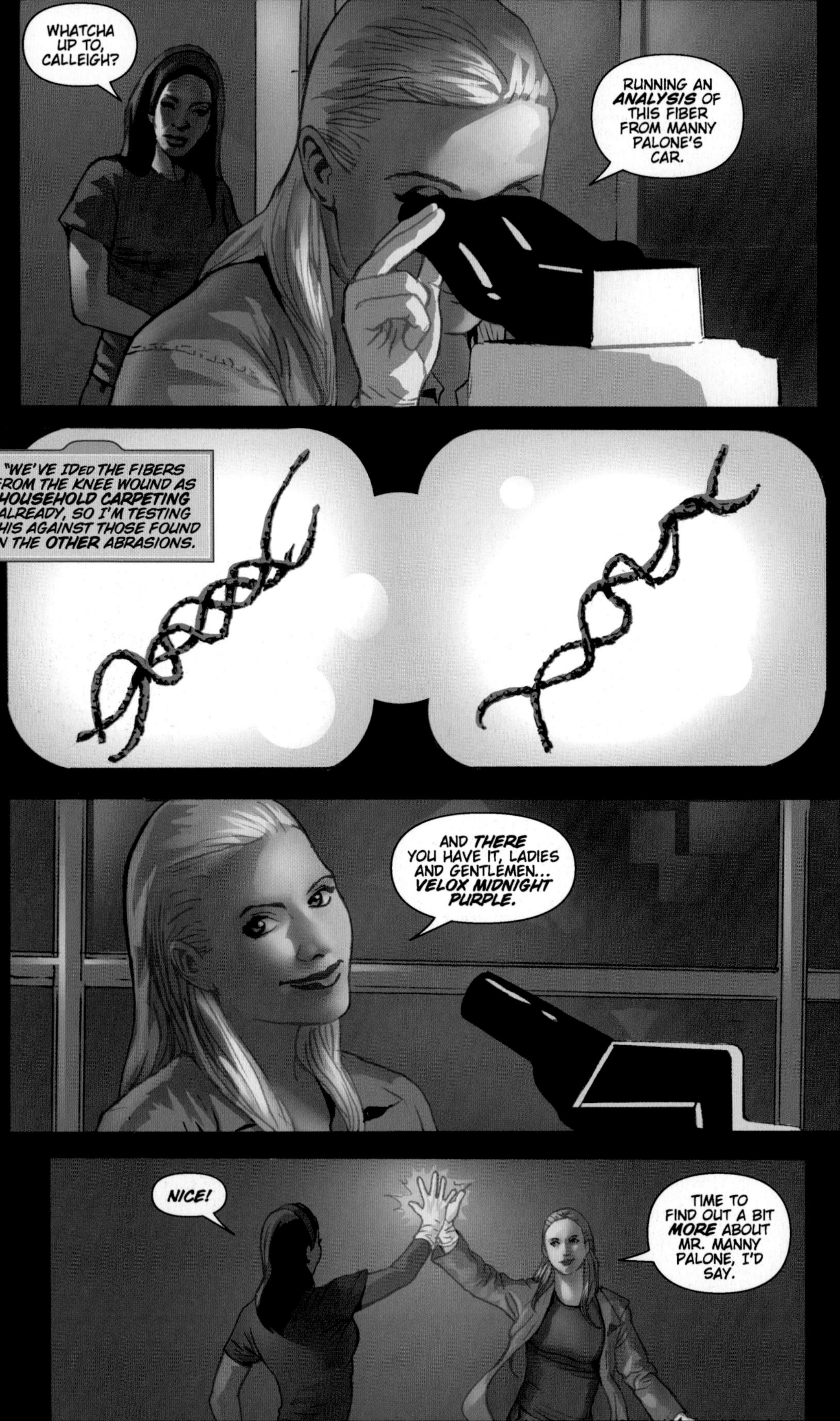
WHATCHA UP TO, CALLEIGH?
RUNNING AN ANALYSIS OF THIS FIBER FROM MANNY PALONE'S CAR.
"WE'VE IDed THE FIBERS FROM THE KNEE WOUND AS HOUSEHOLD CARPETING ALREADY, SO I'M TESTING THIS AGAINST THOSE FOUND IN THE OTHER ABRASIONS.
AND THERE YOU HAVE IT, LADIES AND GENTLEMEN... VELOX MIDNIGHT PURPLE.
NICE!
TIME TO FIND OUT A BIT MORE ABOUT MR. MANNY PALONE, I'D SAY.

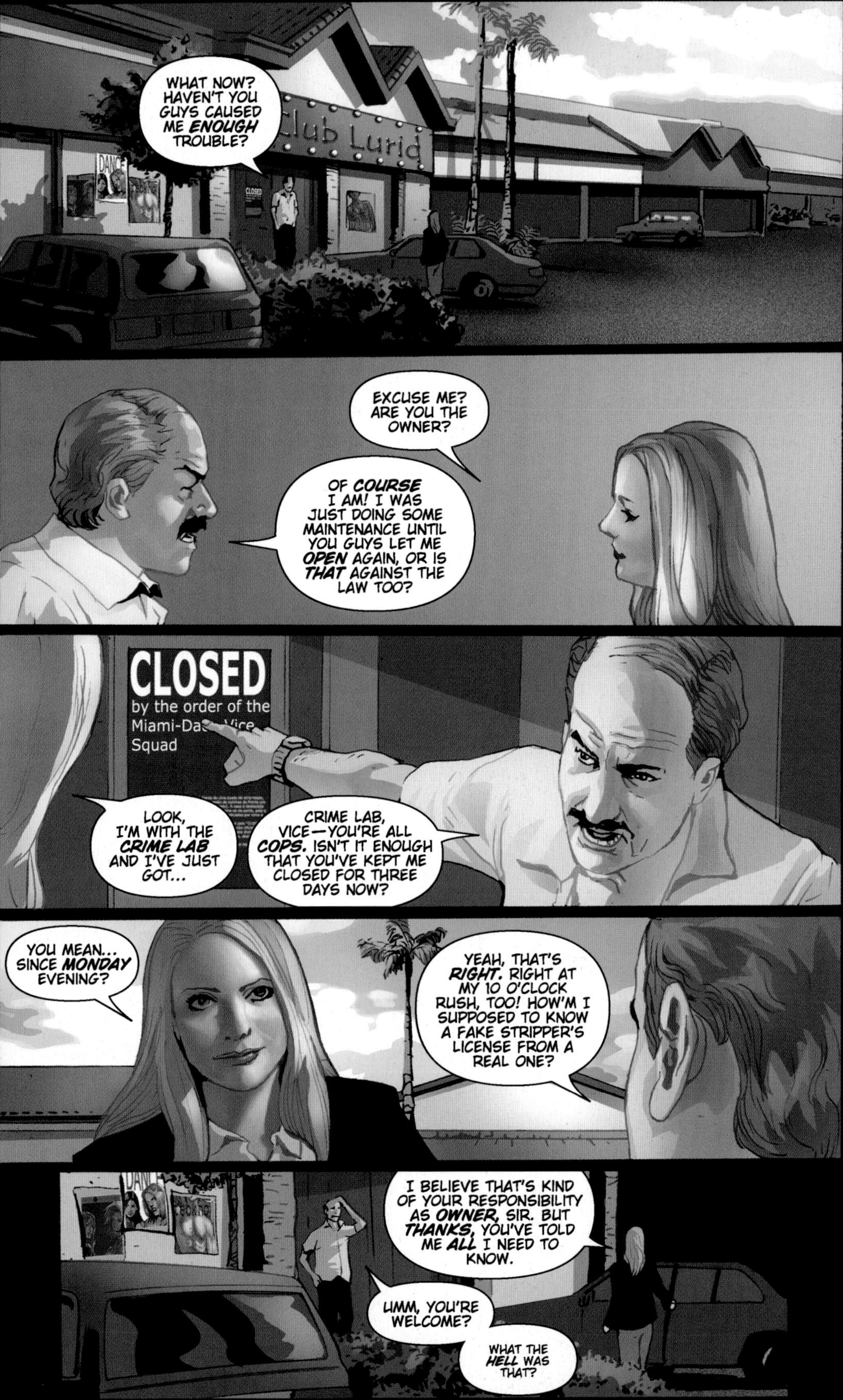

WHAT NOW? HAVEN'T YOU GUYS CAUSED ME *ENOUGH* TROUBLE?
Club Lurid
EXCUSE ME? ARE YOU THE OWNER?
OF *COURSE* I AM! I WAS JUST DOING SOME MAINTENANCE UNTIL YOU GUYS LET ME *OPEN* AGAIN, OR IS *THAT* AGAINST THE LAW TOO?
CLOSED
by the order of the
Squad
LOOK, I'M WITH THE *CRIME LAB* AND I'VE JUST GOT...
CRIME LAB, VICE—YOU'RE ALL *COPS.* ISN'T IT ENOUGH THAT YOU'VE KEPT ME CLOSED FOR THREE DAYS NOW?
YOU MEAN... SINCE *MONDAY* EVENING?
YEAH, THAT'S *RIGHT.* RIGHT AT MY 10 O'CLOCK RUSH, TOO! HOW'M I SUPPOSED TO KNOW A FAKE STRIPPER'S LICENSE FROM A REAL ONE?
I BELIEVE THAT'S KIND OF YOUR RESPONSIBILITY AS *OWNER,* SIR. BUT *THANKS,* YOU'VE TOLD ME *ALL* I NEED TO KNOW.
UMM, YOU'RE WELCOME?
WHAT THE *HELL* WAS THAT?

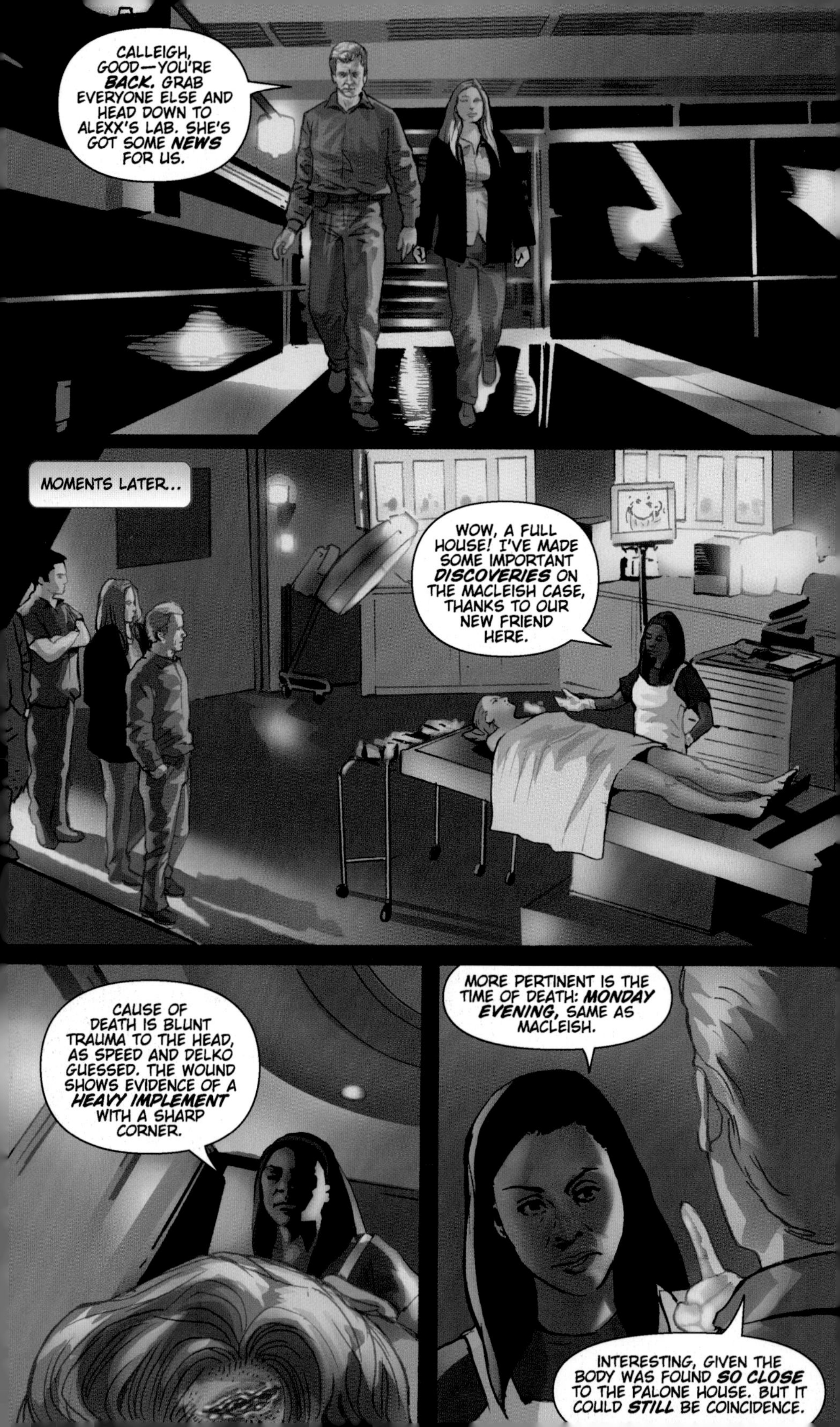
CALLEIGH, GOOD—YOU'RE BACK. GRAB EVERYONE ELSE AND HEAD DOWN TO ALEXX'S LAB. SHE'S GOT SOME NEWS FOR US.
MOMENTS LATER..
WOW, A FULL HOUSE! I'VE MADE SOME IMPORTANT DISCOVERIES ON THE MACLEISH CASE, THANKS TO OUR NEW FRIEND HERE.
CAUSE OF DEATH IS BLUNT TRAUMA TO THE HEAD, AS SPEED AND DELKO GUESSED. THE WOUND SHOWS EVIDENCE OF A HEAVY IMPLEMENT WITH A SHARP CORNER.
MORE PERTINENT IS THE TIME OF DEATH: MONDAY EVENING, SAME AS MACLEISH.
INTERESTING, GIVEN THE BODY WAS FOUND SO CLOSE TO THE PALONE HOUSE. BUT IT COULD STILL BE COINCIDENCE.

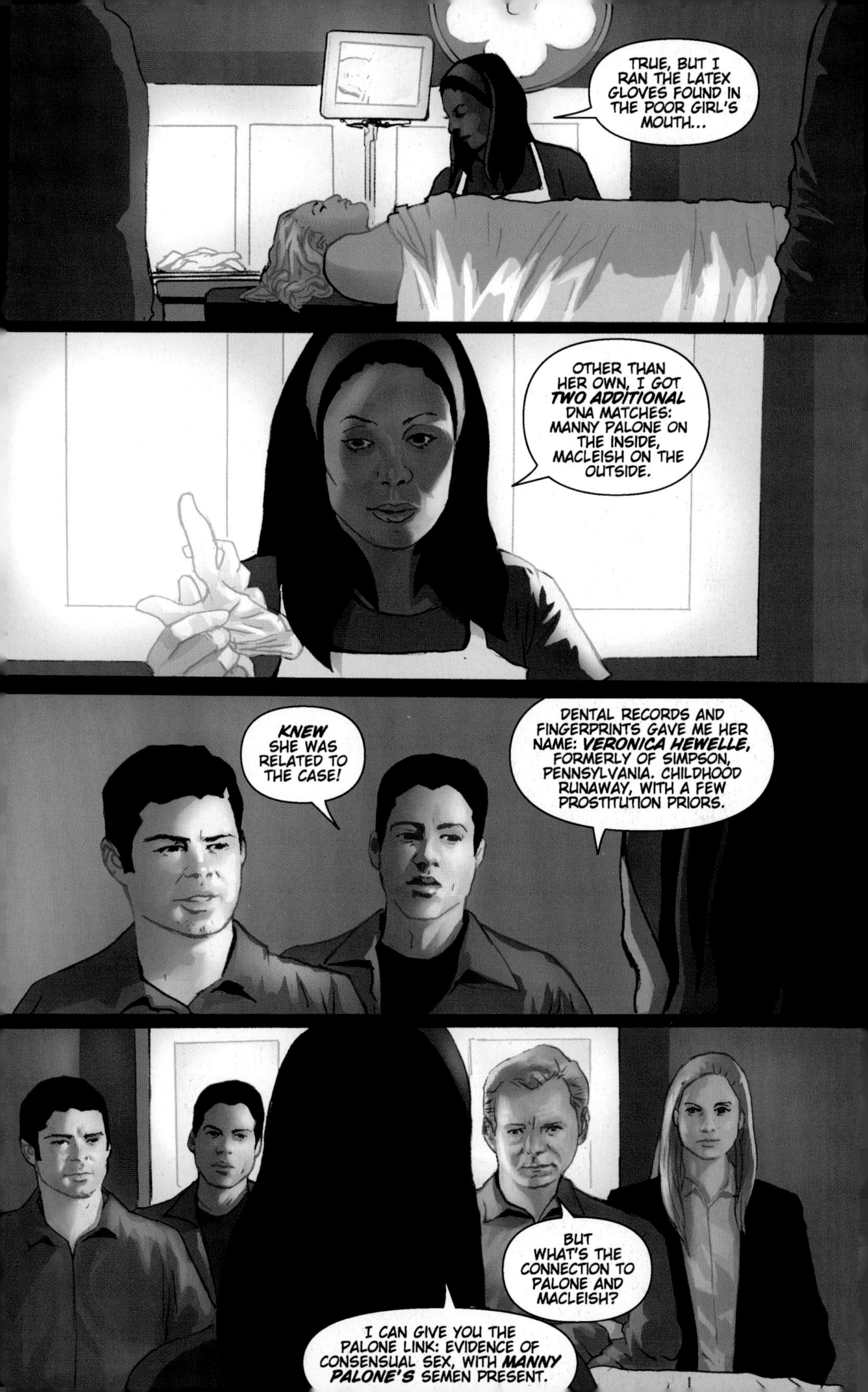
TRUE, BUT I RAN THE LATEX GLOVES FOUND IN THE POOR GIRL'S MOUTH...
OTHER THAN HER OWN, I GOT TWO ADDITIONAL DNA MATCHES: MANNY PALONE ON THE INSIDE, MACLEISH ON THE OUTSIDE.
KNEW SHE WAS RELATED TO THE CASE!
DENTAL RECORDS AND FINGERPRINTS GAVE ME HER NAME: VERONICA HEWELLE, FORMERLY OF SIMPSON, PENNSYLVANIA. CHILDHOOD RUNAWAY, WITH A FEW PROSTITUTION PRIORS.
BUT WHAT'S THE CONNECTION TO PALONE AND MACLEISH?
I CAN GIVE YOU THE PALONE LINK: EVIDENCE OF CONSENSUAL SEX, WITH MANNY PALONE'S SEMEN PRESENT.

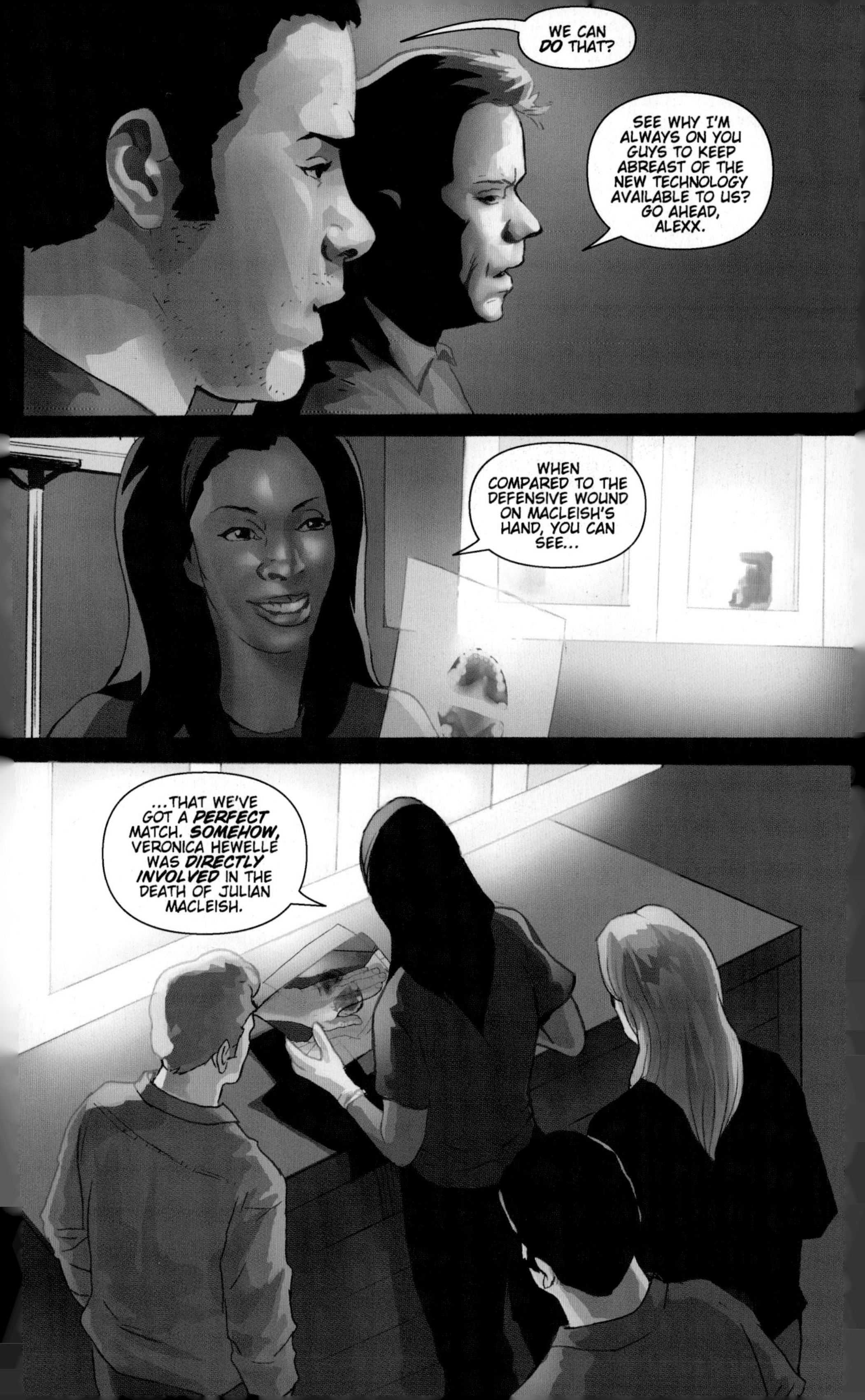
WE CAN DO THAT?
SEE WHY I'M ALWAYS ON YOU GUYS TO KEEP ABREAST OF THE NEW TECHNOLOGY AVAILABLE TO US? GO AHEAD, ALEXX.
WHEN COMPARED TO THE DEFENSIVE WOUND ON MACLEISH'S HAND, YOU CAN SEE...
...THAT WE'VE GOT A PERFECT MATCH. SOMEHOW, VERONICA HEWELLE WAS DIRECTLY INVOLVED IN THE DEATH OF JULIAN MACLEISH.

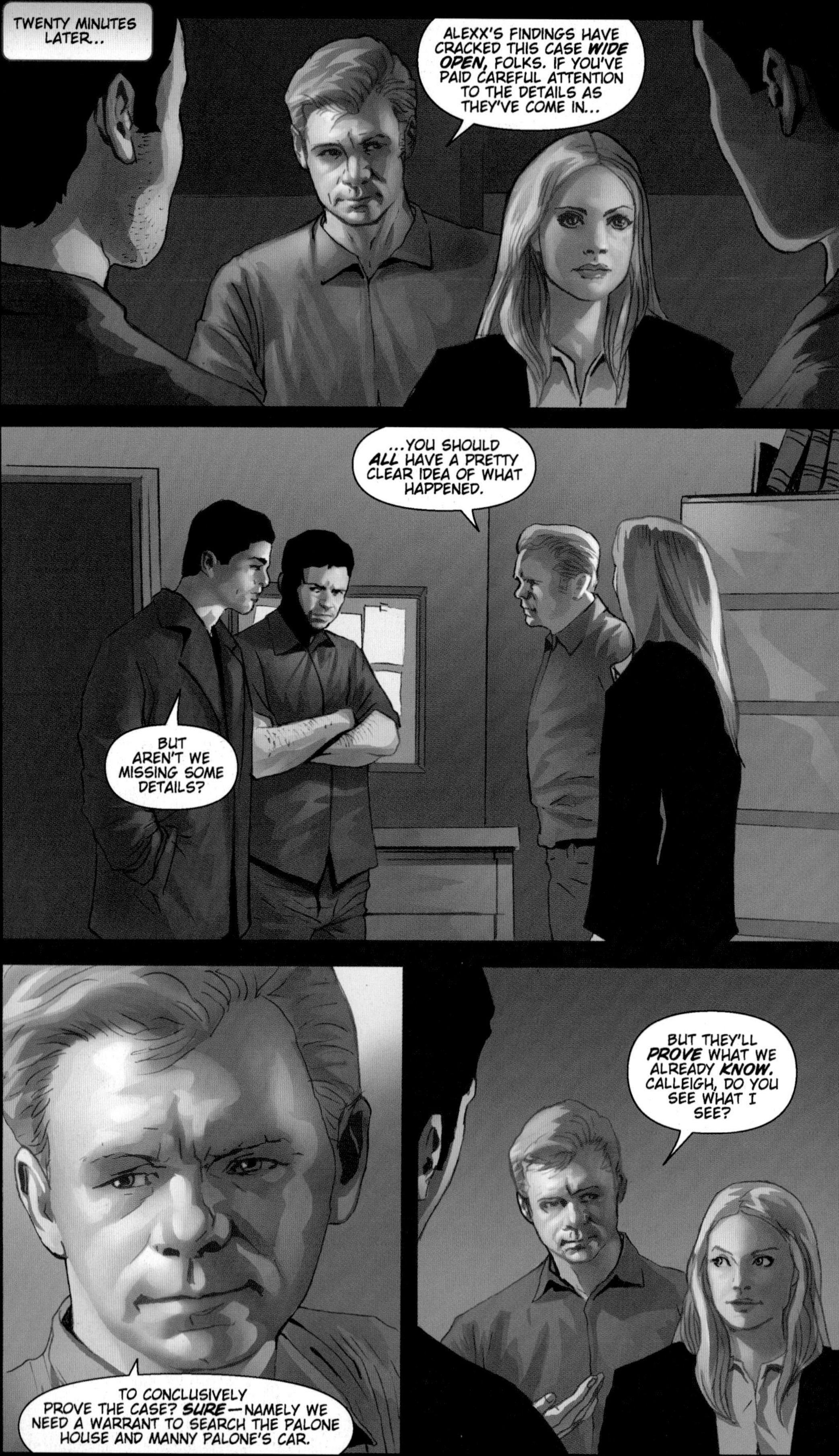
TWENTY MINUTES LATER...
ALEXX'S FINDINGS HAVE CRACKED THIS CASE WIDE OPEN, FOLKS. IF YOU'VE PAID CAREFUL ATTENTION TO THE DETAILS AS THEY'VE COME IN...
...YOU SHOULD ALL HAVE A PRETTY CLEAR IDEA OF WHAT HAPPENED.
BUT AREN'T WE MISSING SOME DETAILS?
TO CONCLUSIVELY PROVE THE CASE? SURE—NAMELY WE NEED A WARRANT TO SEARCH THE PALONE HOUSE AND MANNY PALONE'S CAR.
BUT THEY'LL PROVE WHAT WE ALREADY KNOW. CALLEIGH, DO YOU SEE WHAT I SEE?

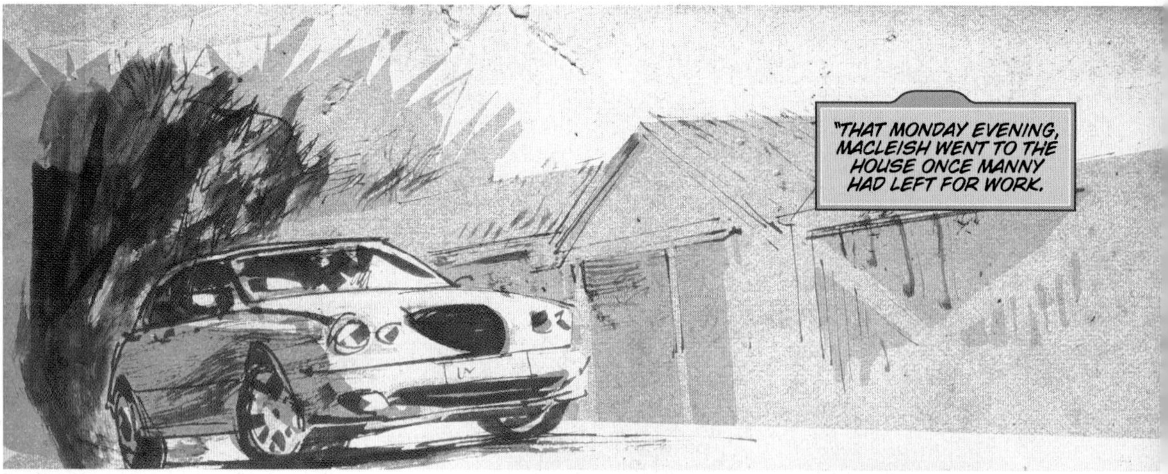
"THAT MONDAY EVENING, MACLEISH WENT TO THE HOUSE ONCE MANNY HAD LEFT FOR WORK.

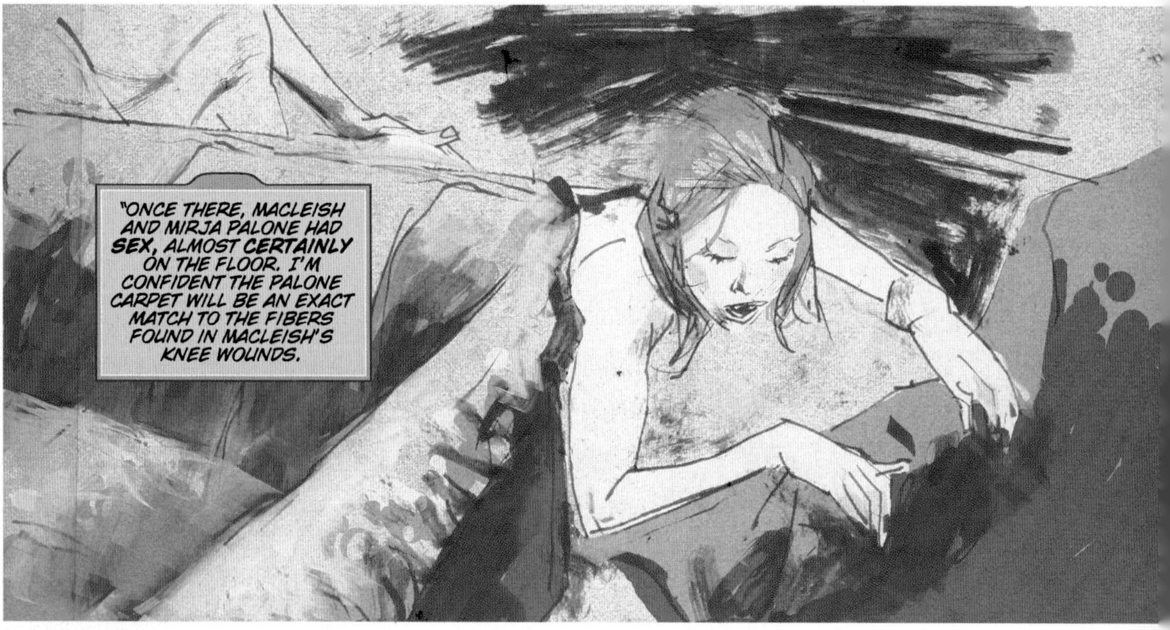
"ONCE THERE, MACLEISH AND MIRJA PALONE HAD SEX, ALMOST CERTAINLY ON THE FLOOR. I'M CONFIDENT THE PALONE CARPET WILL BE AN EXACT MATCH TO THE FIBERS FOUND IN MACLEISH'S KNEE WOUNDS.

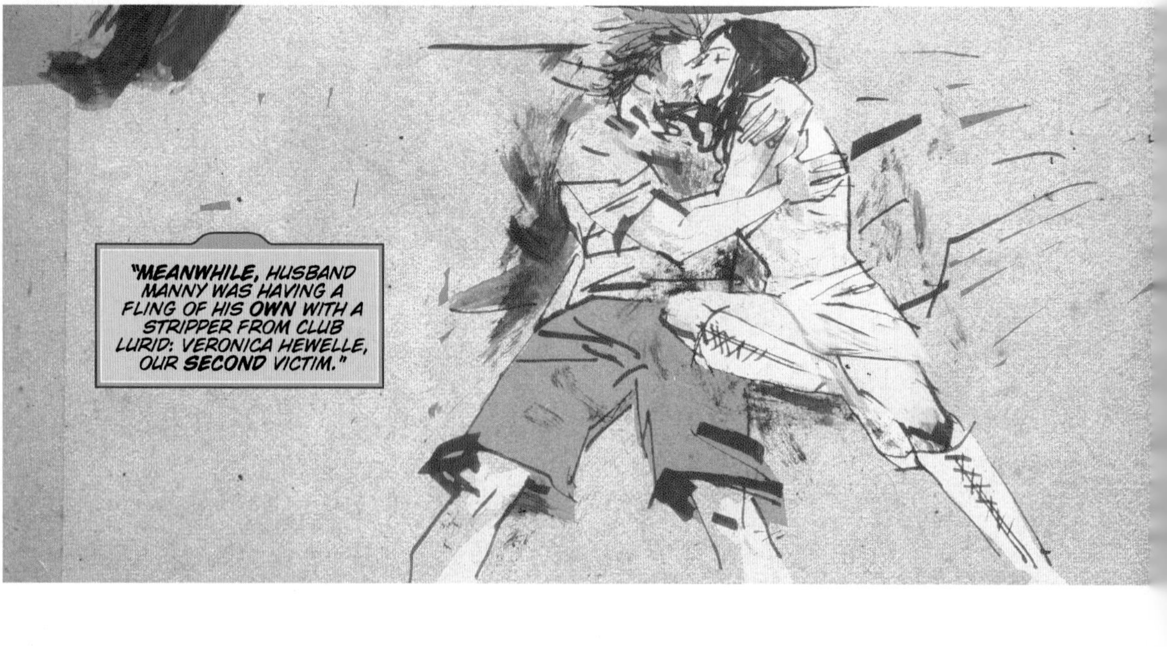
"MEANWHILE, HUSBAND MANNY WAS HAVING A FLING OF HIS OWN WITH A STRIPPER FROM CLUB LURID: VERONICA HEWELLE, OUR SECOND VICTIM."

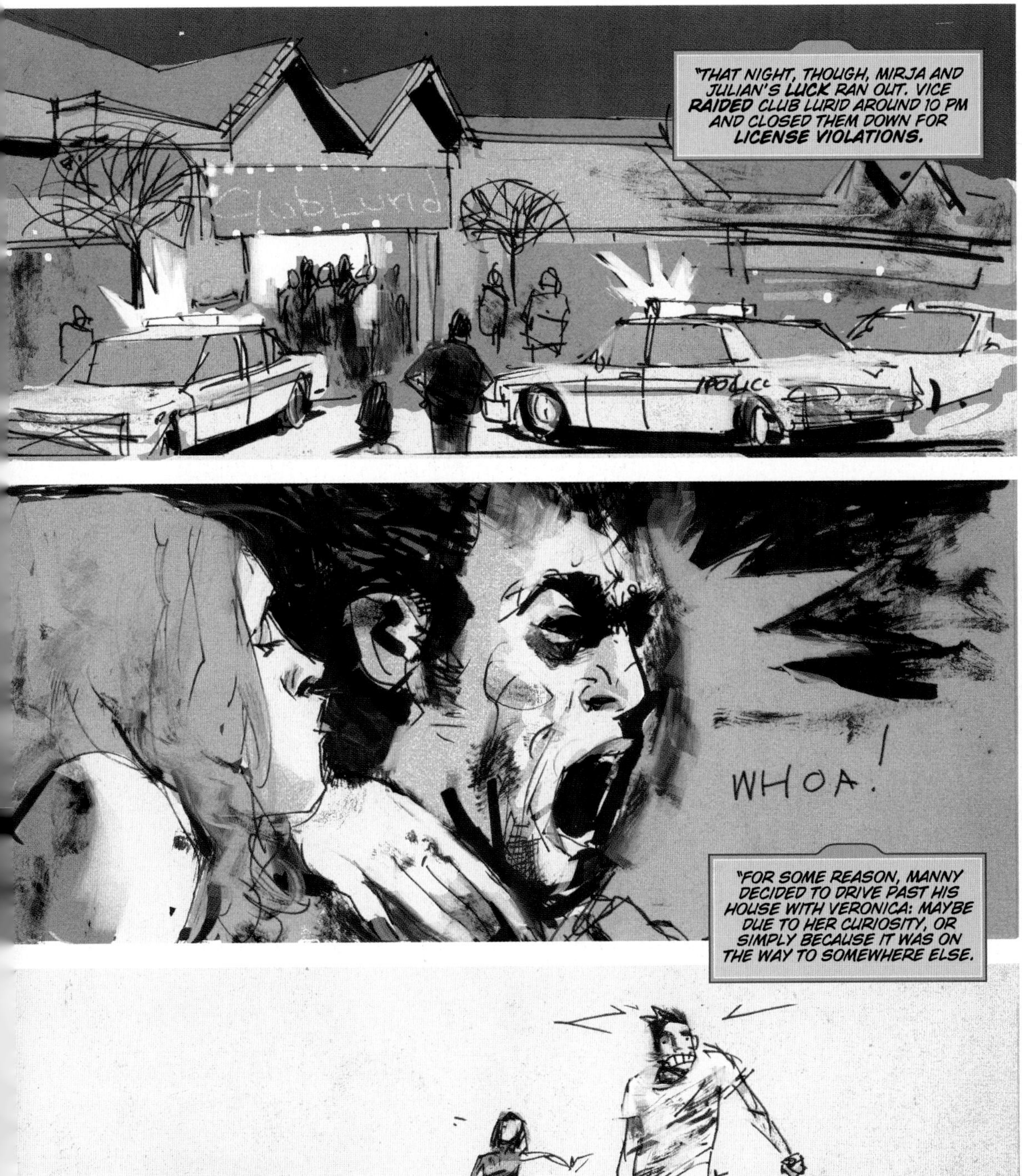
"THAT NIGHT, THOUGH, MIRJA AND JULIAN'S LUCK RAN OUT. VICE RAIDED CLUB LURID AROUND 10 PM AND CLOSED THEM DOWN FOR LICENSE VIOLATIONS.
ClubLurid
POLICE
WHOA!
"FOR SOME REASON, MANNY DECIDED TO DRIVE PAST HIS HOUSE WITH VERONICA: MAYBE DUE TO HER CURIOSITY, OR SIMPLY BECAUSE IT WAS ON THE WAY TO SOMEWHERE ELSE.
"IN ANY CASE, MANNY MUST'VE RECOGNIZED MIRJA'S BOSS'S CAR PARKED OUTSIDE AND THE LIGHTS ON IN THE HOUSE, AND PASSION TOOK OVER."

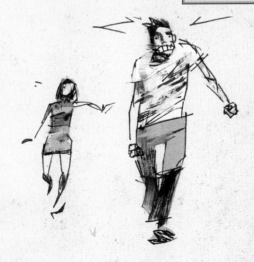

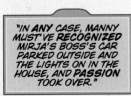

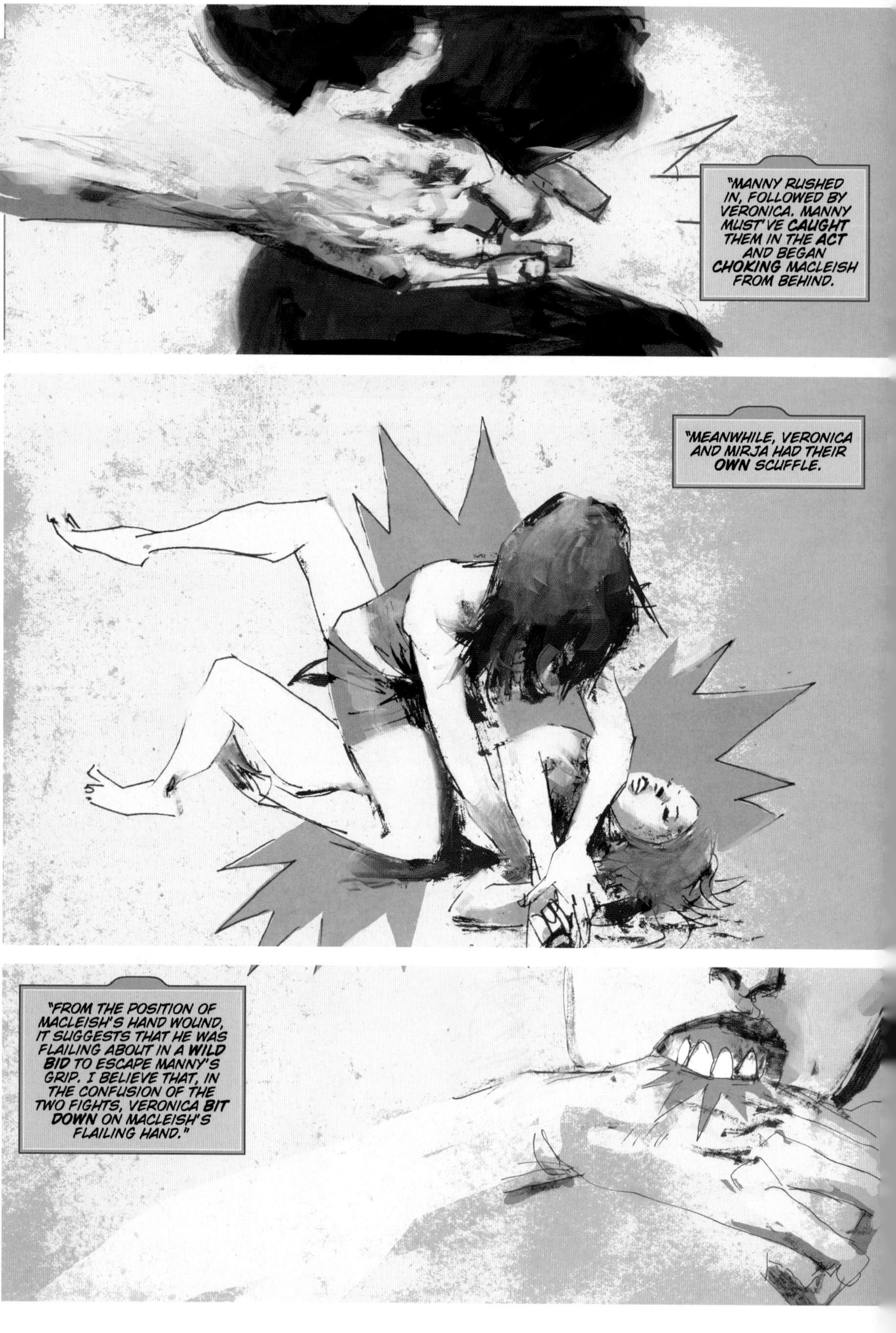
"MANNY RUSHED IN, FOLLOWED BY VERONICA. MANNY MUST'VE CAUGHT THEM IN THE ACT AND BEGAN CHOKING MACLEISH FROM BEHIND.
"MEANWHILE, VERONICA AND MIRJA HAD THEIR OWN SCUFFLE.
"FROM THE POSITION OF MACLEISH'S HAND WOUND, IT SUGGESTS THAT HE WAS FLAILING ABOUT IN A WILD BID TO ESCAPE MANNY'S GRIP. I BELIEVE THAT, IN THE CONFUSION OF THE TWO FIGHTS, VERONICA BIT DOWN ON MACLEISH'S FLAILING HAND."

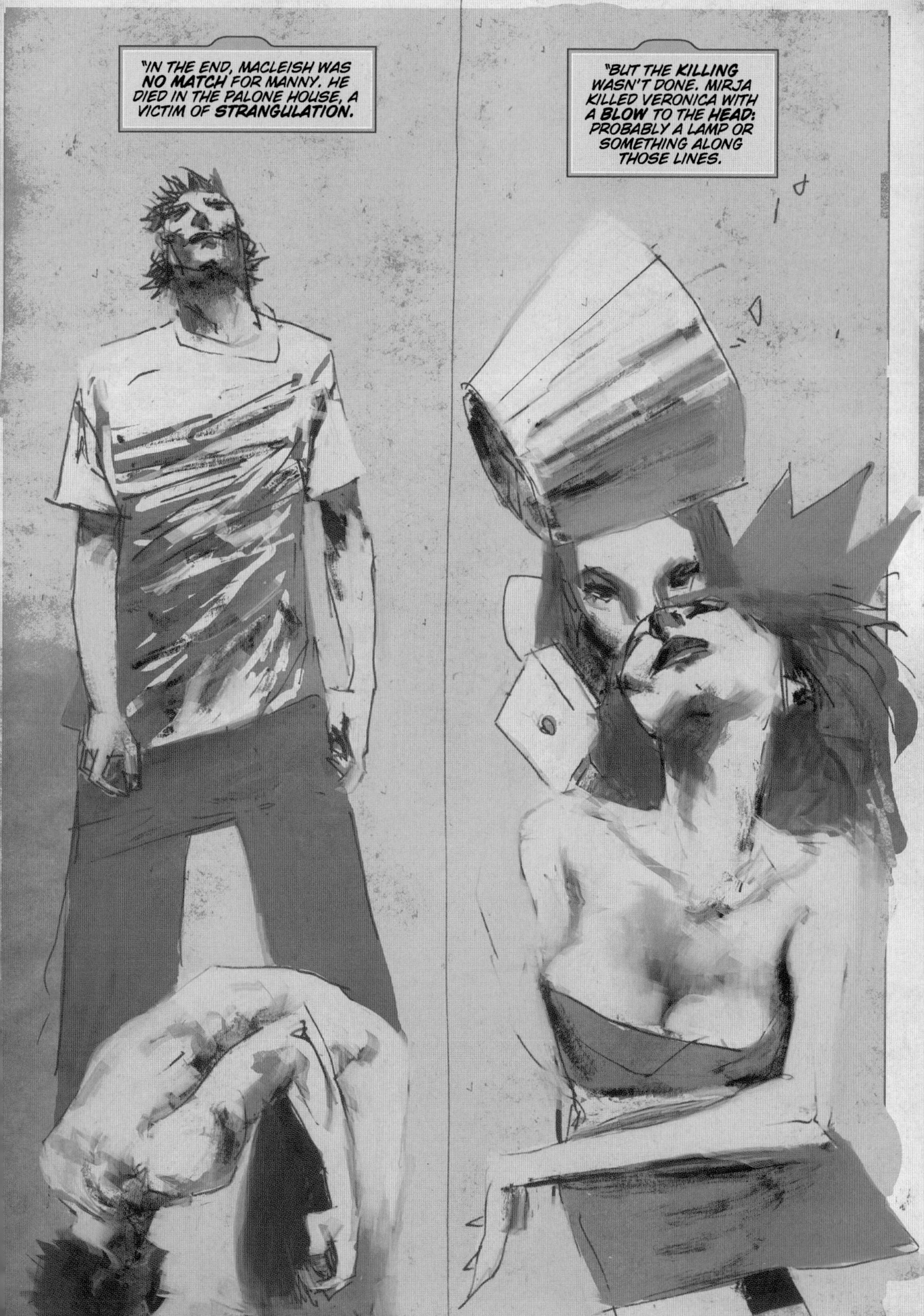
"IN THE END, MACLEISH WAS NO MATCH FOR MANNY. HE DIED IN THE PALONE HOUSE, A VICTIM OF STRANGULATION.
"BUT THE KILLING WASN'T DONE. MIRJA KILLED VERONICA WITH A BLOW TO THE HEAD: PROBABLY A LAMP OR SOMETHING ALONG THOSE LINES.

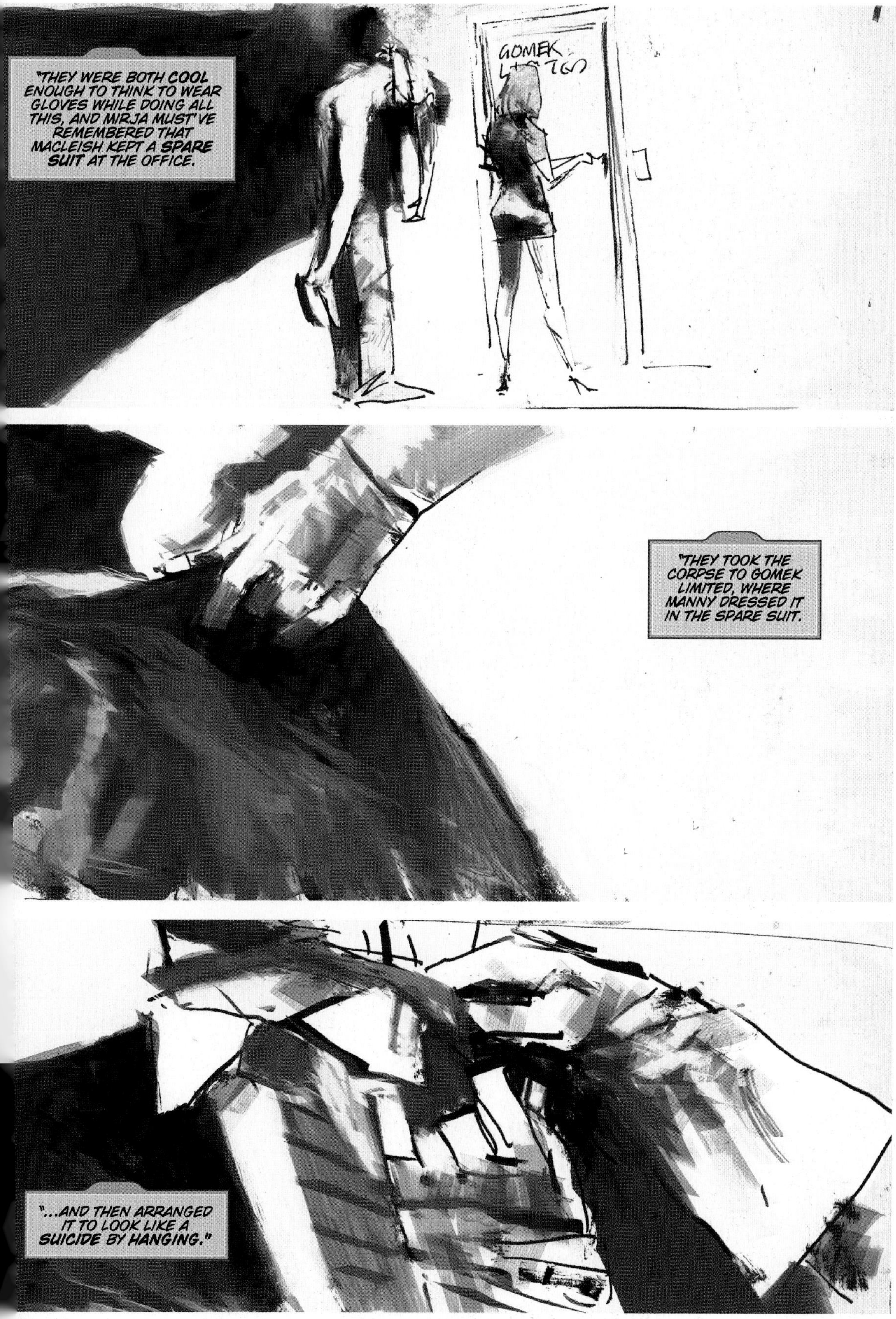
"THEY WERE BOTH COOL ENOUGH TO THINK TO WEAR GLOVES WHILE DOING ALL THIS, AND MIRJA MUST'VE REMEMBERED THAT MACLEISH KEPT A SPARE SUIT AT THE OFFICE.
GOMEK
"THEY TOOK THE CORPSE TO GOMEK LIMITED, WHERE MANNY DRESSED IT IN THE SPARE SUIT.
"...AND THEN ARRANGED IT TO LOOK LIKE A SUICIDE BY HANGING."

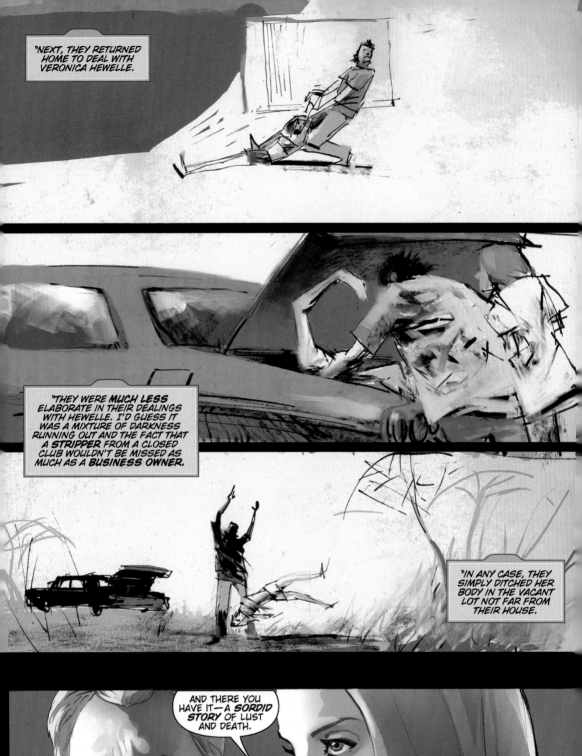

"NEXT, THEY RETURNED HOME TO DEAL WITH VERONICA HEWELLE.

"THEY WERE MUCH LESS ELABORATE IN THEIR DEALINGS WITH HEWELLE. I'D GUESS IT WAS A MIXTURE OF DARKNESS RUNNING OUT AND THE FACT THAT A STRIPPER FROM A CLOSED CLUB WOULDN'T BE MISSED AS MUCH AS A BUSINESS OWNER.

"IN ANY CASE, THEY SIMPLY DITCHED HER BODY IN THE VACANT LOT NOT FAR FROM THEIR HOUSE.

AND THERE YOU HAVE IT—A SORDID STORY OF LUST AND DEATH.

LET'S NOT FORGET THAT THERE ARE TWO VERY REAL, VERY DEAD PEOPLE AS A RESULT OF THIS STORY, CALLEIGH.

BUT GOOD JOB WITH THE CALL, NONETHELESS.

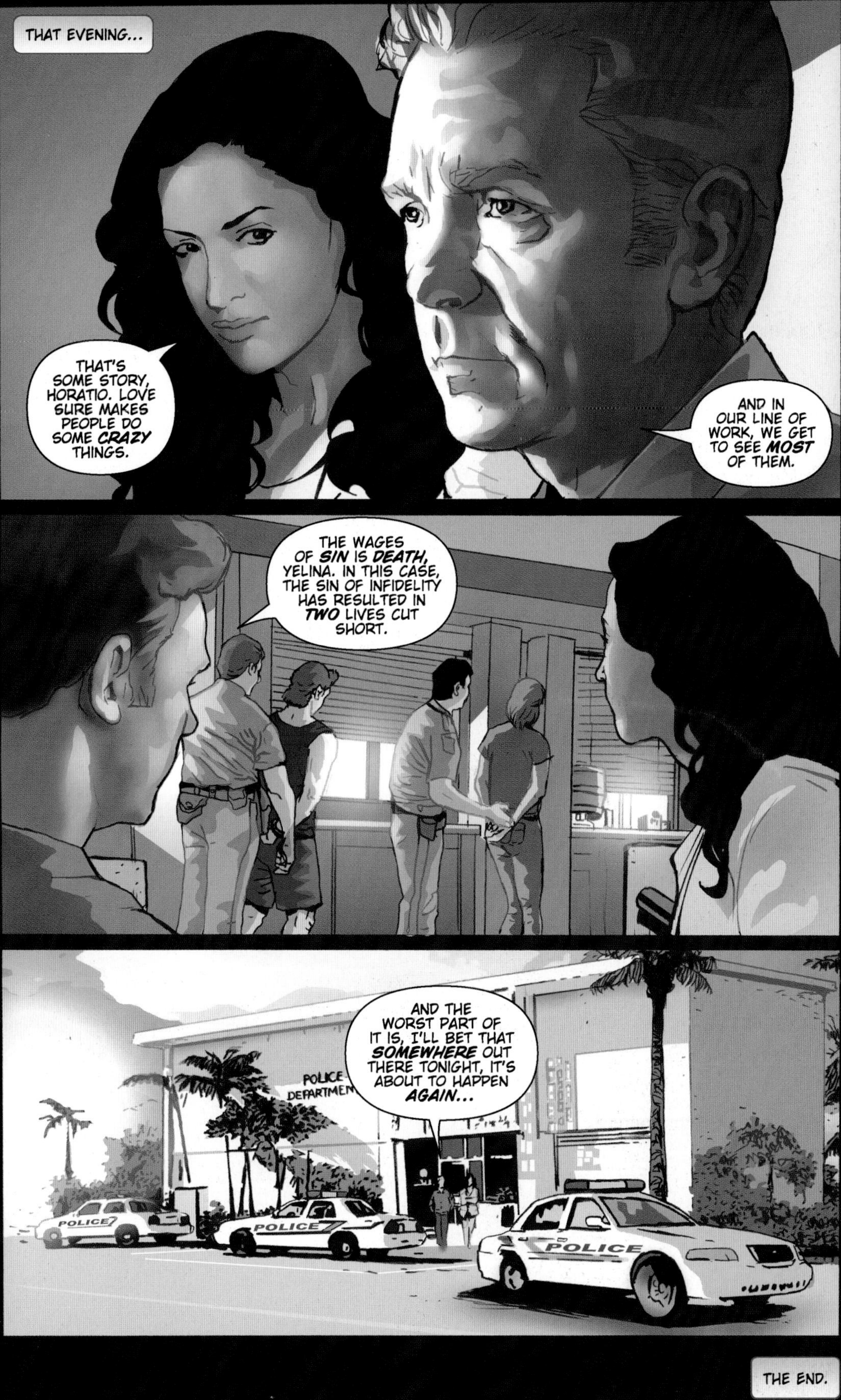
THAT EVENING...
THAT'S SOME STORY, HORATIO. LOVE SURE MAKES PEOPLE DO SOME CRAZY THINGS.
AND IN OUR LINE OF WORK, WE GET TO SEE MOST OF THEM.
THE WAGES OF SIN IS DEATH, YELINA. IN THIS CASE, THE SIN OF INFIDELITY HAS RESULTED IN TWO LIVES CUT SHORT.
POLICE DEPARTMEN
AND THE WORST PART OF IT IS, I'LL BET THAT SOMEWHERE OUT THERE TONIGHT, IT'S ABOUT TO HAPPEN AGAIN...
POLICE
POLICE
POLICE
THE END.

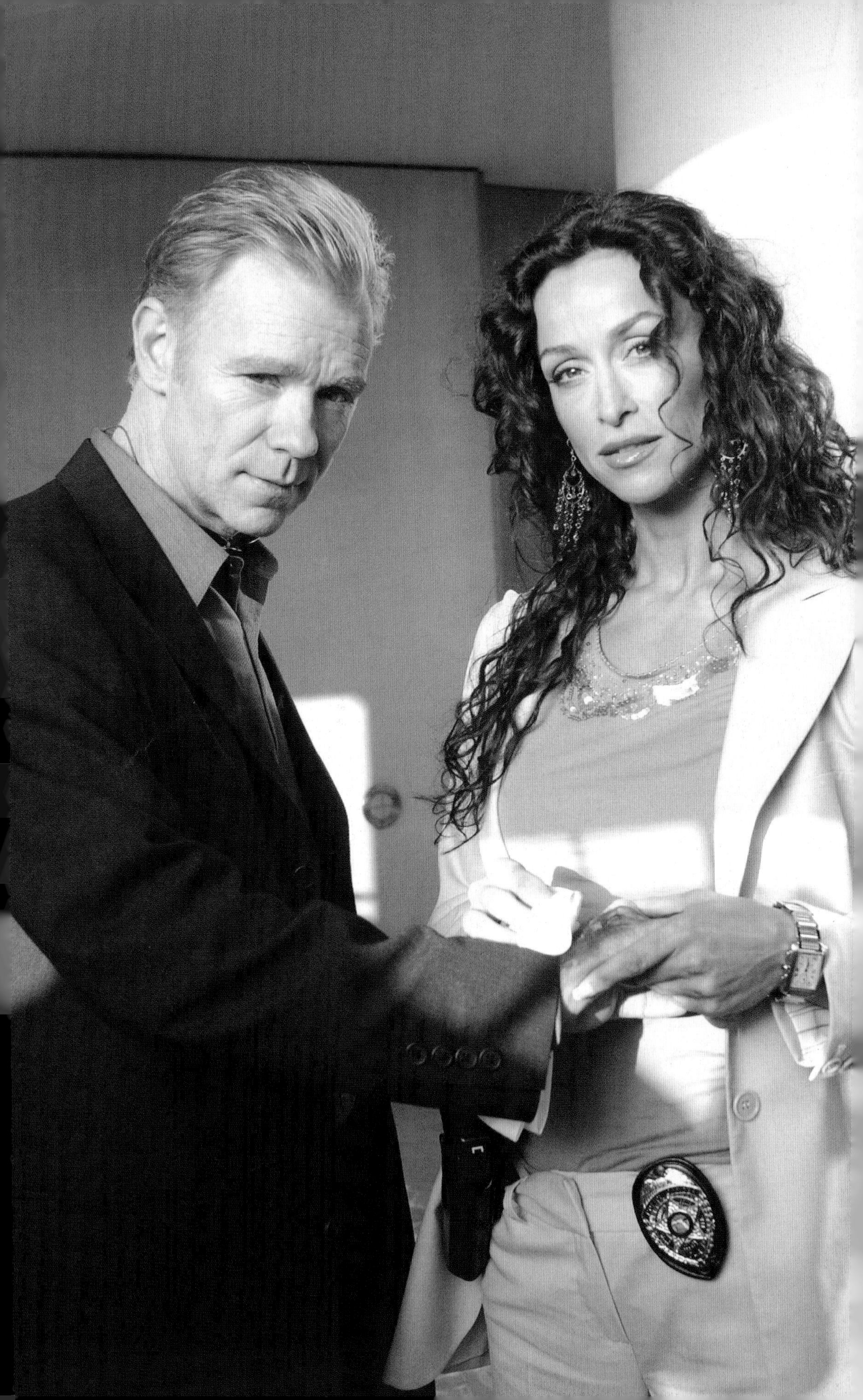

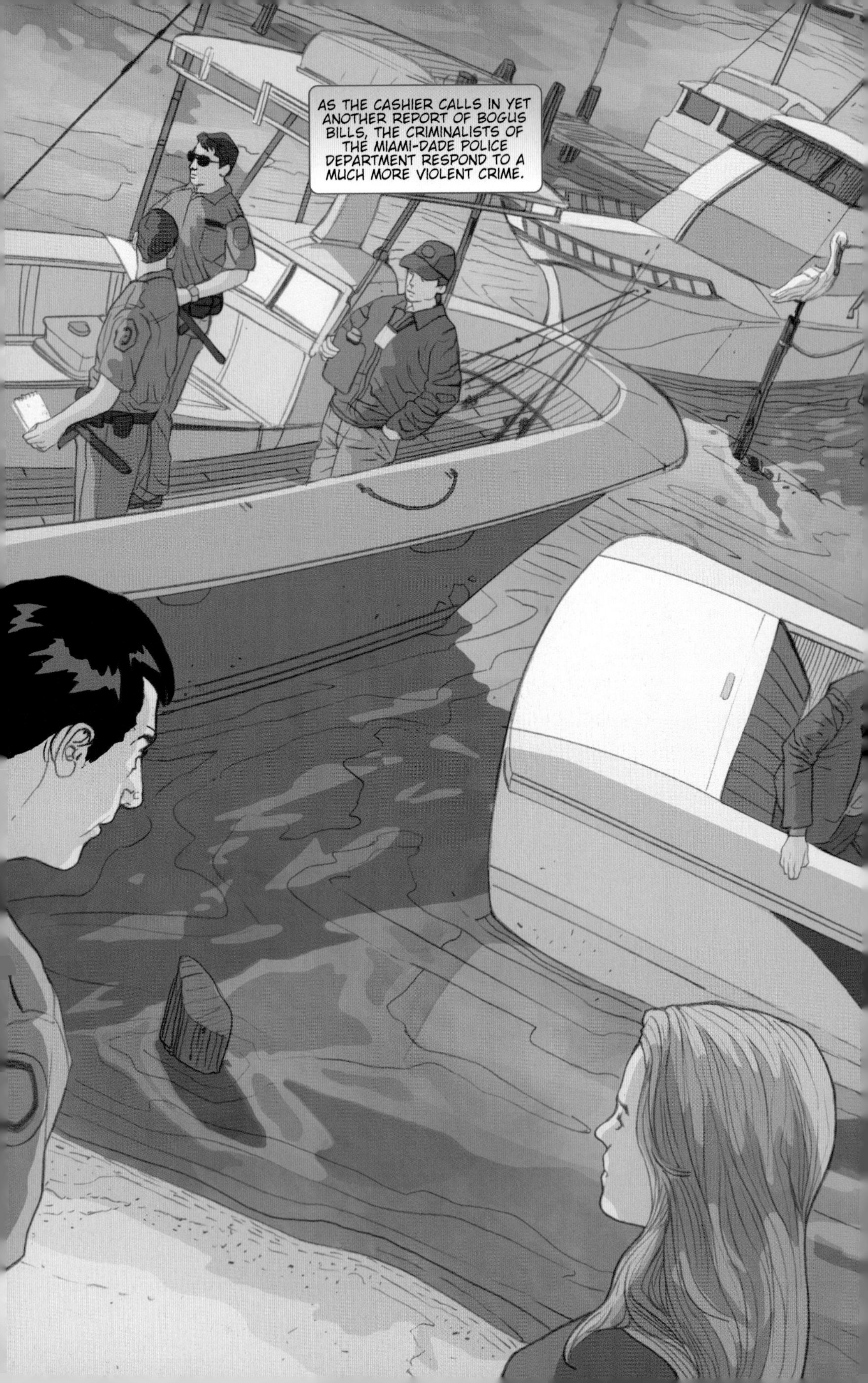
AS THE CASHIER CALLS IN YET ANOTHER REPORT OF BOGUS BILLS, THE CRIMINALISTS OF THE MIAMI-DADE POLICE DEPARTMENT RESPOND TO A MUCH MORE VIOLENT CRIME.

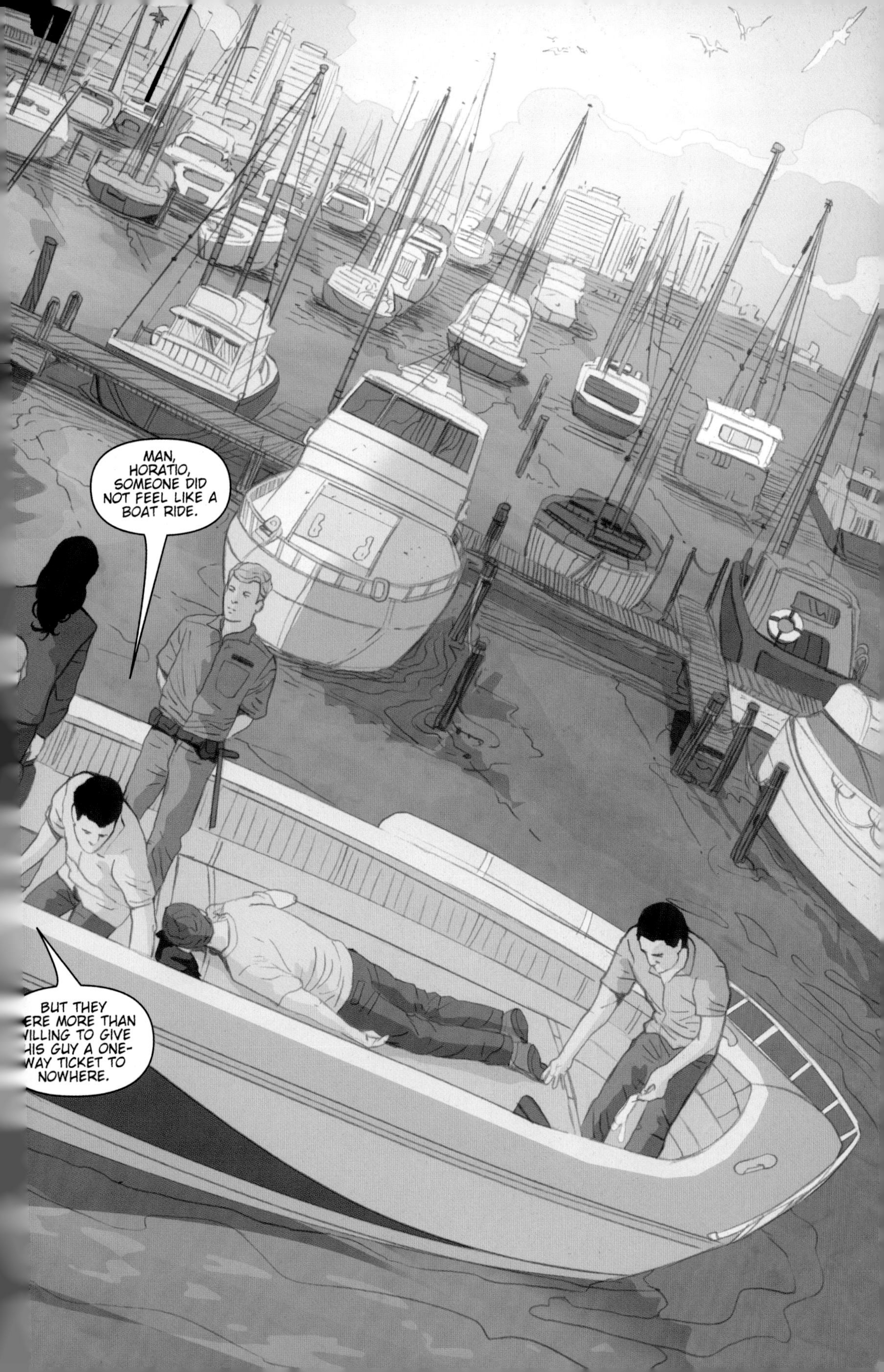
MAN, HORATIO, SOMEONE DID NOT FEEL LIKE A BOAT RIDE.
BUT THEY ERE MORE THAN VILLING TO GIVE HIS GUY A ONE-WAY TICKET TO NOWHERE.

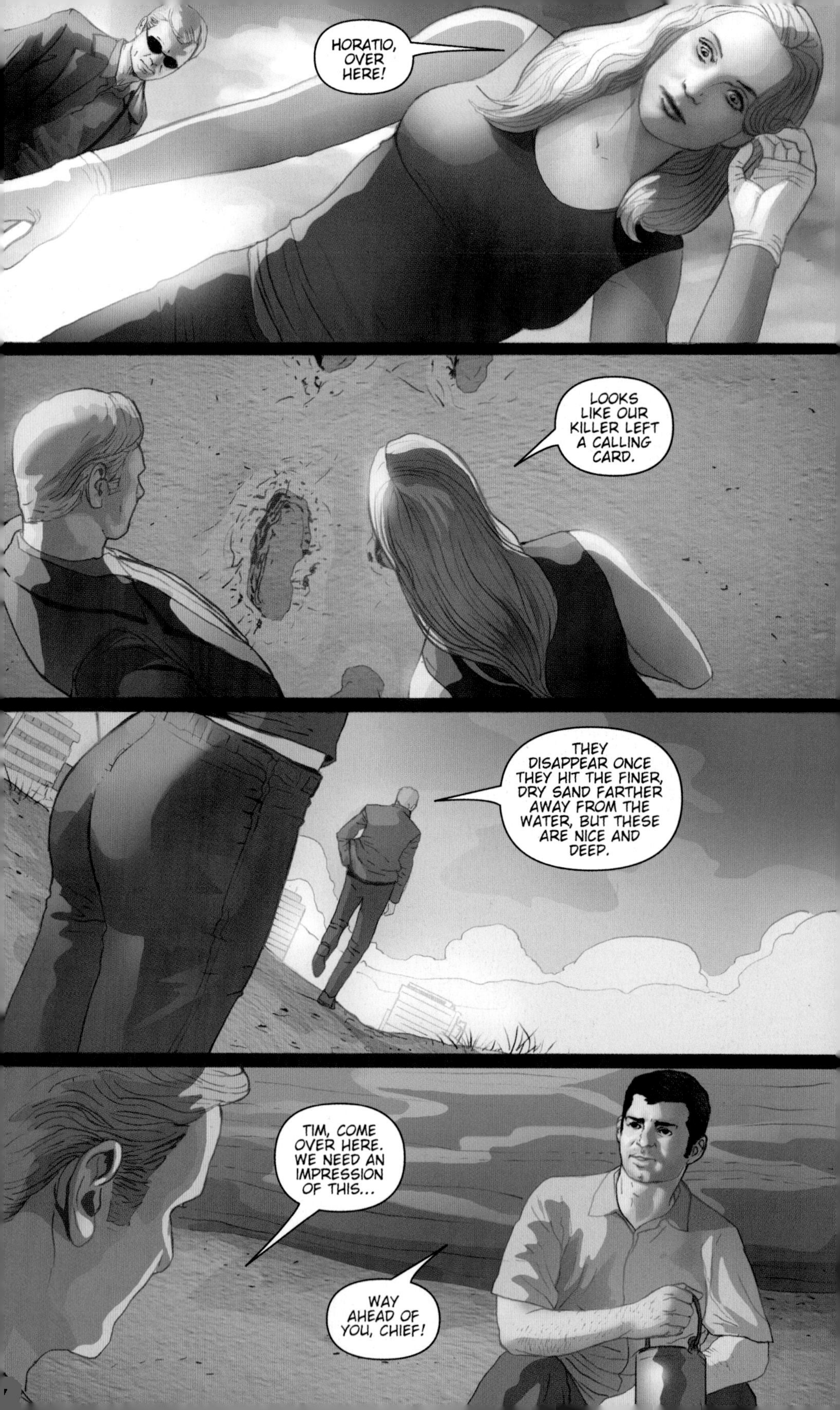
HORATIO, OVER HERE!
LOOKS LIKE OUR KILLER LEFT A CALLING CARD.
THEY DISAPPEAR ONCE THEY HIT THE FINER, DRY SAND FARTHER AWAY FROM THE WATER, BUT THESE ARE NICE AND DEEP.
TIM, COME OVER HERE. WE NEED AN IMPRESSION OF THIS...
WAY AHEAD OF YOU, CHIEF!

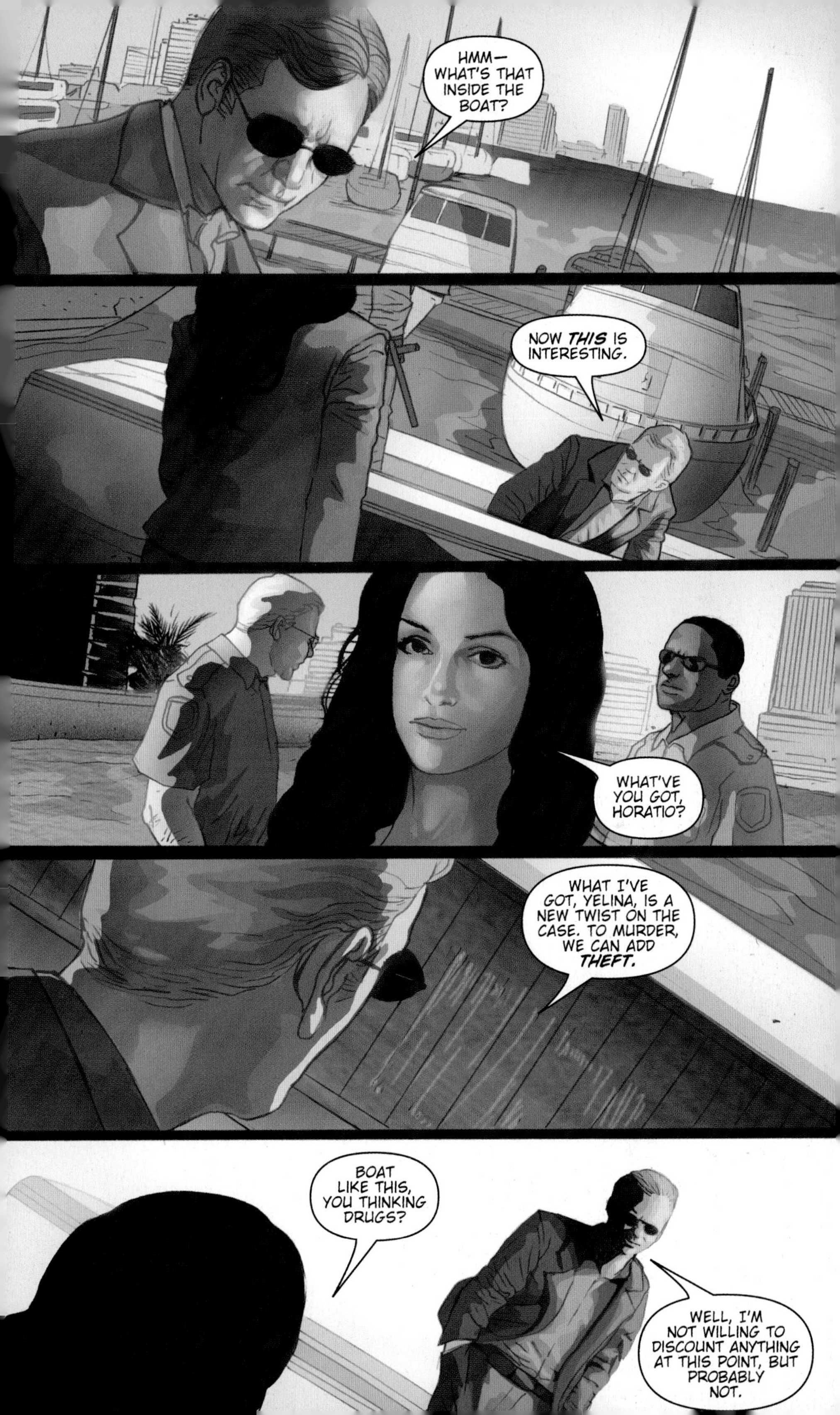
HMM— WHAT'S THAT INSIDE THE BOAT?
NOW THIS IS INTERESTING.
WHAT'VE YOU GOT, HORATIO?
WHAT I'VE GOT, YELINA, IS A NEW TWIST ON THE CASE. TO MURDER, WE CAN ADD THEFT.
BOAT LIKE THIS, YOU THINKING DRUGS?
WELL, I'M NOT WILLING TO DISCOUNT ANYTHING AT THIS POINT, BUT PROBABLY NOT.

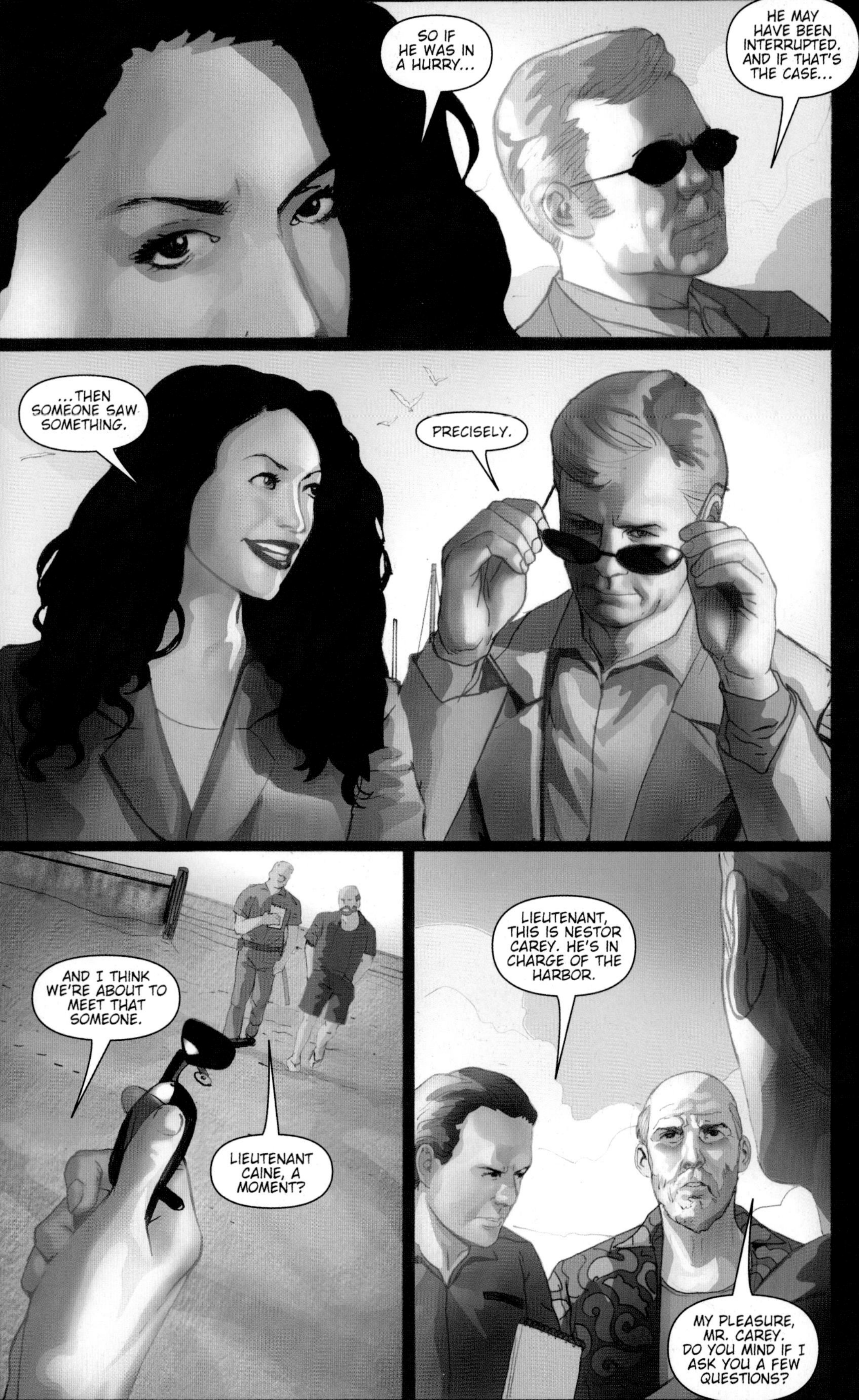
SO IF HE WAS IN A HURRY...
HE MAY HAVE BEEN INTERRUPTED. AND IF THAT'S THE CASE...
...THEN SOMEONE SAW SOMETHING.
PRECISELY.
AND I THINK WE'RE ABOUT TO MEET THAT SOMEONE.
LIEUTENANT CAINE, A MOMENT?
LIEUTENANT, THIS IS NESTOR CAREY. HE'S IN CHARGE OF THE HARBOR.
MY PLEASURE, MR. CAREY. DO YOU MIND IF I ASK YOU A FEW QUESTIONS?

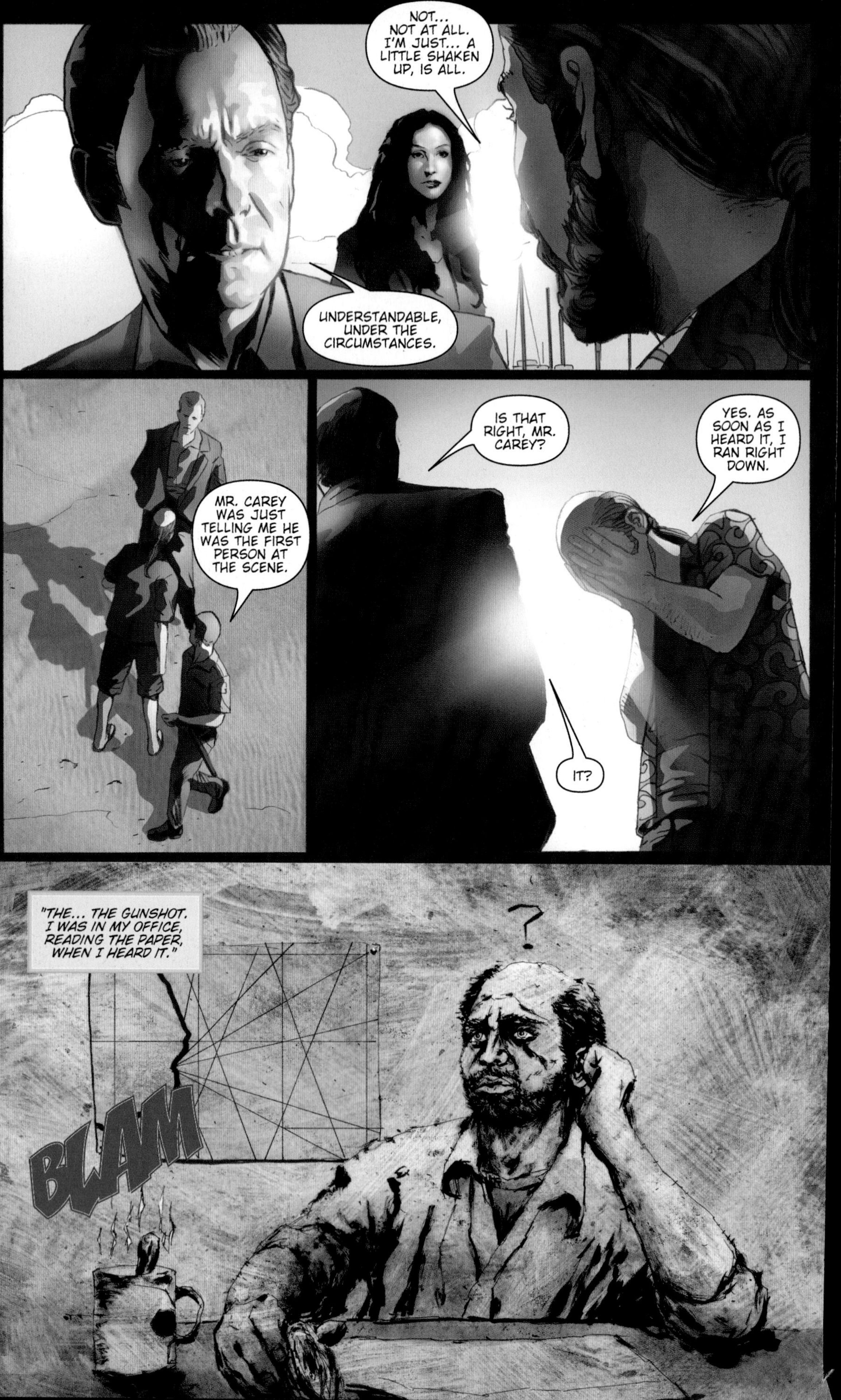
NOT... NOT AT ALL. I'M JUST... A LITTLE SHAKEN UP, IS ALL.
UNDERSTANDABLE, UNDER THE CIRCUMSTANCES.
MR. CAREY WAS JUST TELLING ME HE WAS THE FIRST PERSON AT THE SCENE.
IS THAT RIGHT, MR. CAREY?
YES. AS SOON AS I HEARD IT, I RAN RIGHT DOWN.
IT?
"THE... THE GUNSHOT. I WAS IN MY OFFICE, READING THE PAPER, WHEN I HEARD IT."
?
BLAM

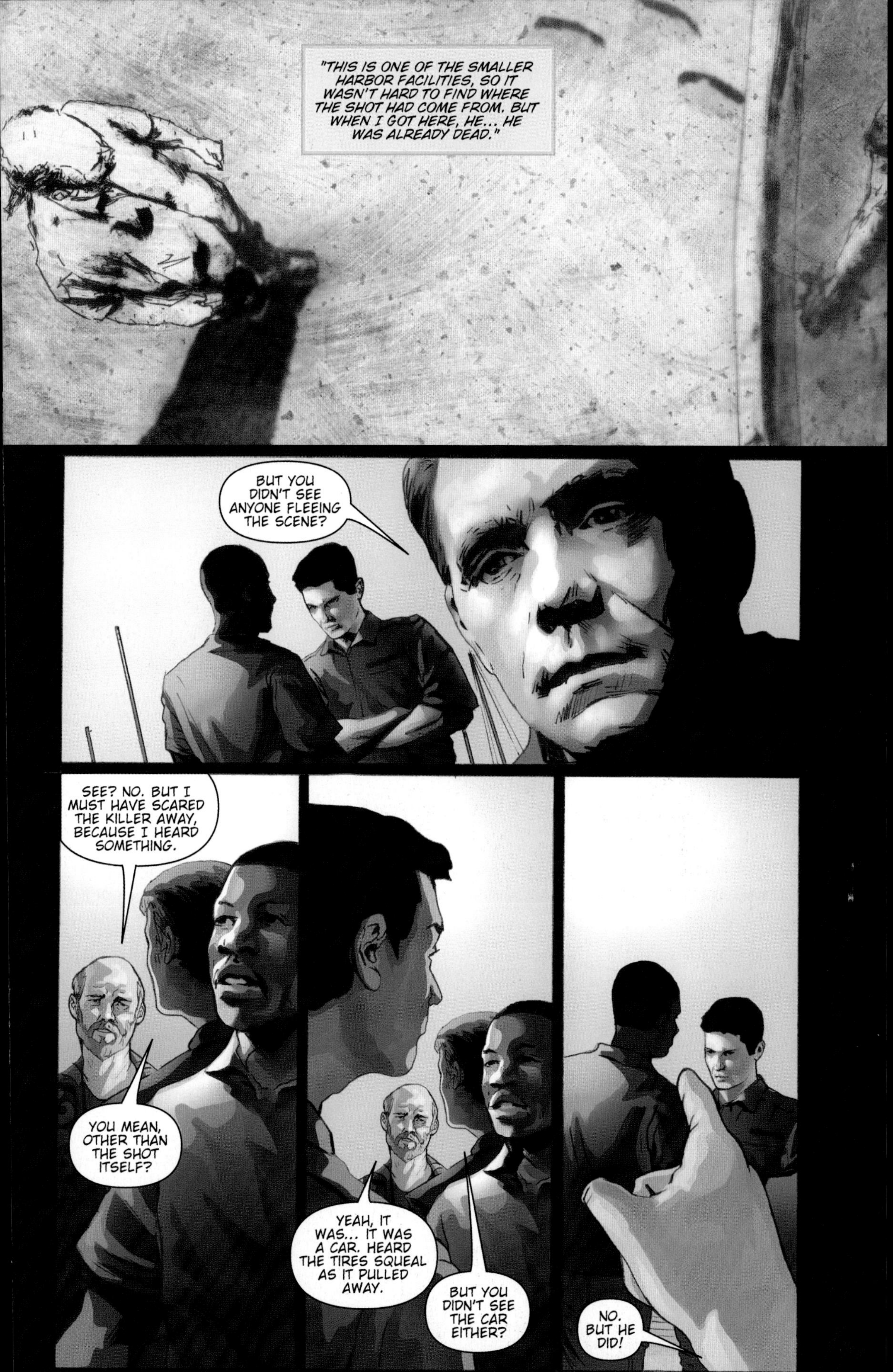
"THIS IS ONE OF THE SMALLER HARBOR FACILITIES, SO IT WASN'T HARD TO FIND WHERE THE SHOT HAD COME FROM. BUT WHEN I GOT HERE, HE... HE WAS ALREADY DEAD."
BUT YOU DIDN'T SEE ANYONE FLEEING THE SCENE?
SEE? NO. BUT I MUST HAVE SCARED THE KILLER AWAY, BECAUSE I HEARD SOMETHING.
YOU MEAN, OTHER THAN THE SHOT ITSELF?
YEAH, IT WAS... IT WAS A CAR. HEARD THE TIRES SQUEAL AS IT PULLED AWAY.
BUT YOU DIDN'T SEE THE CAR EITHER?
NO. BUT HE DID!

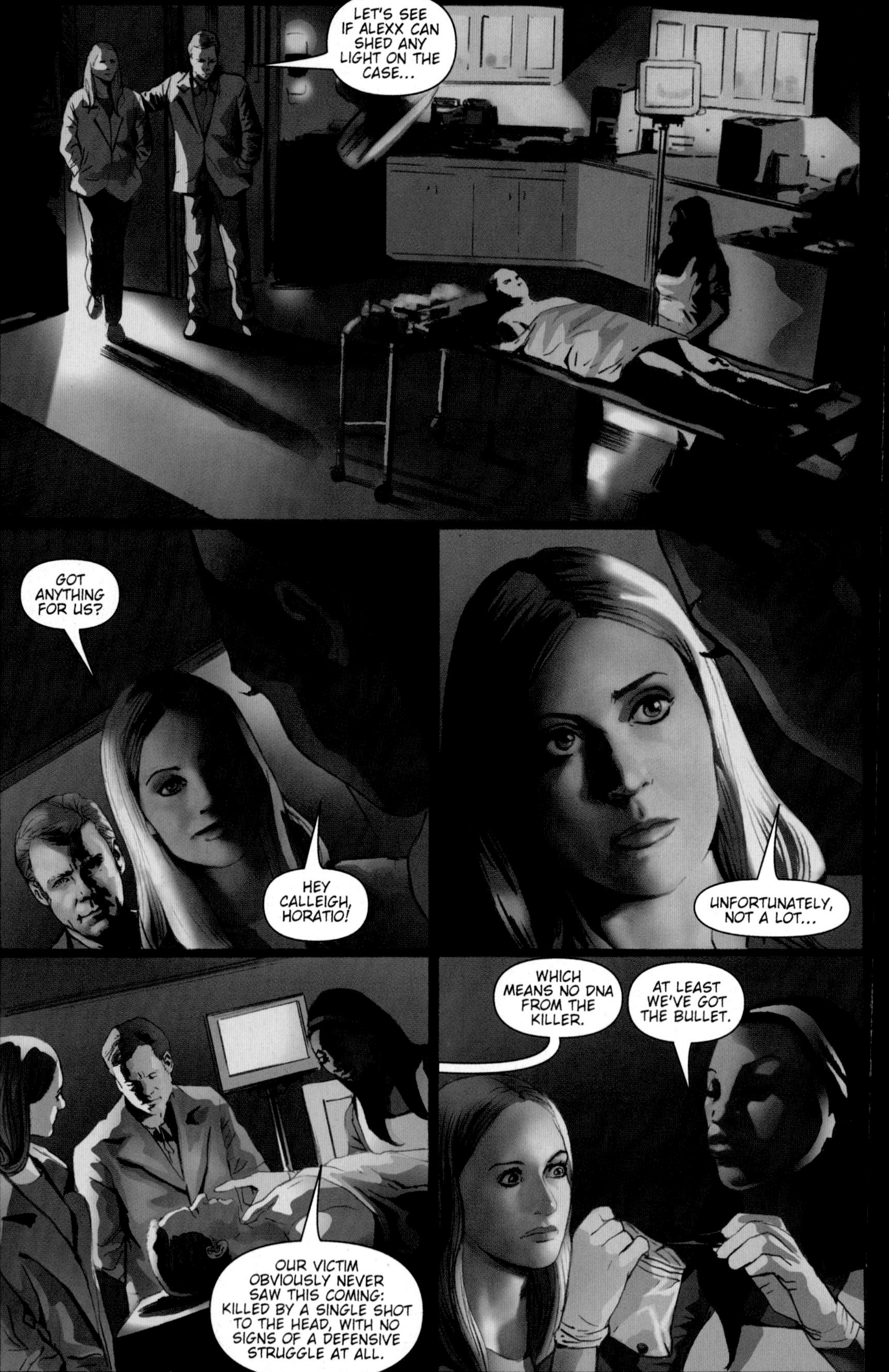
LET'S SEE IF ALEXX CAN SHED ANY LIGHT ON THE CASE...
GOT ANYTHING FOR US?
HEY CALLEIGH, HORATIO!
UNFORTUNATELY, NOT A LOT...
OUR VICTIM OBVIOUSLY NEVER SAW THIS COMING: KILLED BY A SINGLE SHOT TO THE HEAD, WITH NO SIGNS OF A DEFENSIVE STRUGGLE AT ALL.
WHICH MEANS NO DNA FROM THE KILLER.
AT LEAST WE'VE GOT THE BULLET.

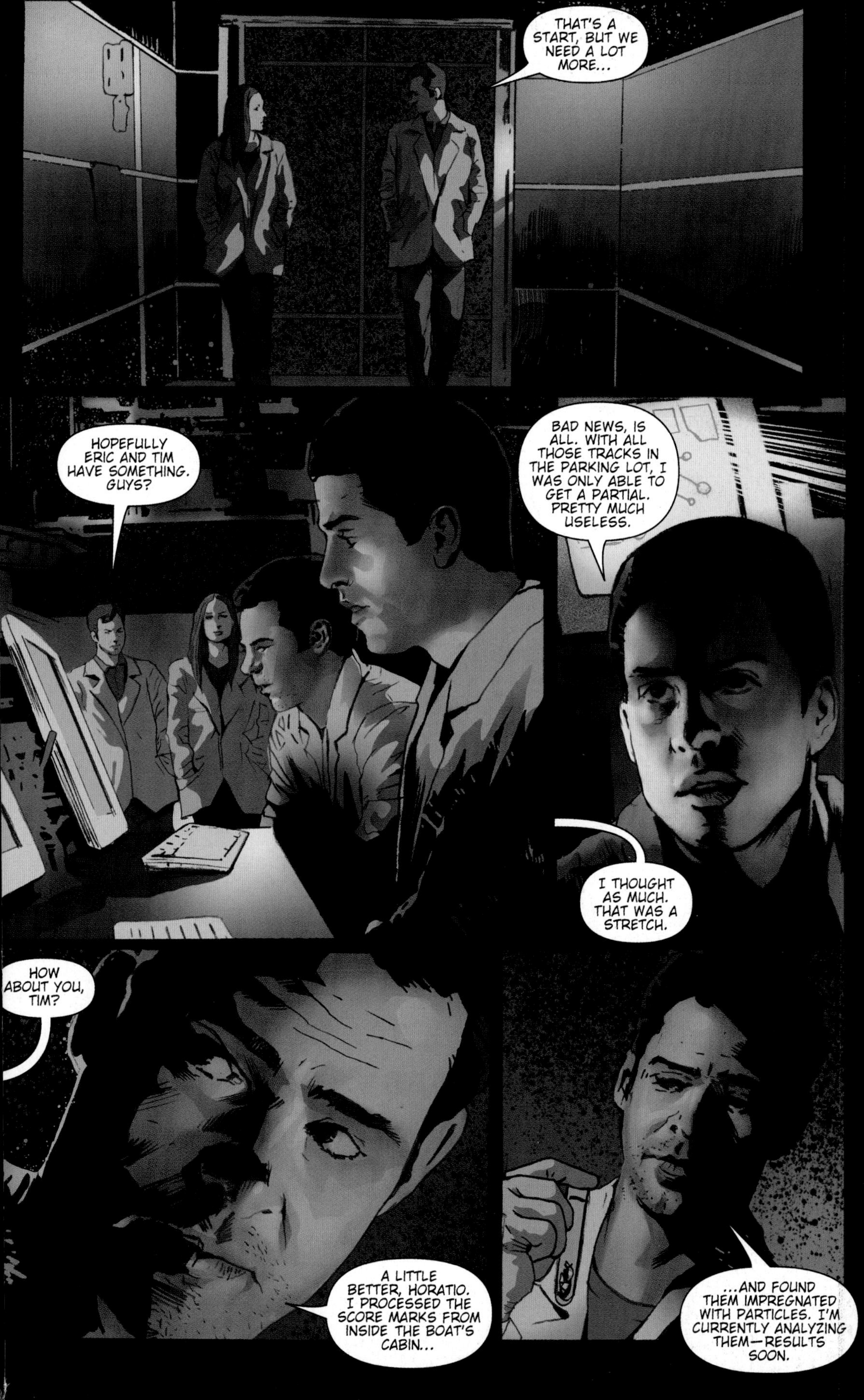
THAT'S A START, BUT WE NEED A LOT MORE...
HOPEFULLY ERIC AND TIM HAVE SOMETHING. GUYS?
BAD NEWS, IS ALL. WITH ALL THOSE TRACKS IN THE PARKING LOT, I WAS ONLY ABLE TO GET A PARTIAL. PRETTY MUCH USELESS.
I THOUGHT AS MUCH. THAT WAS A STRETCH.
HOW ABOUT YOU, TIM?
A LITTLE BETTER, HORATIO. I PROCESSED THE SCORE MARKS FROM INSIDE THE BOAT'S CABIN...
...AND FOUND THEM IMPREGNATED WITH PARTICLES. I'M CURRENTLY ANALYZING THEM—RESULTS SOON.

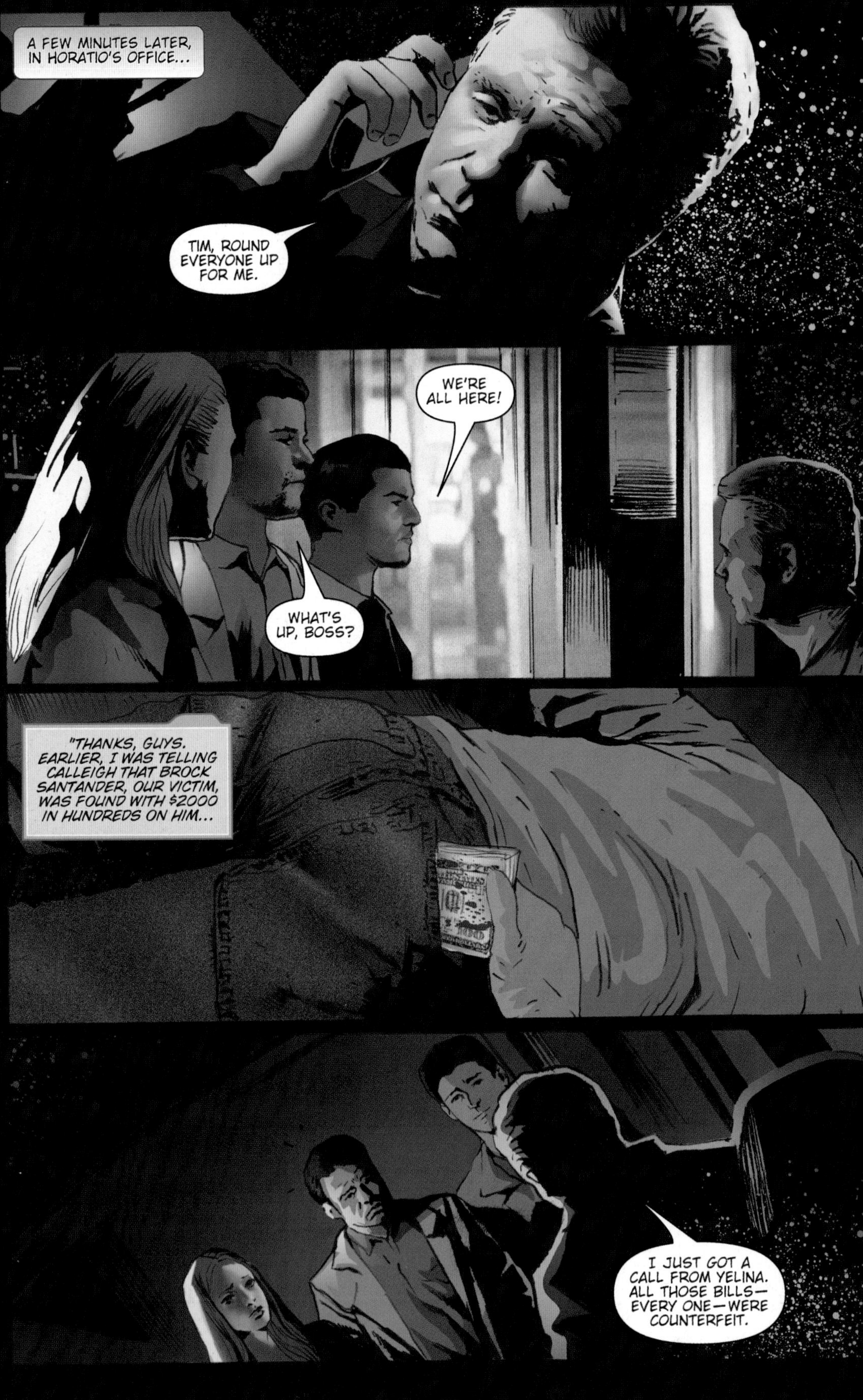
A FEW MINUTES LATER, IN HORATIO'S OFFICE...
TIM, ROUND EVERYONE UP FOR ME.
WE'RE ALL HERE!
WHAT'S UP, BOSS?
"THANKS, GUYS. EARLIER, I WAS TELLING CALLEIGH THAT BROCK SANTANDER, OUR VICTIM, WAS FOUND WITH $2000 IN HUNDREDS ON HIM...
I JUST GOT A CALL FROM YELINA. ALL THOSE BILLS—EVERY ONE—WERE COUNTERFEIT.

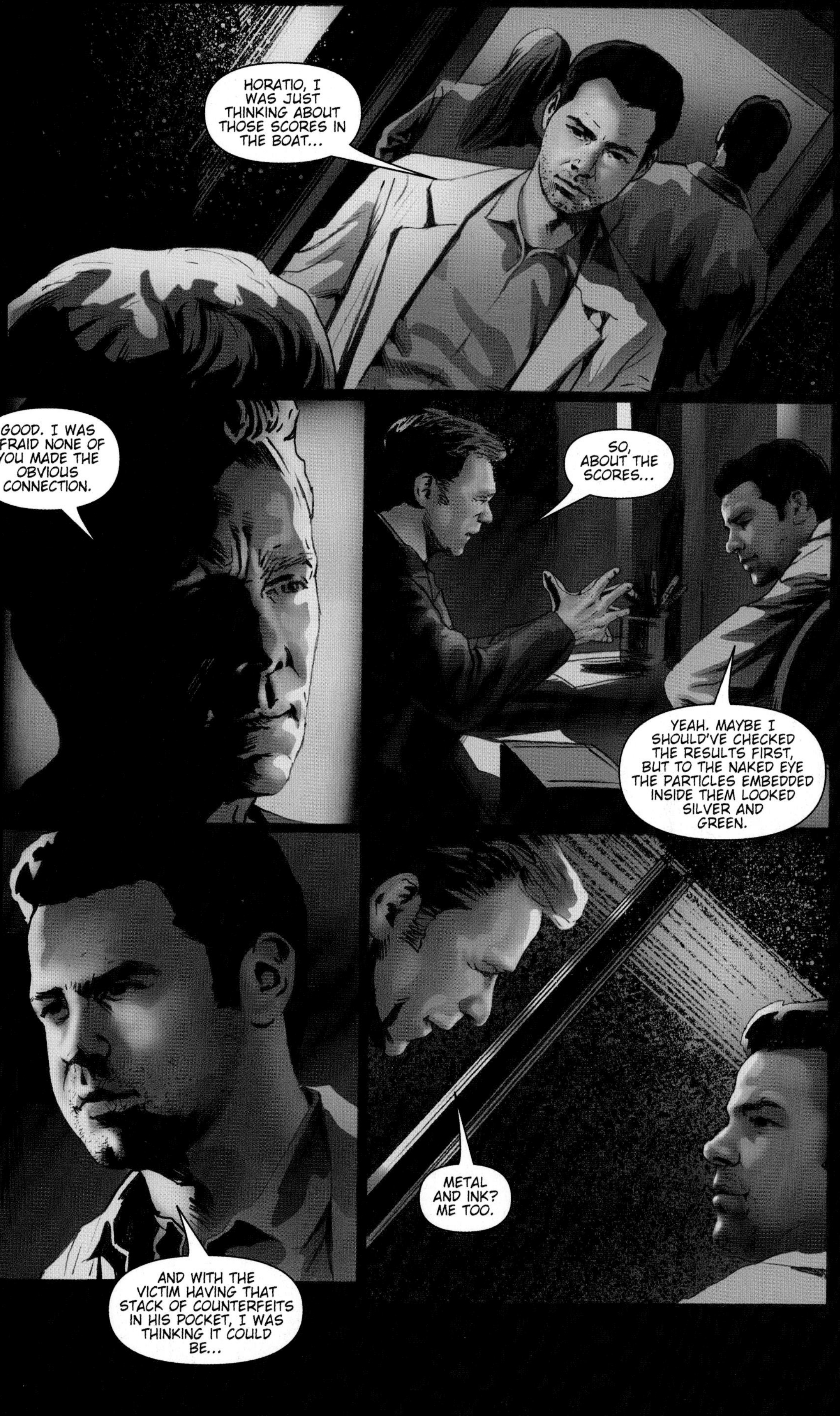
HORATIO, I WAS JUST THINKING ABOUT THOSE SCORES IN THE BOAT...
GOOD. I WAS AFRAID NONE OF YOU MADE THE OBVIOUS CONNECTION.
SO, ABOUT THE SCORES...
YEAH. MAYBE I SHOULD'VE CHECKED THE RESULTS FIRST, BUT TO THE NAKED EYE THE PARTICLES EMBEDDED INSIDE THEM LOOKED SILVER AND GREEN.
AND WITH THE VICTIM HAVING THAT STACK OF COUNTERFEITS IN HIS POCKET, I WAS THINKING IT COULD BE...
METAL AND INK? ME TOO.

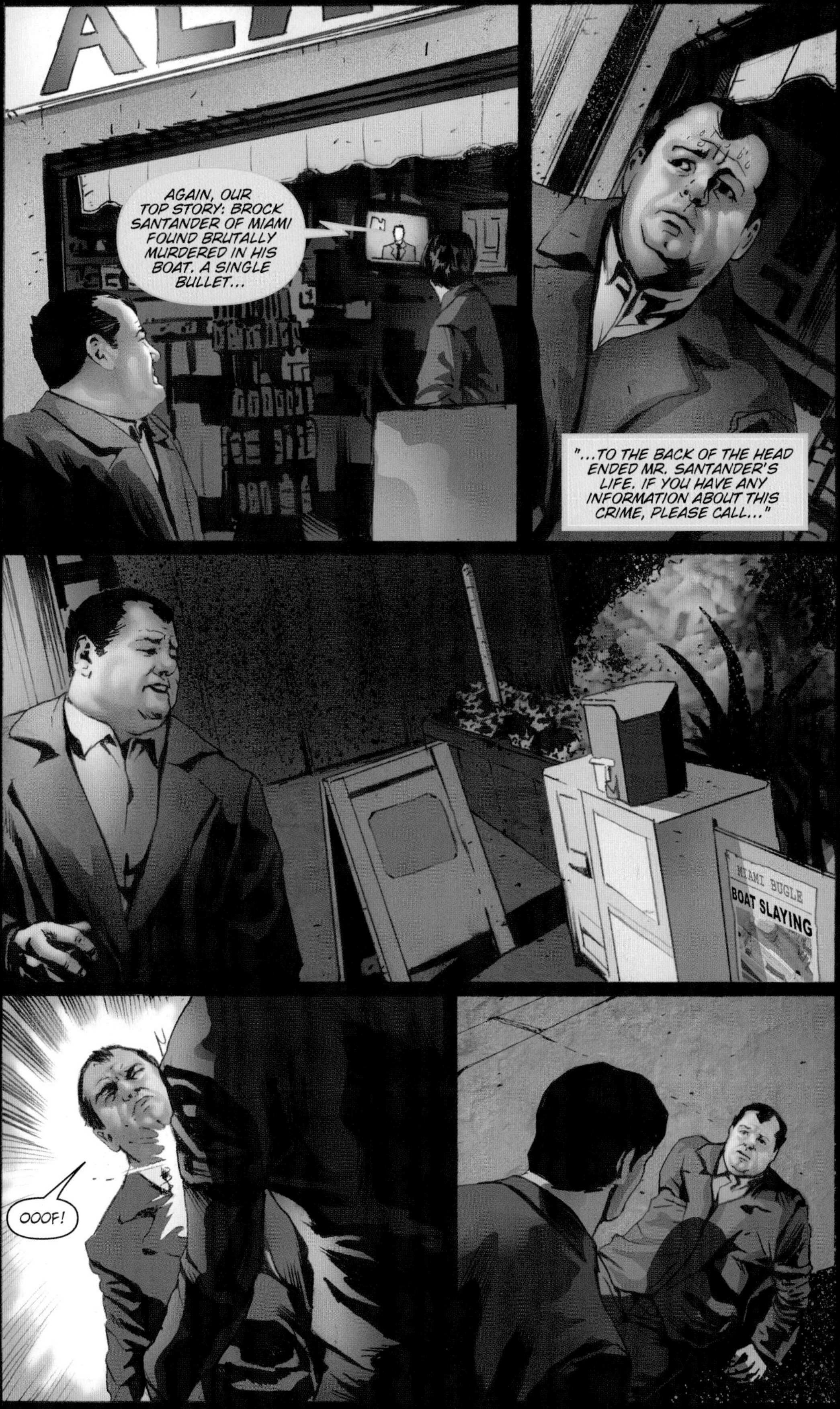
AGAIN, OUR TOP STORY: BROCK SANTANDER OF MIAMI FOUND BRUTALLY MURDERED IN HIS BOAT. A SINGLE BULLET...
"...TO THE BACK OF THE HEAD ENDED MR. SANTANDER'S LIFE. IF YOU HAVE ANY INFORMATION ABOUT THIS CRIME, PLEASE CALL..."
MIAMI BUGLE
BOAT SLAYING
OOOF!

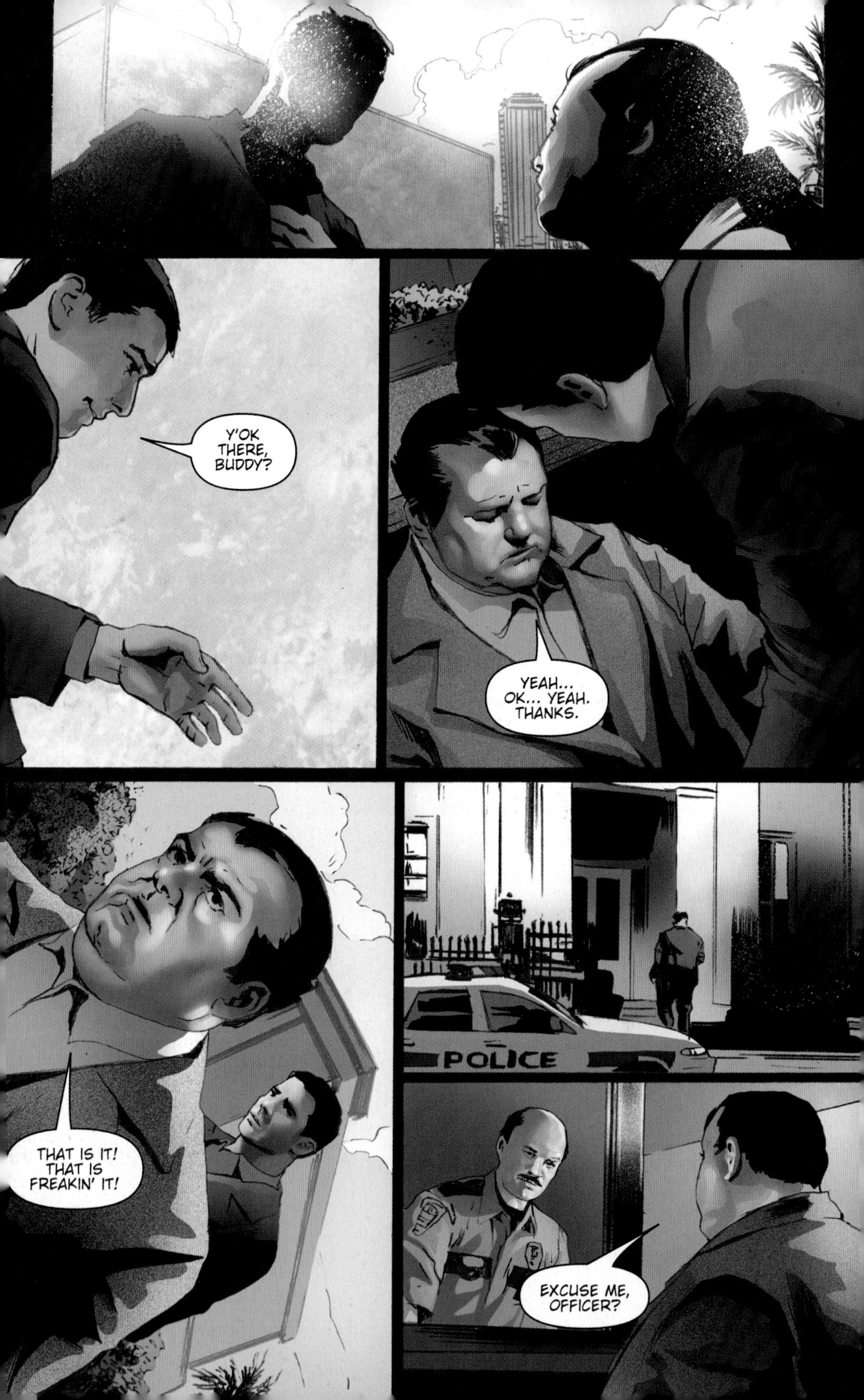
Y'OK THERE, BUDDY?
YEAH... OK... YEAH. THANKS.
THAT IS IT! THAT IS FREAKIN' IT!
POLICE
EXCUSE ME, OFFICER?

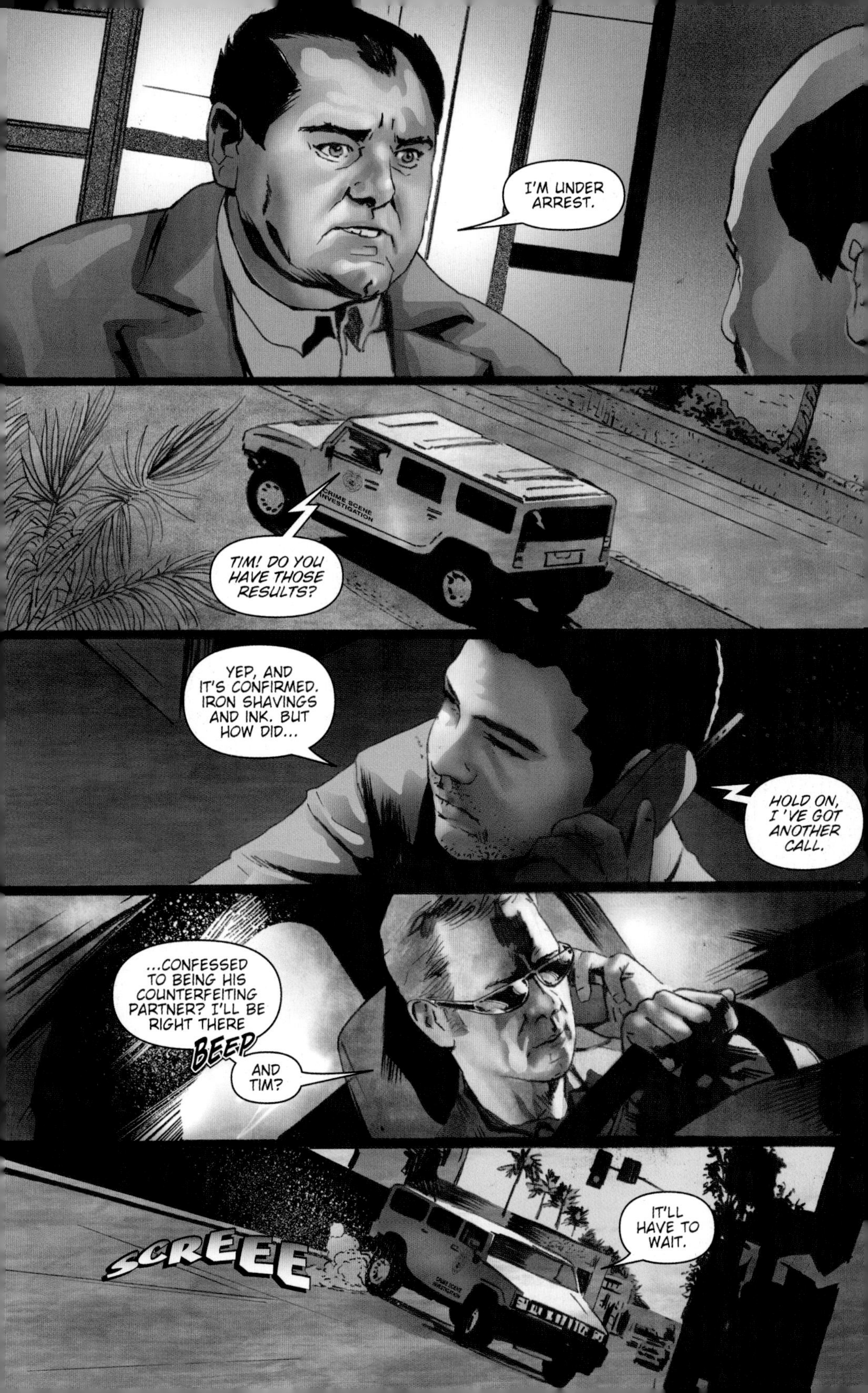
I'M UNDER ARREST.
TIM! DO YOU HAVE THOSE RESULTS?
YEP, AND IT'S CONFIRMED. IRON SHAVINGS AND INK. BUT HOW DID...
HOLD ON, I'VE GOT ANOTHER CALL.
...CONFESSED TO BEING HIS COUNTERFEITING PARTNER? I'LL BE RIGHT THERE
BEEP
AND TIM?
SCREEEE
IT'LL HAVE TO WAIT.

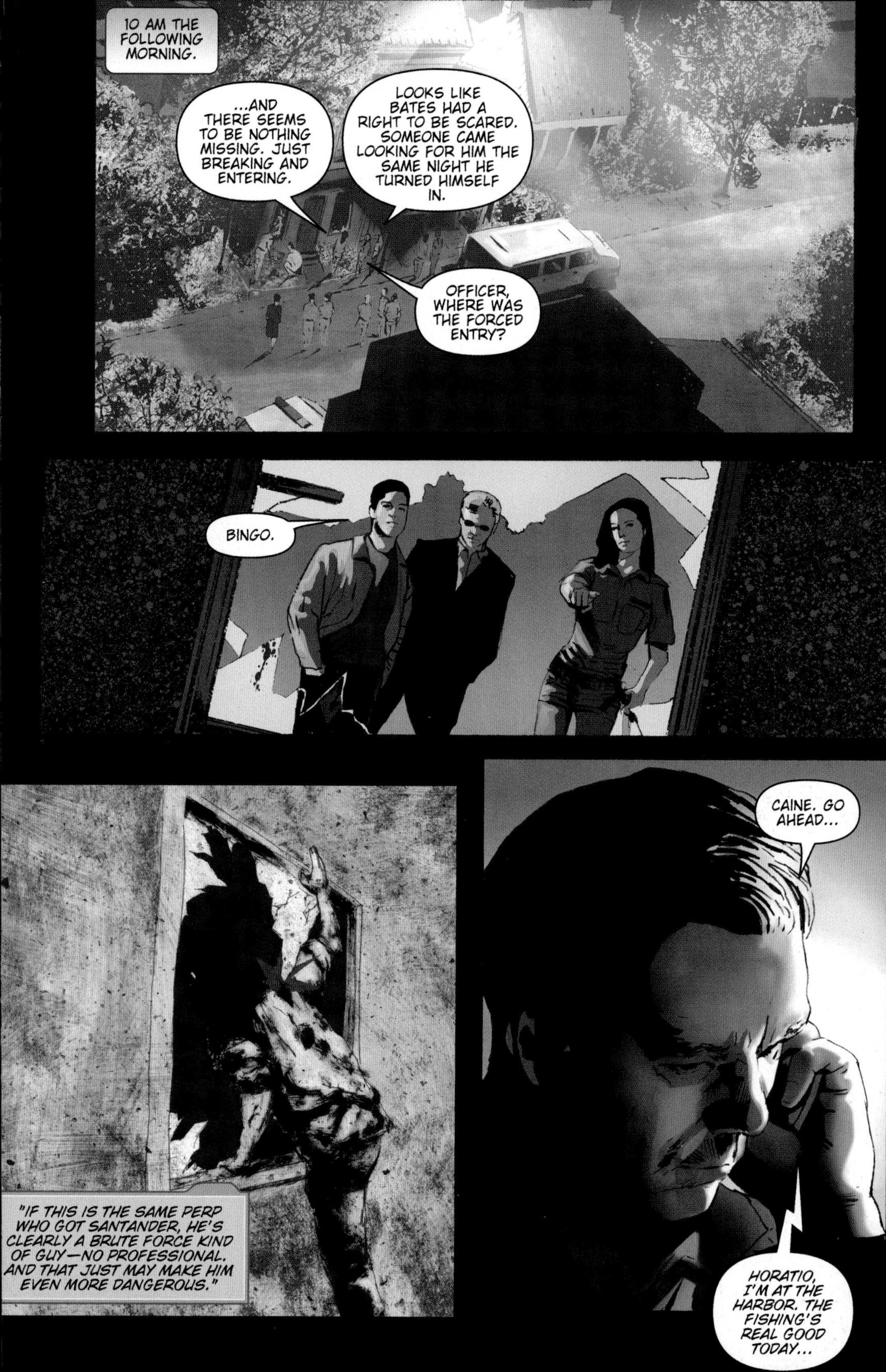
10 AM THE FOLLOWING MORNING.
...AND THERE SEEMS TO BE NOTHING MISSING. JUST BREAKING AND ENTERING.
LOOKS LIKE BATES HAD A RIGHT TO BE SCARED. SOMEONE CAME LOOKING FOR HIM THE SAME NIGHT HE TURNED HIMSELF IN.
OFFICER, WHERE WAS THE FORCED ENTRY?
BINGO.
"IF THIS IS THE SAME PERP WHO GOT SANTANDER, HE'S CLEARLY A BRUTE FORCE KIND OF GUY—NO PROFESSIONAL. AND THAT JUST MAY MAKE HIM EVEN MORE DANGEROUS."
CAINE. GO AHEAD...
HORATIO, I'M AT THE HARBOR. THE FISHING'S REAL GOOD TODAY...

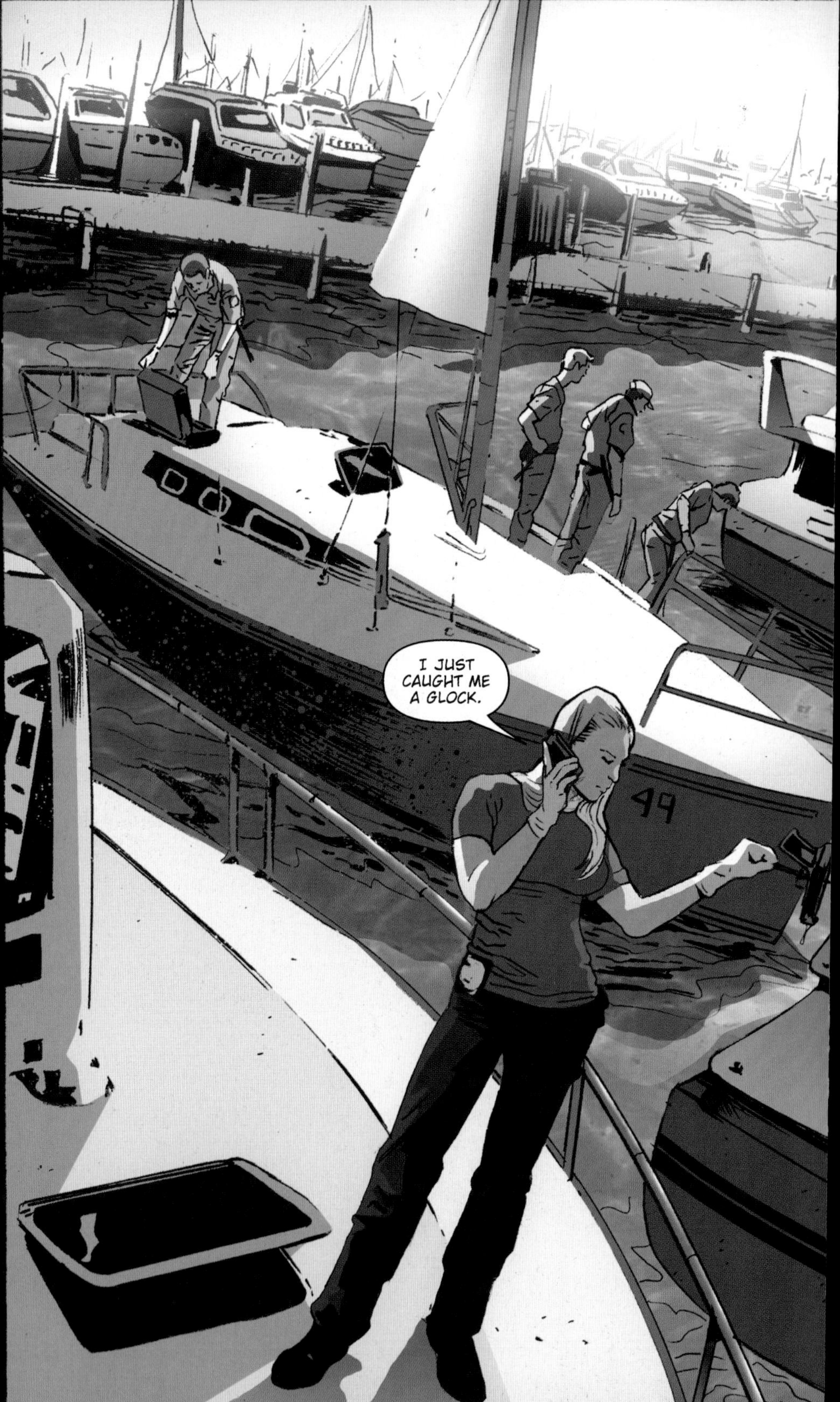
I JUST CAUGHT ME A GLOCK.

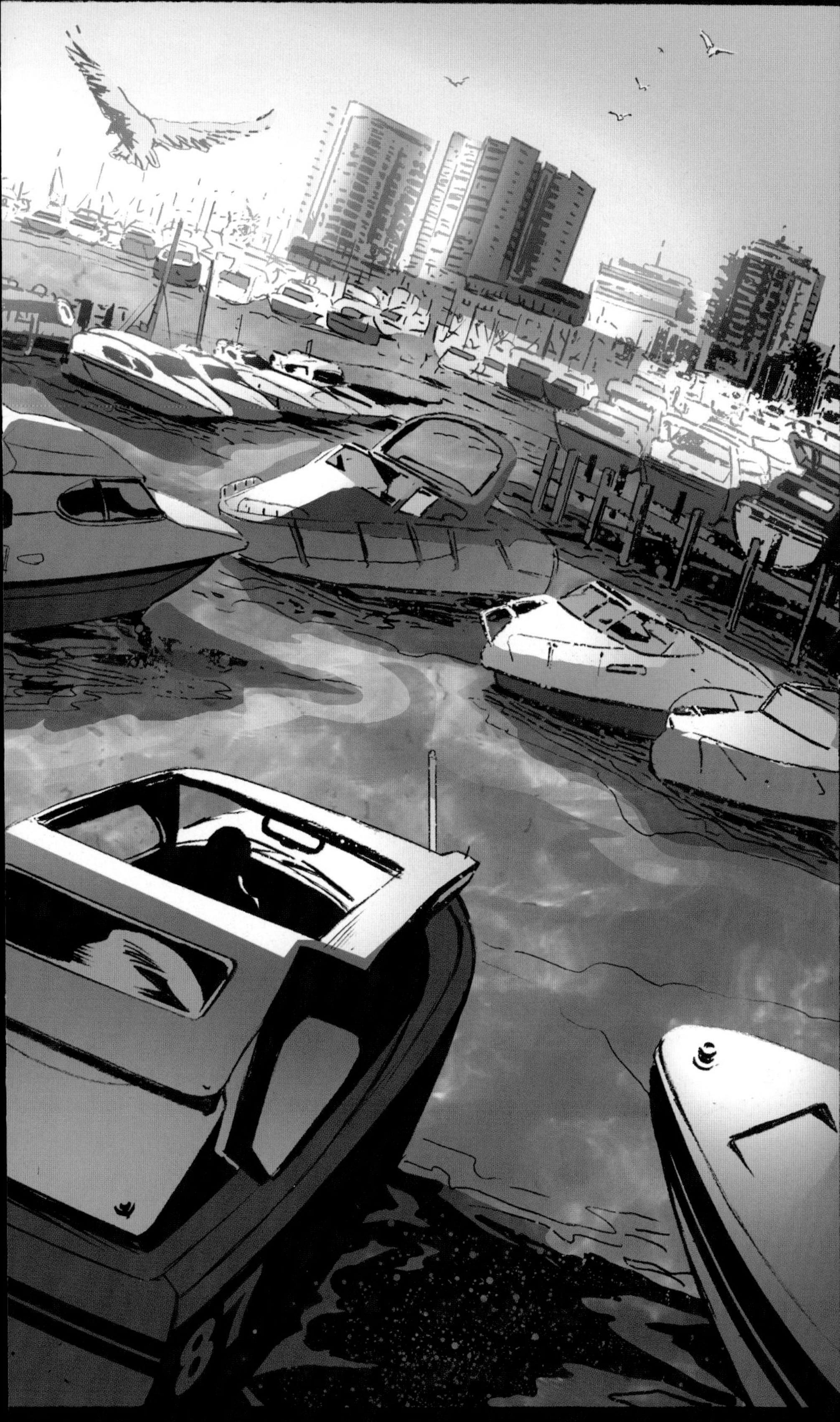

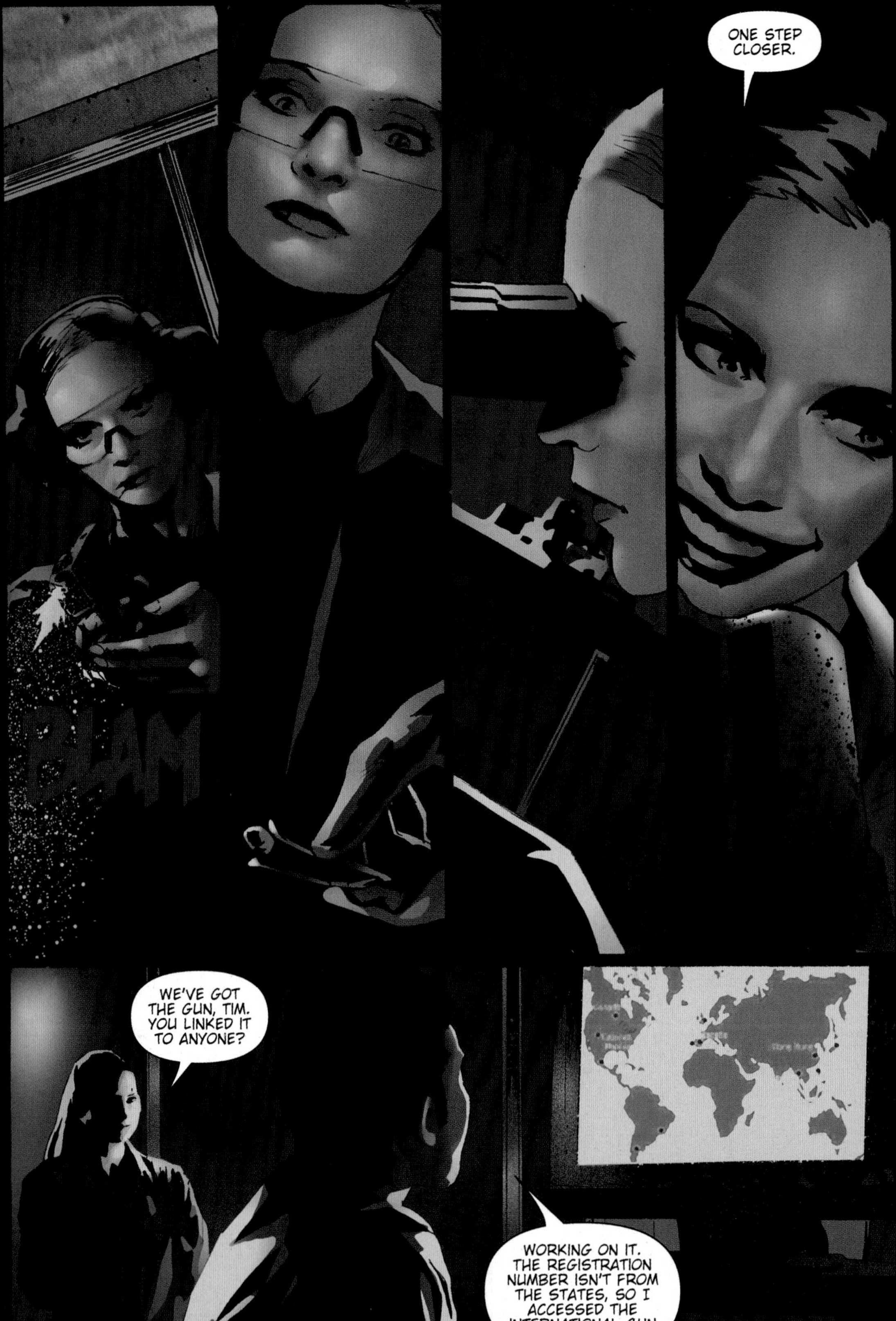
ONE STEP CLOSER.
WE'VE GOT THE GUN, TIM. YOU LINKED IT TO ANYONE?
WORKING ON IT. THE REGISTRATION NUMBER ISN'T FROM THE STATES, SO I ACCESSED THE INTERNATIONAL GUN REGISTRY.

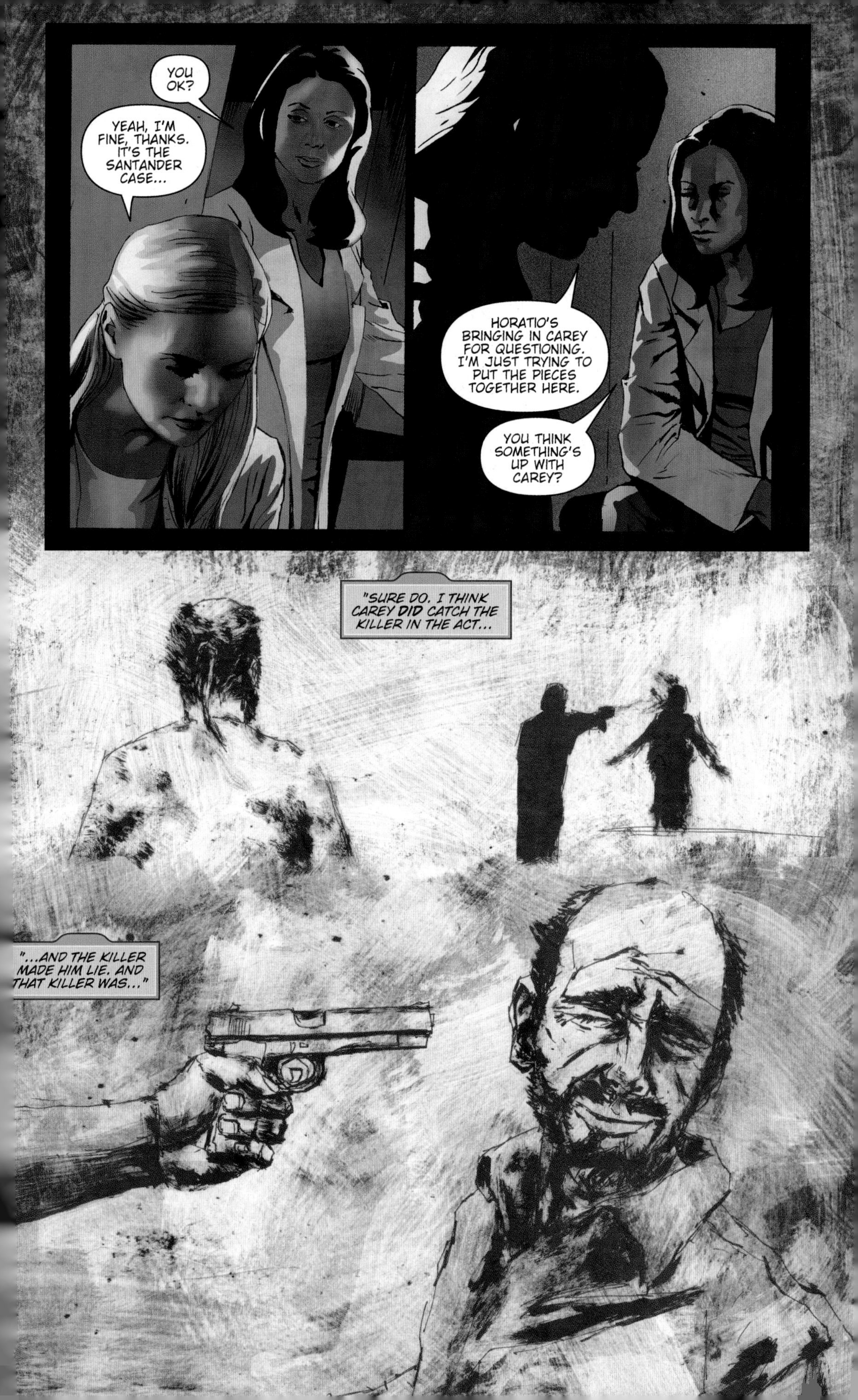
YOU OK?
YEAH, I'M FINE, THANKS. IT'S THE SANTANDER CASE...
HORATIO'S BRINGING IN CAREY FOR QUESTIONING. I'M JUST TRYING TO PUT THE PIECES TOGETHER HERE.
YOU THINK SOMETHING'S UP WITH CAREY?
"SURE DO. I THINK CAREY DID CATCH THE KILLER IN THE ACT...
"...AND THE KILLER MADE HIM LIE. AND THAT KILLER WAS..."

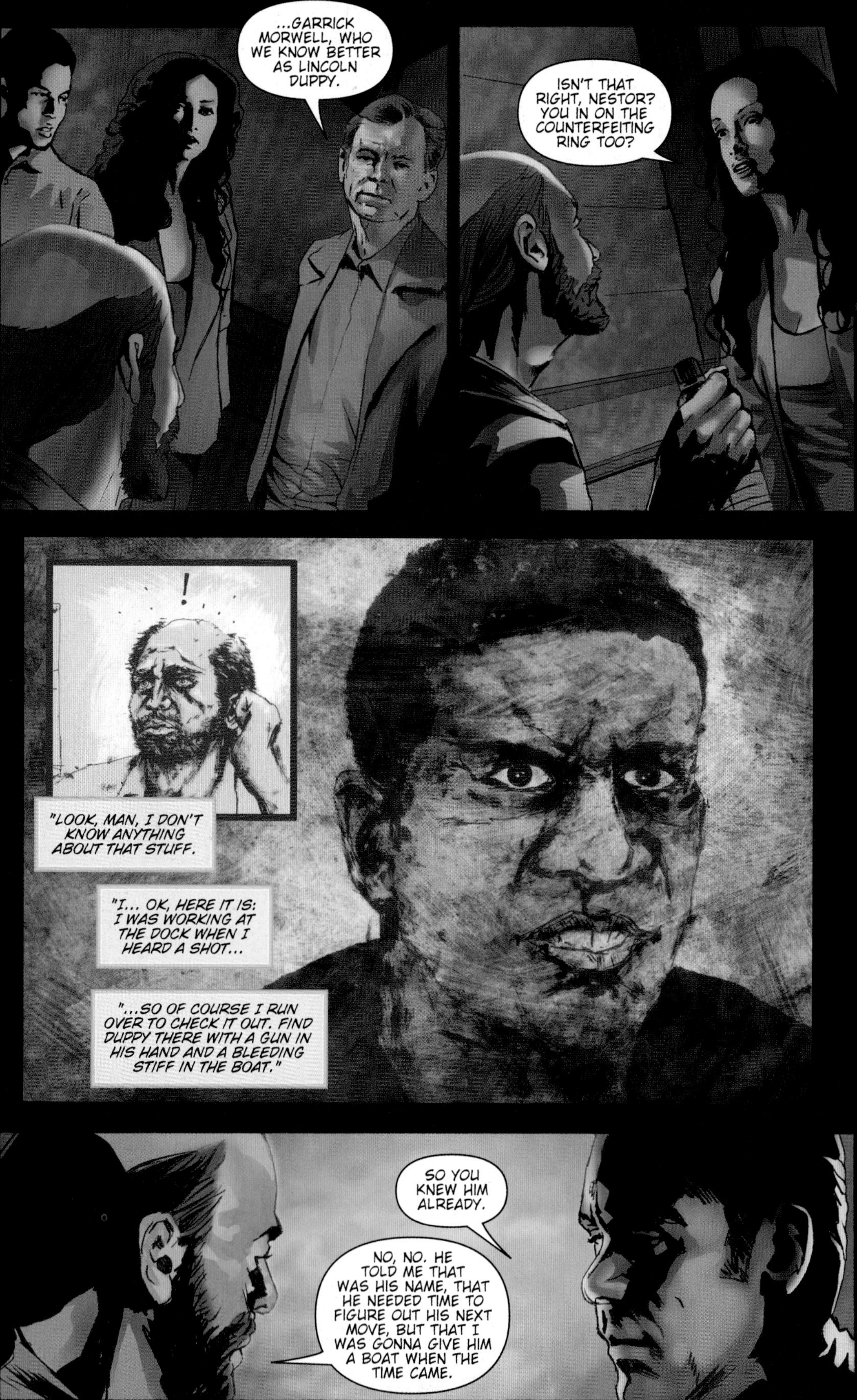
...GARRICK MORWELL, WHO WE KNOW BETTER AS LINCOLN DUPPY.
ISN'T THAT RIGHT, NESTOR? YOU IN ON THE COUNTERFEITING RING TOO?
!
"LOOK, MAN, I DON'T KNOW ANYTHING ABOUT THAT STUFF.
"I... OK, HERE IT IS: I WAS WORKING AT THE DOCK WHEN I HEARD A SHOT...
"...SO OF COURSE I RUN OVER TO CHECK IT OUT. FIND DUPPY THERE WITH A GUN IN HIS HAND AND A BLEEDING STIFF IN THE BOAT."
SO YOU KNEW HIM ALREADY.
NO, NO. HE TOLD ME THAT WAS HIS NAME, THAT HE NEEDED TIME TO FIGURE OUT HIS NEXT MOVE, BUT THAT I WAS GONNA GIVE HIM A BOAT WHEN THE TIME CAME.

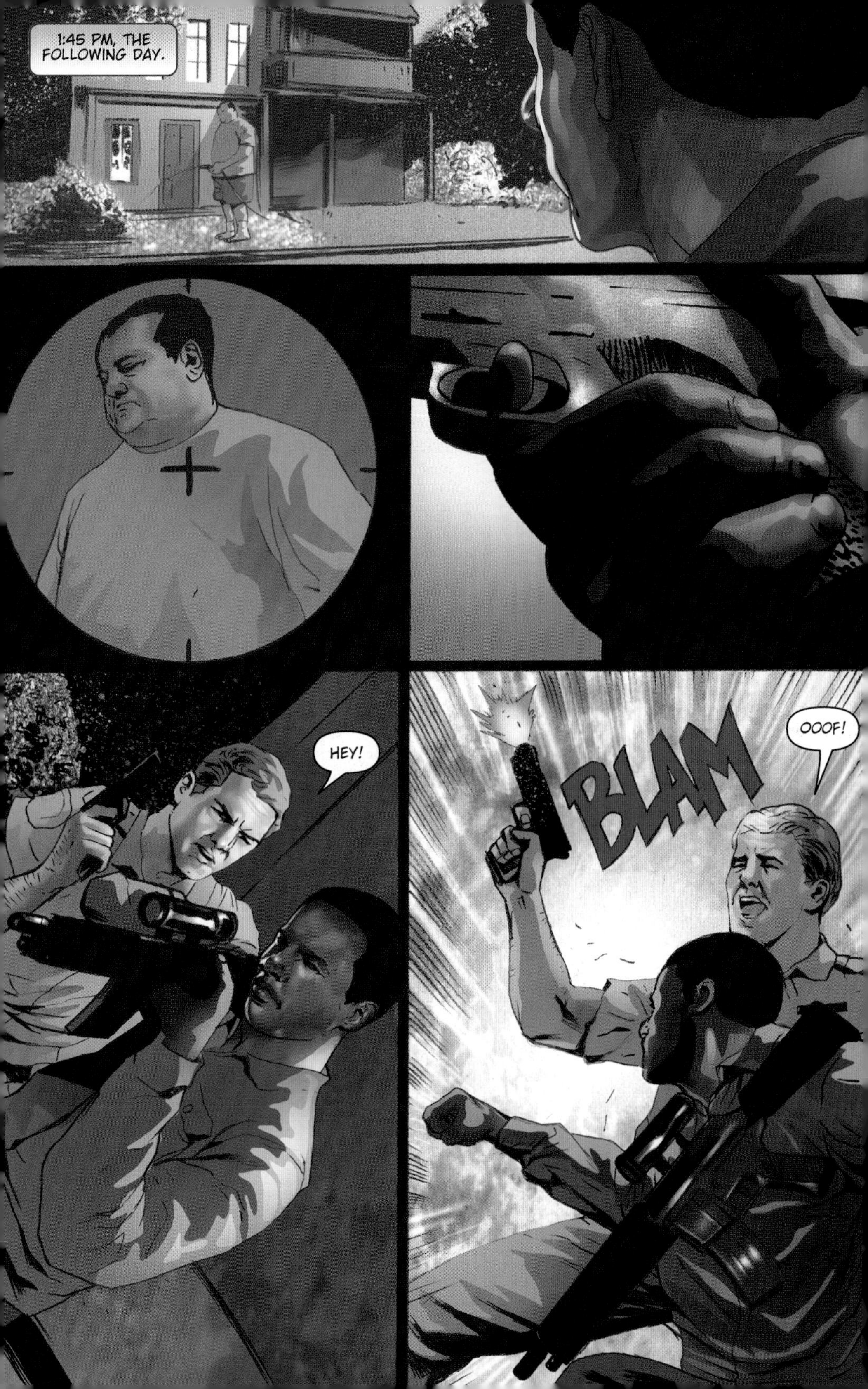
1:45 PM, THE FOLLOWING DAY.
HEY!
BLAM
OOOF!

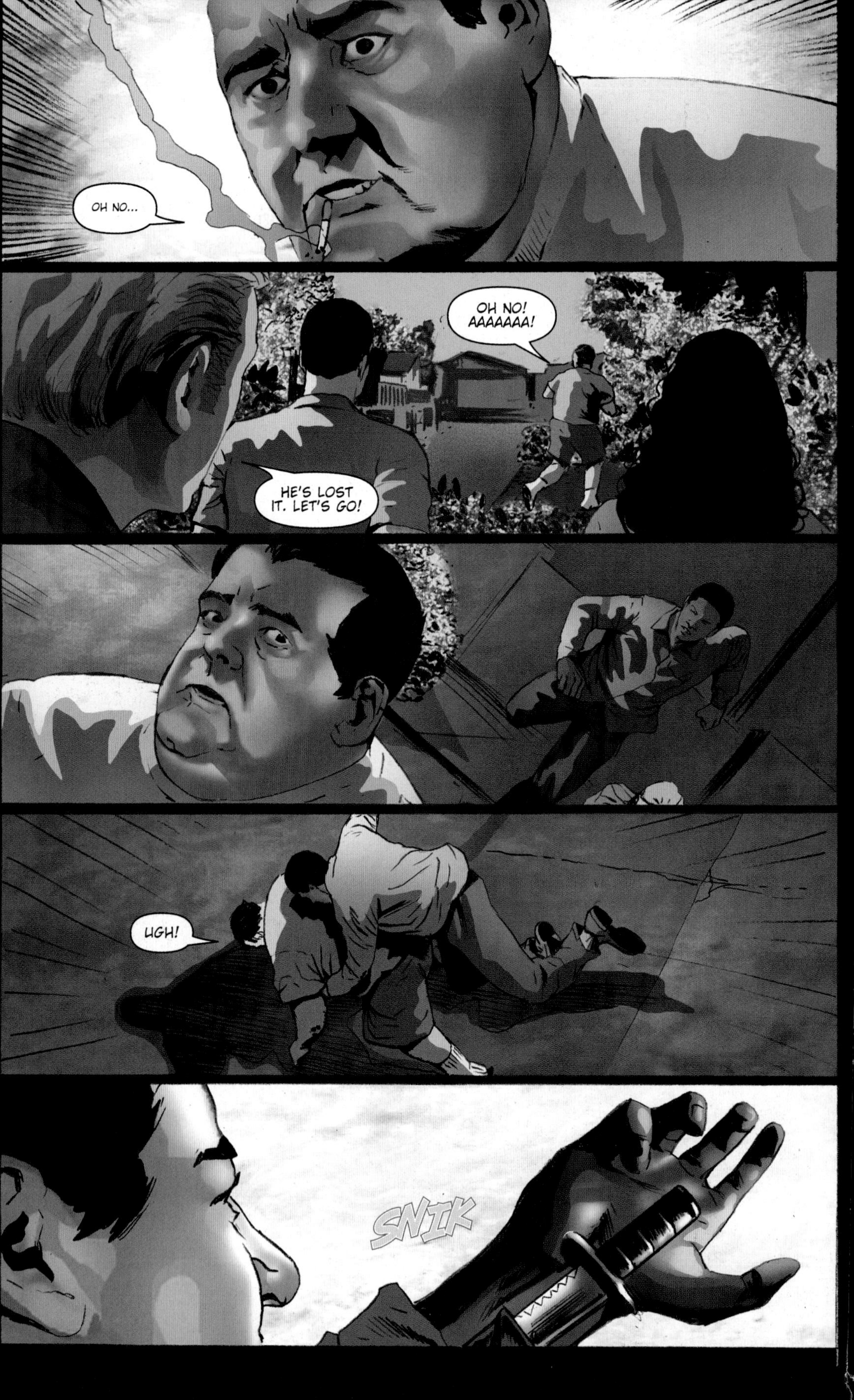
OH NO...
OH NO! AAAAAAA!
HE'S LOST IT. LET'S GO!
UGH!
SNIK

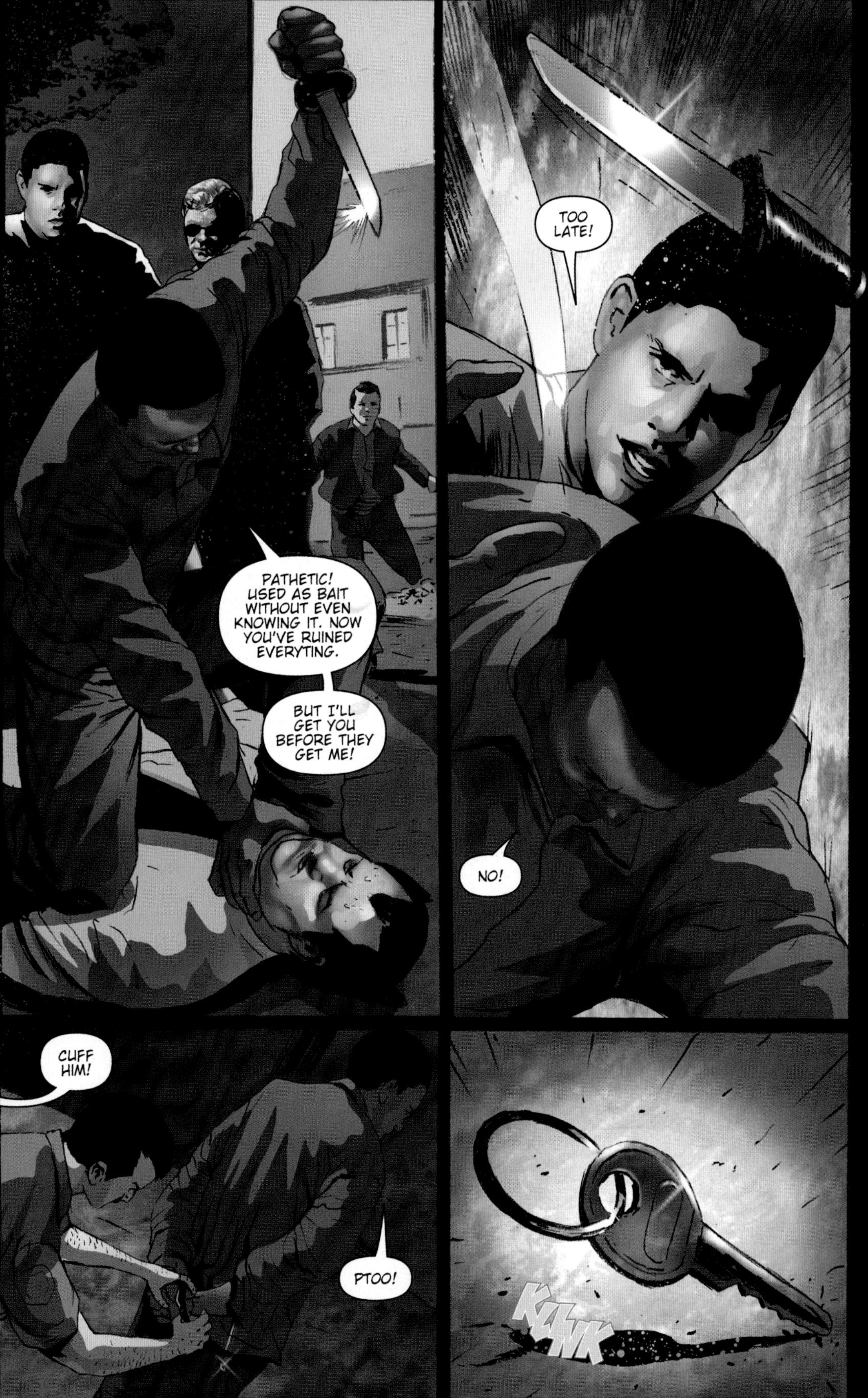
PATHETIC! USED AS BAIT WITHOUT EVEN KNOWING IT. NOW YOU'VE RUINED EVERYTING.
BUT I'LL GET YOU BEFORE THEY GET ME!
TOO LATE!
NO!
CUFF HIM!
PTOO!
KLINK

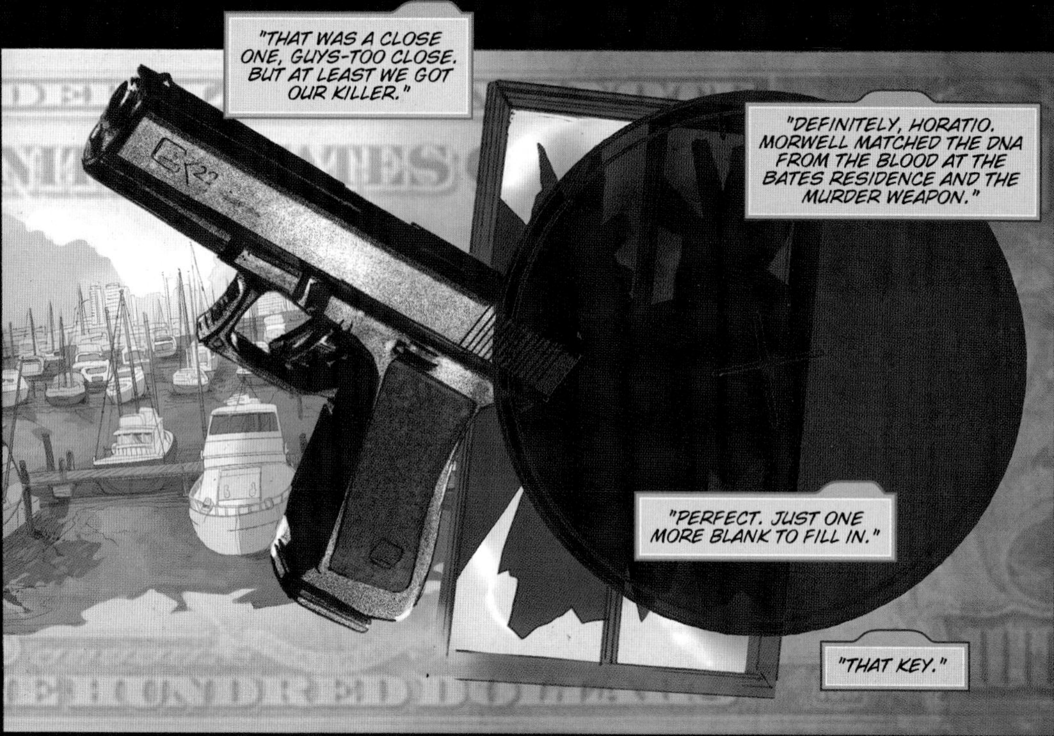
"THAT WAS A CLOSE ONE, GUYS-TOO CLOSE. BUT AT LEAST WE GOT OUR KILLER."
"DEFINITELY, HORATIO. MORWELL MATCHED THE DNA FROM THE BLOOD AT THE BATES RESIDENCE AND THE MURDER WEAPON."
"PERFECT. JUST ONE MORE BLANK TO FILL IN."
"THAT KEY."

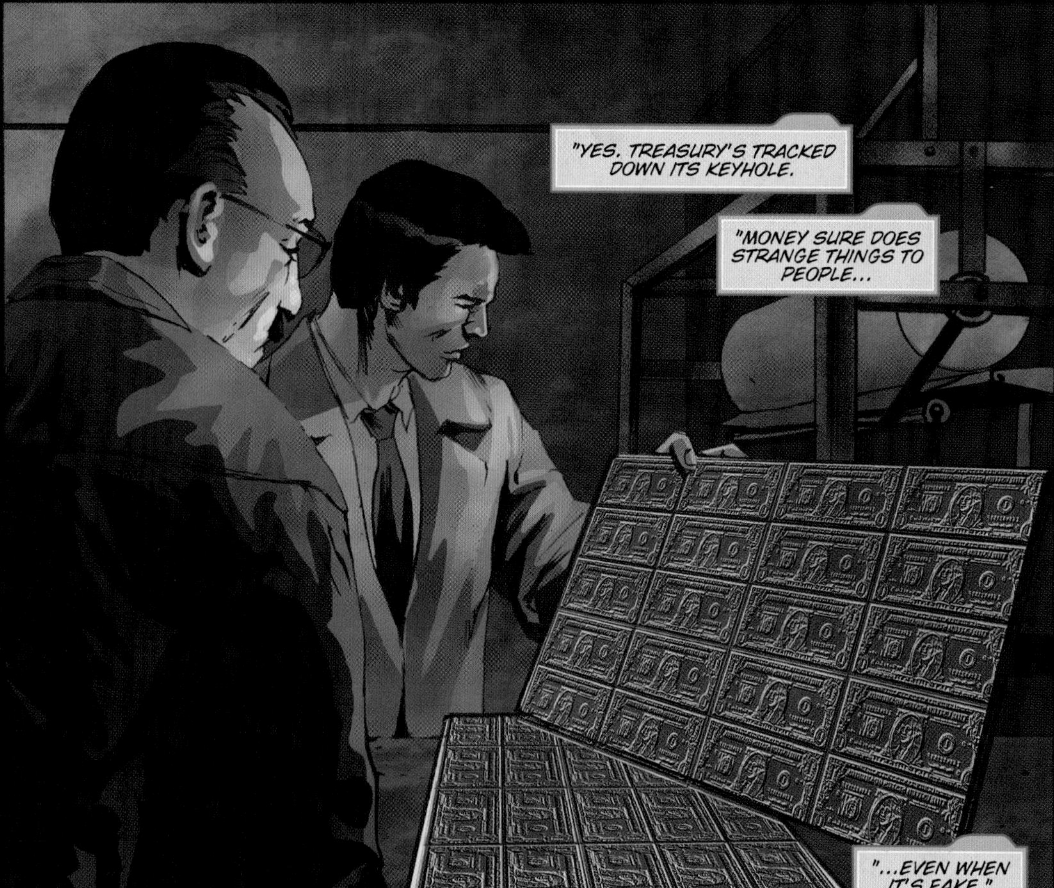
"YES. TREASURY'S TRACKED DOWN ITS KEYHOLE.
"MONEY SURE DOES STRANGE THINGS TO PEOPLE...
"...EVEN WHEN IT'S FAKE."

THE END.

IDW

$6.99

CSI: Miami

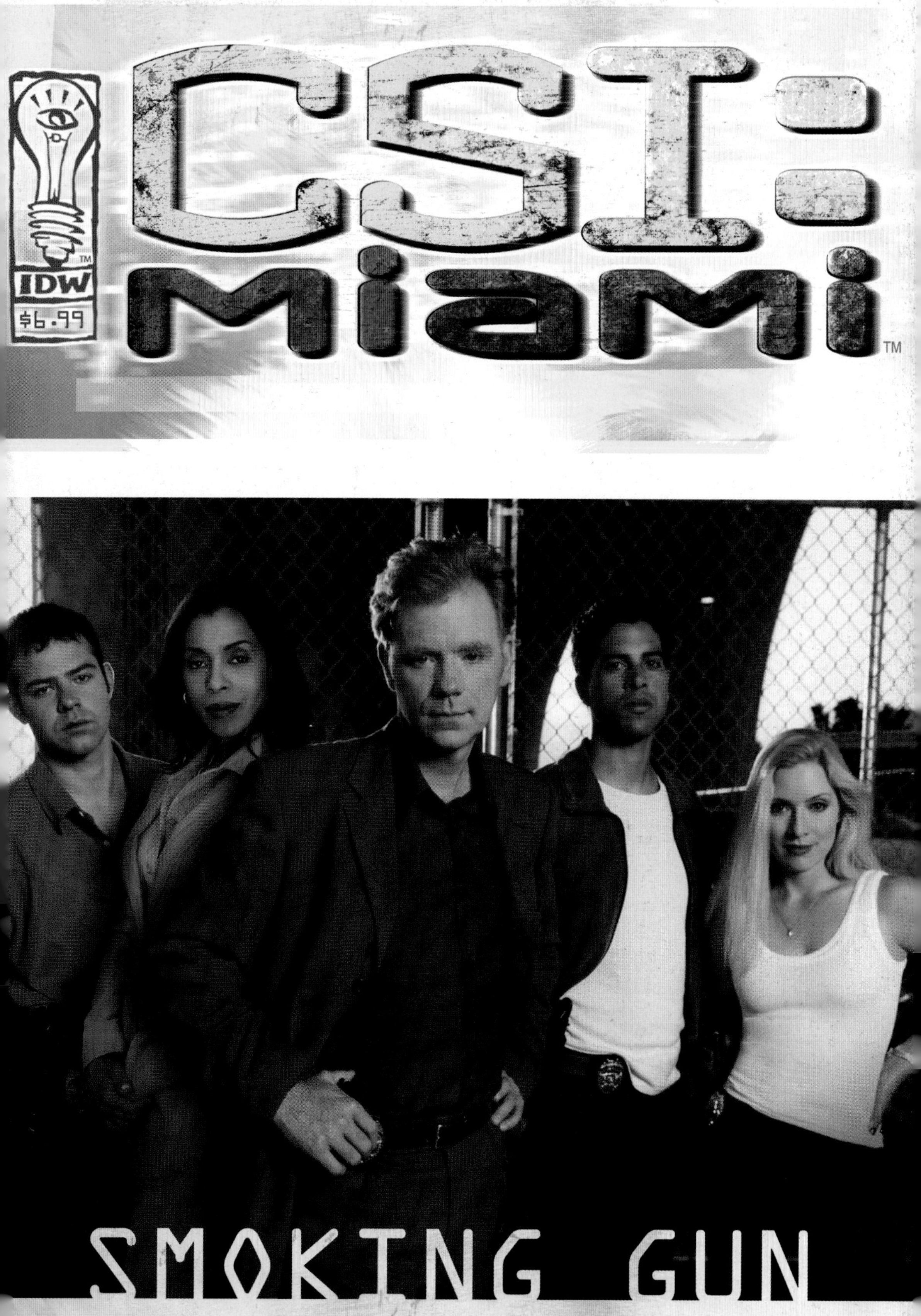

SMOKING GUN

MARIOTTE • AVILÉS • WOOD

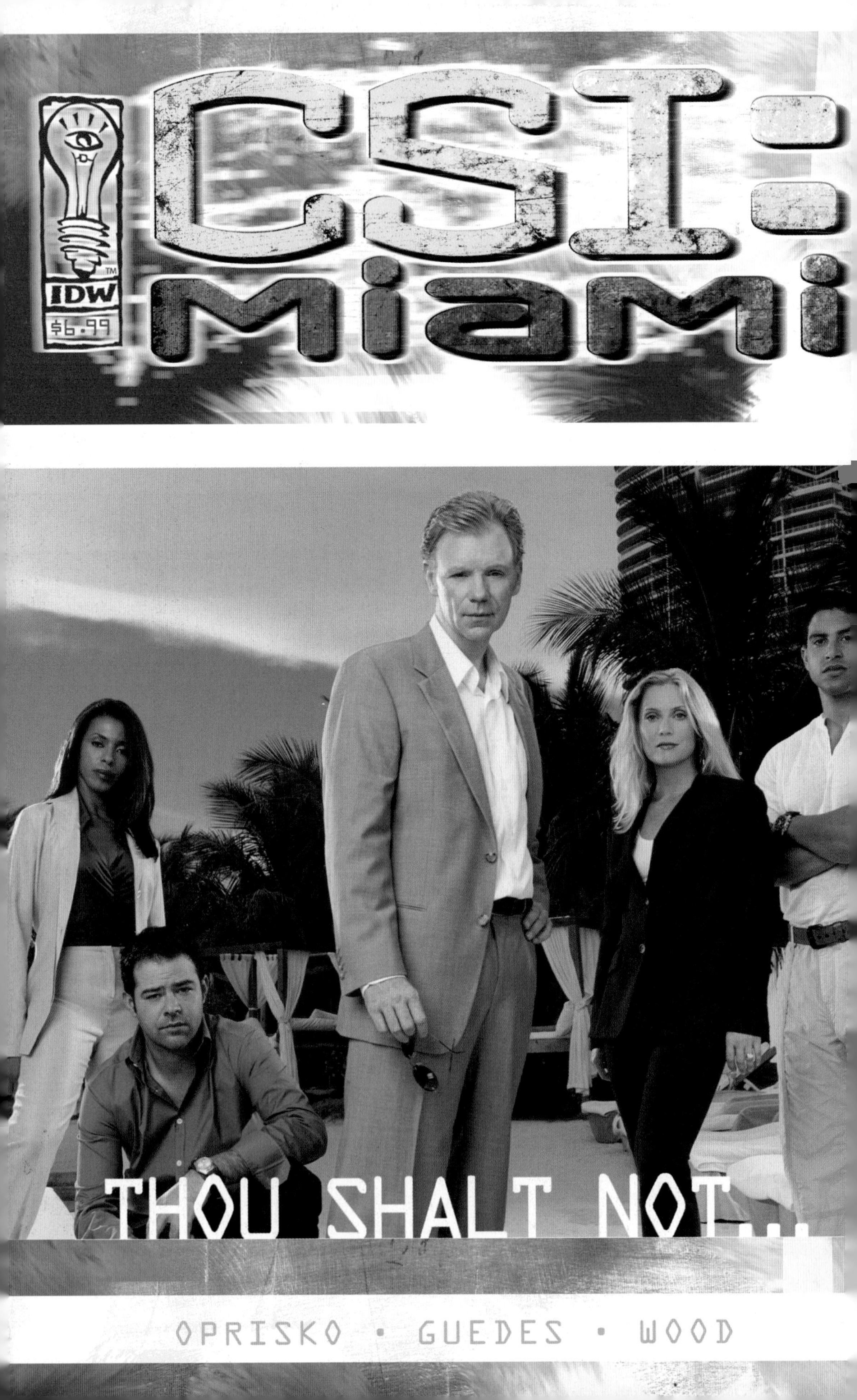
IDW
$6.99
CSI:
Miami
THOU SHALT NOT...
OPRISKO · GUEDES · WOOD

IDW

$6.99

CSI: MIAMI™

BLOOD/MONEY

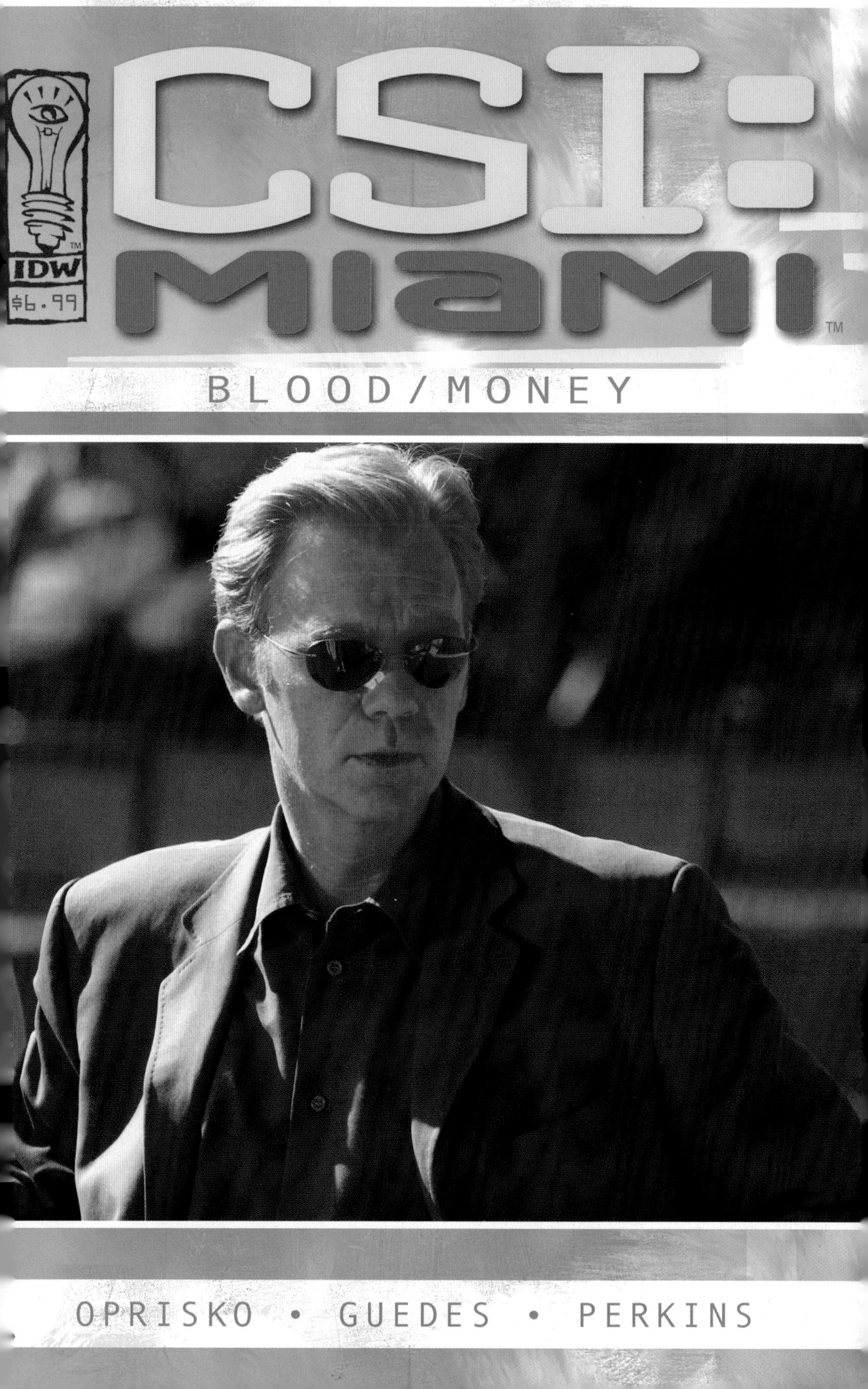

OPRISKO • GUEDES • PERKINS

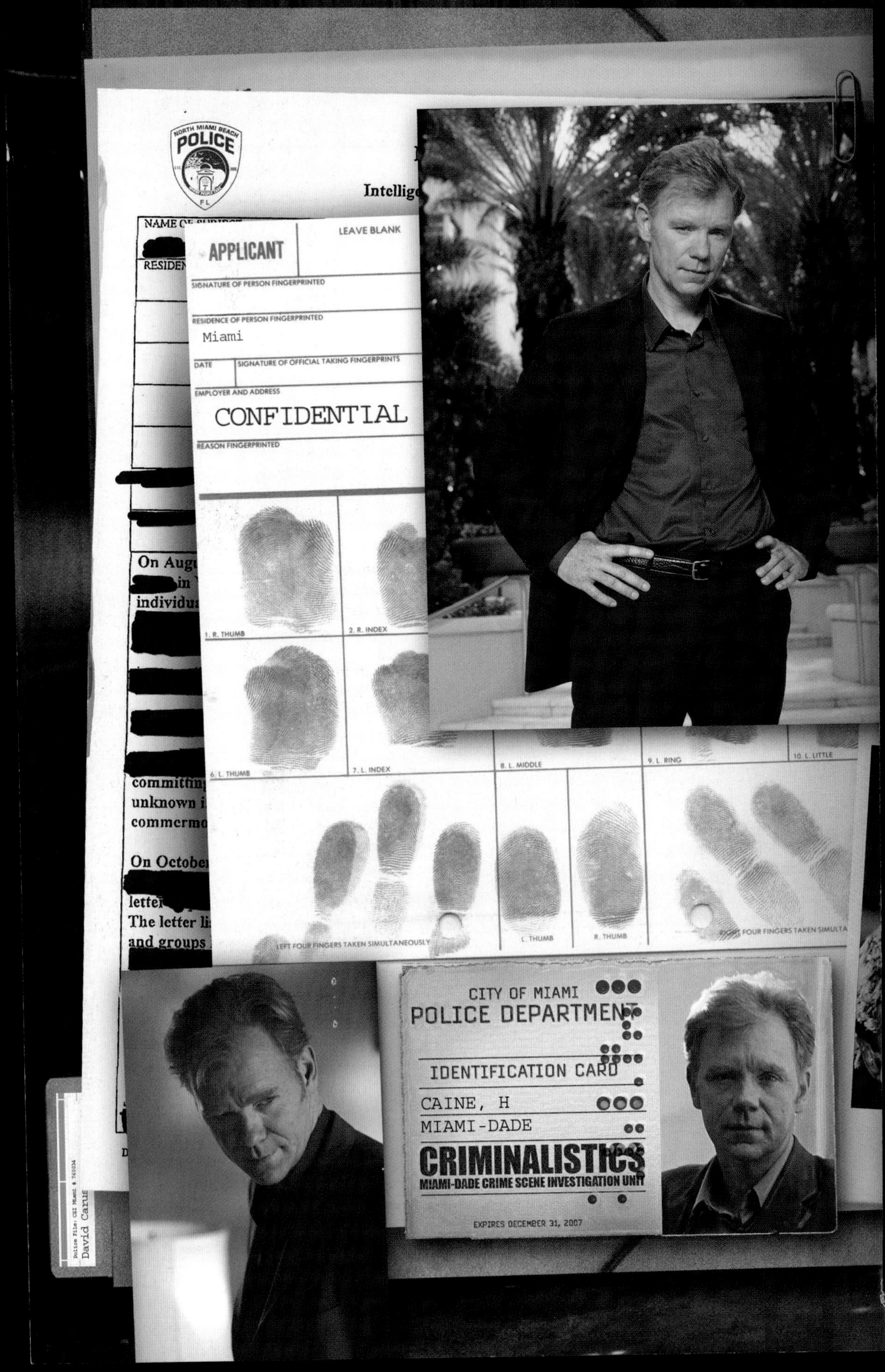

NORTH MIAMI BEACH POLICE
FL

NAME OF SUBJECT

RESIDEN

APPLICANT

LEAVE BLANK

SIGNATURE OF PERSON FINGERPRINTED

RESIDENCE OF PERSON FINGERPRINTED

Miami

DATE   SIGNATURE OF OFFICIAL TAKING FINGERPRINTS

EMPLOYER AND ADDRESS

CONFIDENTIAL

REASON FINGERPRINTED

1. R. THUMB   2. R. INDEX

6. L. THUMB   7. L. INDEX   8. L. MIDDLE   9. L. RING   10. L. LITTLE

LEFT FOUR FINGERS TAKEN SIMULTANEOUSLY   L. THUMB   R. THUMB   RIGHT FOUR FINGERS TAKEN SIMULTA

On Augu
in
individua

committing
unknown i
commermo

On October

letter
The letter li
and groups

Police File: CSI Miami # 760034

David Caine

D

CITY OF MIAMI
POLICE DEPARTMENT

IDENTIFICATION CARD

CAINE, H

MIAMI-DADE

CRIMINALISTICS
MIAMI-DADE CRIME SCENE INVESTIGATION UNIT

EXPIRES DECEMBER 31, 2007

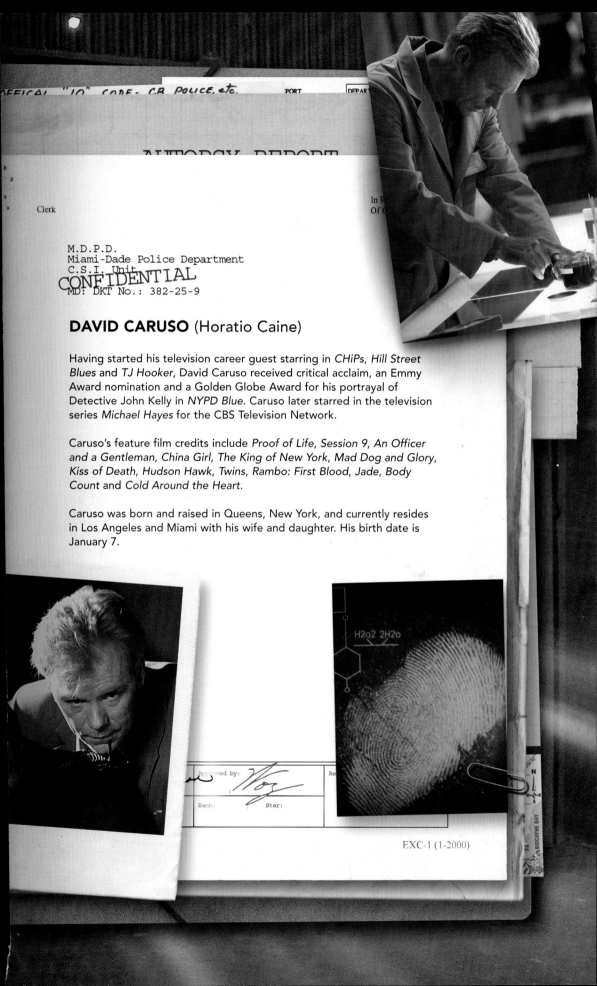

OFFICAL "10" CODE - CB POLICE, etc.

Clerk

M.D.P.D.
Miami-Dade Police Department
C.S.I. Unit
CONFIDENTIAL
MD: DKT No.: 382-25-9

DAVID CARUSO (Horatio Caine)

Having started his television career guest starring in *CHiPs*, *Hill Street Blues* and *TJ Hooker*, David Caruso received critical acclaim, an Emmy Award nomination and a Golden Globe Award for his portrayal of Detective John Kelly in *NYPD Blue*. Caruso later starred in the television series *Michael Hayes* for the CBS Television Network.

Caruso's feature film credits include *Proof of Life*, *Session 9*, *An Officer and a Gentleman*, *China Girl*, *The King of New York*, *Mad Dog and Glory*, *Kiss of Death*, *Hudson Hawk*, *Twins*, *Rambo: First Blood*, *Jade*, *Body Count* and *Cold Around the Heart*.

Caruso was born and raised in Queens, New York, and currently resides in Los Angeles and Miami with his wife and daughter. His birth date is January 7.

H2o2 2H2o

Approved by:

Rank: Star:

EXC-1 (1-2000)

Clerk CONFIDENTIAL

In Replying Give Number
Of Case And Names

M.D.P.D.
Miami-Dade Police Department
C.S.I. Unit

MD: DKT No.: 382-25-10

EMILY PROCTER (Calleigh Duquesne)

While studying for a degree in Journalism and Dance at East Carolina University, Emily Procter worked as a weather anchor at WITN in nearby Greenville, NC. Soon after graduating, she moved to Los Angeles to pursue an acting career, quickly landing roles in the feature films *Leaving Las Vegas* and *Jerry Maguire*, and earning her first starring role in the television film *Breast Men*. Procter's additional feature film credits include *Body Shots*, *Tiara Tango* and *Guinevere*.

Most recently, Procter portrayed White House-staffer Ainsley Hayes on the Emmy Award-winning *The West Wing*. She has also guest starred on *Friends*, *Just Shoot Me!*, and as Lana Lang in *Lois & Clark: The New Adventures of Superman*.

Born and raised in Raleigh, North Carolina, Procter currently resides in Los Angeles. Her birth date is October 8.

Encl.

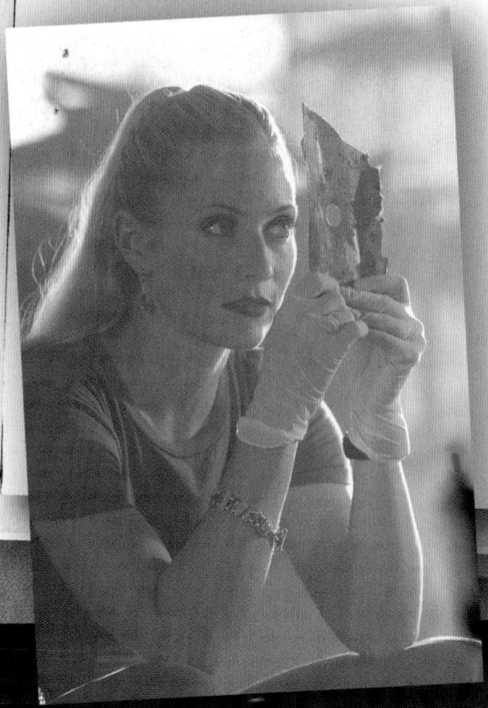

EXC-1 (1-2000)

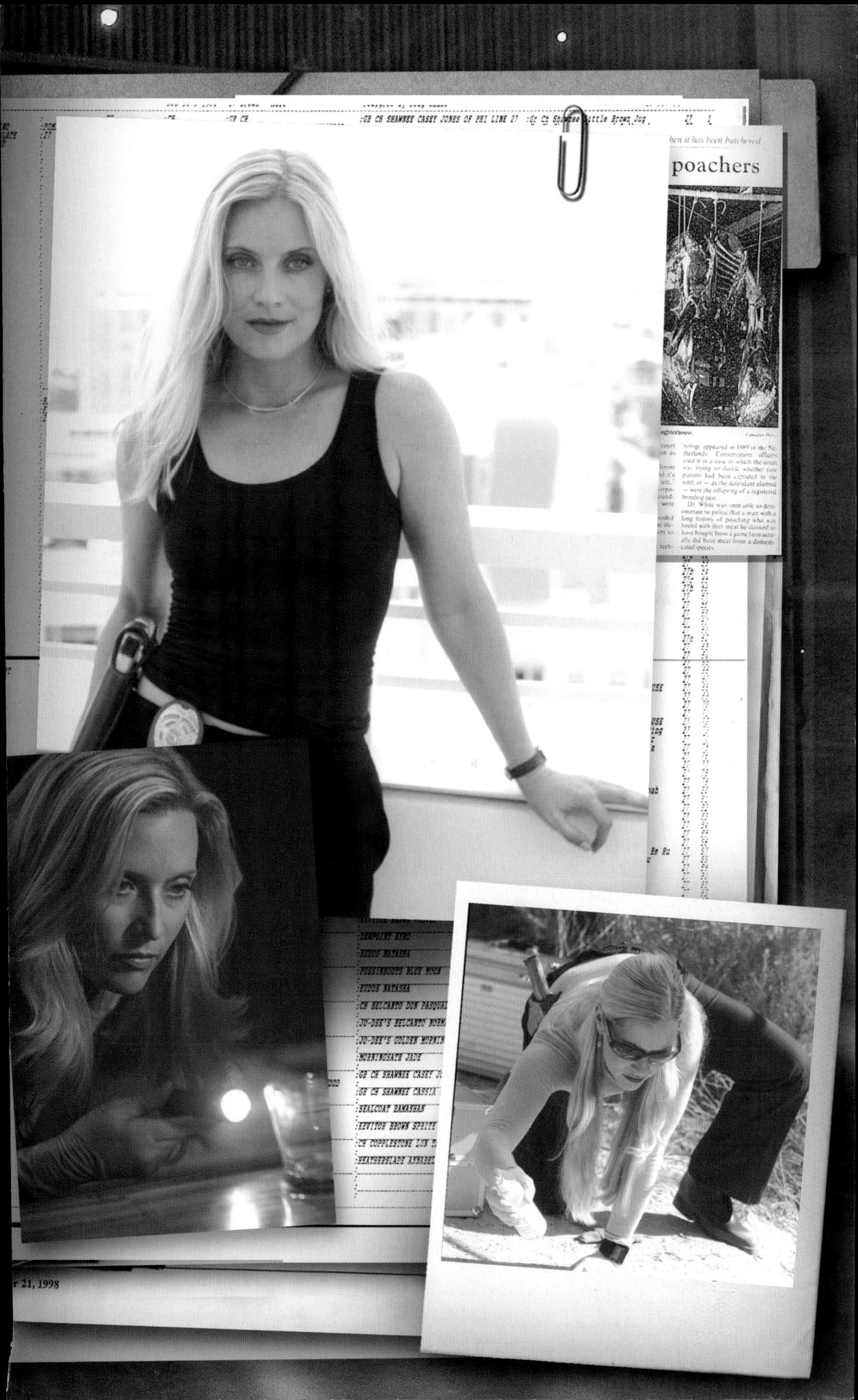

:GB CH SHAWNEE CASEY JONES OF PHI LINE 27 :Gr Ch Shawnee Little Brown Jug
hen it has been butchered
poachers
ughterhouse.
nology appeared in 1989 in the Netherlands. Conservation officers used it in a case in which the court was trying to decide whether rare parrots had been captured in the wild, or — as the defendant claimed — were the offspring of a registered breeding pair.
Dr White was once able to demonstrate to police that a man with a long history of poaching who was found with deer meat he claimed to have bought from a game farm actually did have meat from a domesticated species.
KUDOS NATASHA
PUSSINBOOTS BLUE MOON
KUDOS NATASHA
CH BELCANTO DON PASQUAL
JO-DEE'S BELCANTO NORM
JO-DEE'S GOLDEN MORNIN
MORNINGSATE JADE
GB CH SHAWNEE CASEY J
GB CH SHAWNEE CASSIA
SEALCOAT RAMASHAN
KEVITOR BROWN SPRITE
CH COPPLESTONE LUN
HEATHERSLADE ANNABEL
r 21, 1998

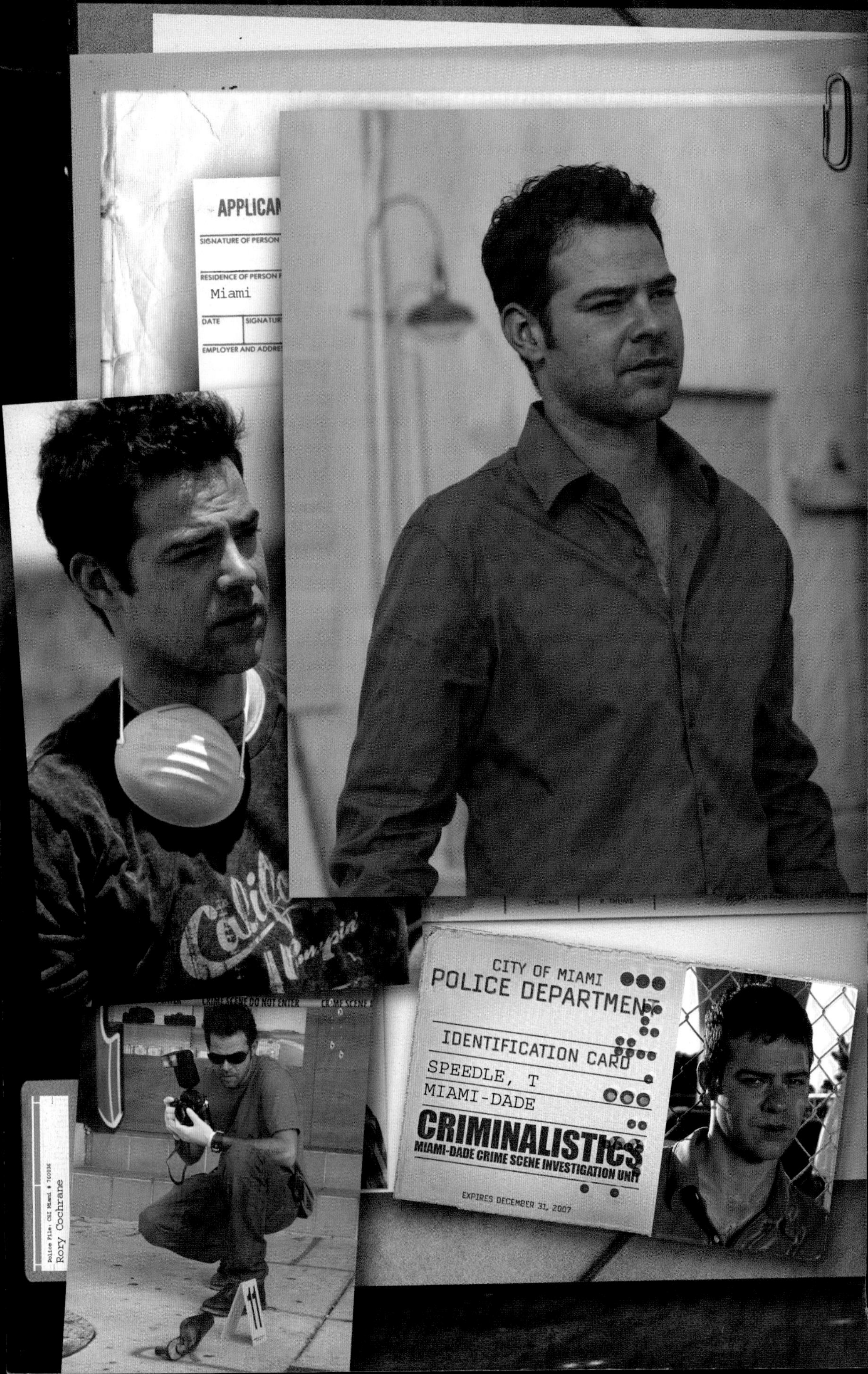
APPLICAN
SIGNATURE OF PERSON
RESIDENCE OF PERSON
Miami
DATE
SIGNATUR
EMPLOYER AND ADDRES
CRIME SCENE DO NOT ENTER
CITY OF MIAMI
POLICE DEPARTMENT
IDENTIFICATION CARD
SPEEDLE, T
MIAMI-DADE
CRIMINALISTICS
MIAMI-DADE CRIME SCENE INVESTIGATION UNIT
EXPIRES DECEMBER 31, 2007
Police File: CSI Miami # 760036
Rory Cochrane

DEPARTURE FROM SPECIFICATION REPORT

DEPARTURE NO.

Clerk

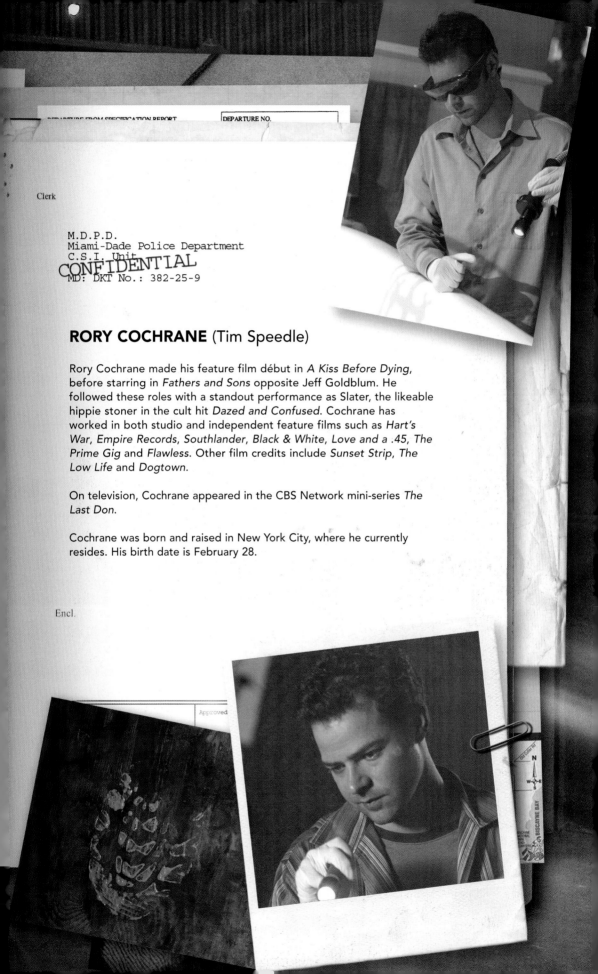

M.D.P.D.
Miami-Dade Police Department
C.S.I. Unit
CONFIDENTIAL
MD: DKT No.: 382-25-9

RORY COCHRANE (Tim Speedle)

Rory Cochrane made his feature film début in *A Kiss Before Dying*, before starring in *Fathers and Sons* opposite Jeff Goldblum. He followed these roles with a standout performance as Slater, the likeable hippie stoner in the cult hit *Dazed and Confused*. Cochrane has worked in both studio and independent feature films such as *Hart's War*, *Empire Records*, *Southlander*, *Black & White*, *Love and a .45*, *The Prime Gig* and *Flawless*. Other film credits include *Sunset Strip*, *The Low Life* and *Dogtown*.

On television, Cochrane appeared in the CBS Network mini-series *The Last Don*.

Cochrane was born and raised in New York City, where he currently resides. His birth date is February 28.

Encl.

Approved

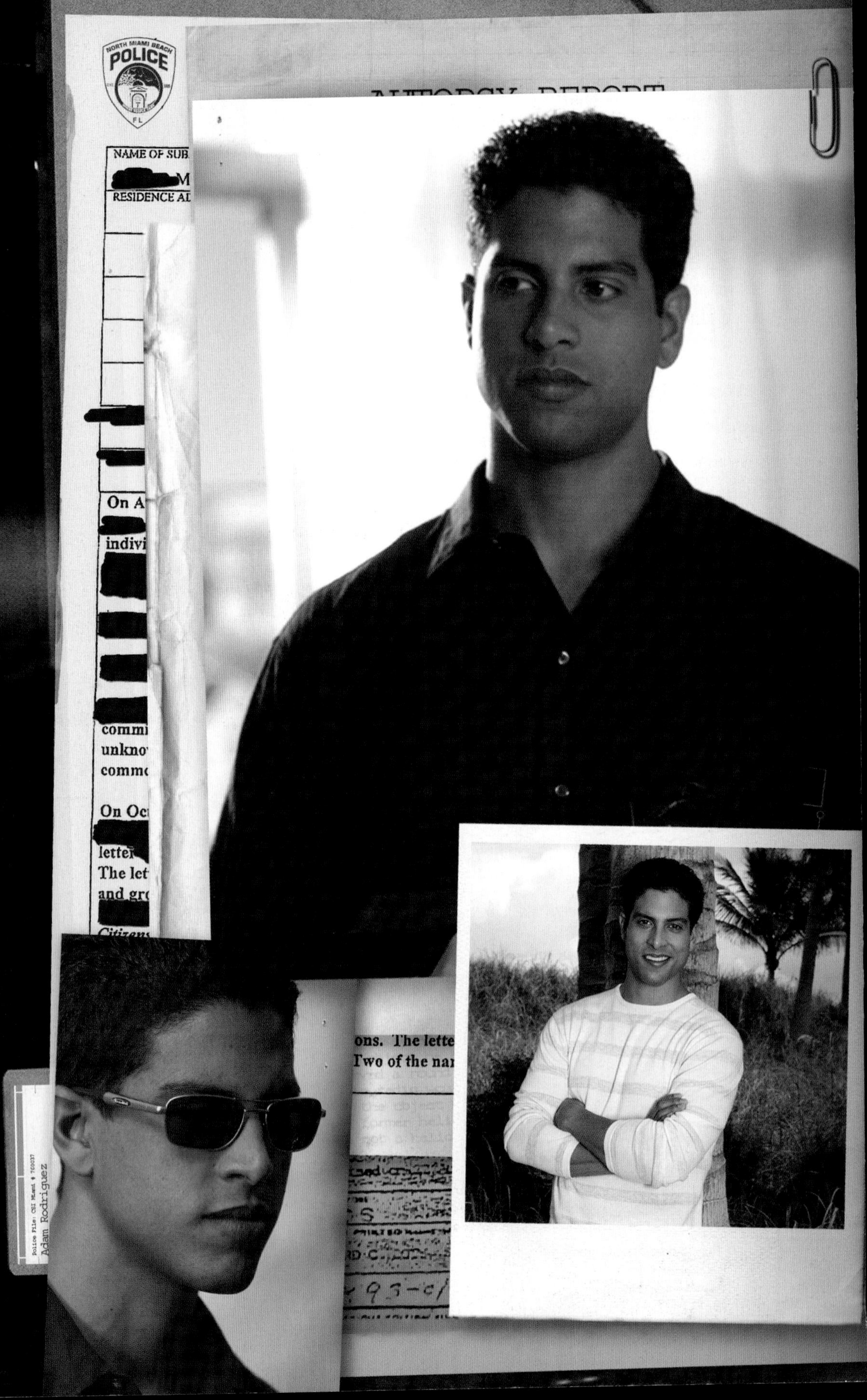
NORTH MIAMI BEACH
POLICE
FL
NAME OF SUB
[redacted] M
RESIDENCE AD
On A
[redacted]
indivi
[redacted]
commi
unkno
comm
On Oc
[redacted]
lette
The le
and gr
[redacted]
ons. The lette
Two of the na
Police File: CSI Miami # 760037
Adam Rodriguez

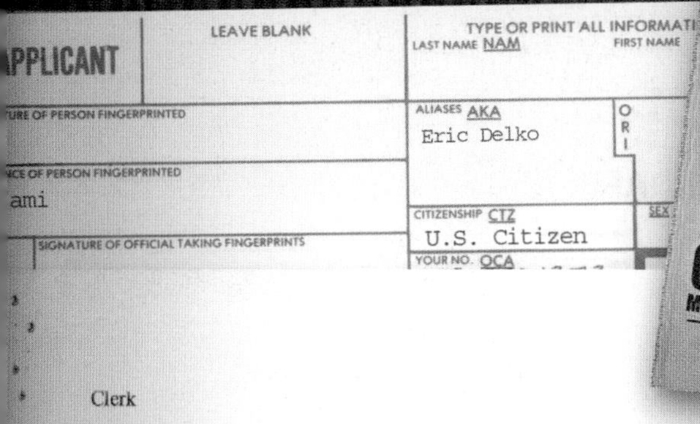
APPLICANT
LEAVE BLANK
TYPE OR PRINT ALL INFORMATI
LAST NAME NAM
FIRST NAME
ALIASES AKA
Eric Delko
CITIZENSHIP CTZ
U.S. Citizen
YOUR NO. OCA
SIGNATURE OF OFFICIAL TAKING FINGERPRINTS
Clerk

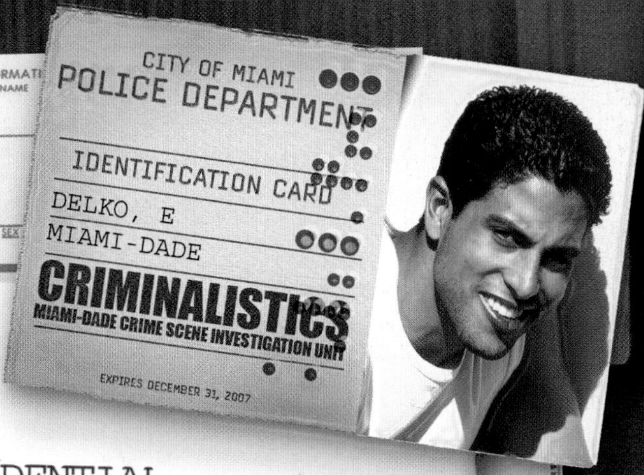
CITY OF MIAMI
POLICE DEPARTMENT
IDENTIFICATION CARD
DELKO, E
MIAMI-DADE
CRIMINALISTICS
MIAMI-DADE CRIME SCENE INVESTIGATION UNIT
EXPIRES DECEMBER 31, 2007

M.D.P.D.
Miami-Dade Police Department
C.S.I. Unit

CONFIDENTIAL

MD: DKT No.: 382-25-9

ADAM RODRIGUEZ (Eric Delko)

When a sports injury sidelined Adam Rodriguez in high school, his dreams of becoming a professional baseball player were put aside and he turned to acting. He had dabbled in children's theatre in his native New York and, at age 10, had auditioned for a role in *The Cosby Show*. His lucky break came when he was cast in a guest-starring role in an episode of *NYPD Blue*.

Rodriguez is also familiar to television audiences from his roles in *Brooklyn South* and *Roswell*. His additional television credits include *All Souls*, *Six Feet Under*, *Resurrection Blvd.*, *Law & Order*, *Felicity* and *Ryan Caulfield: Year One*. He has also appeared in the feature film *The Impostor*, and in Jennifer Lopez's video for 'If You Had My Love'.

Rodriguez currently divides his time between New York and Los Angeles. His birth date is April 2.

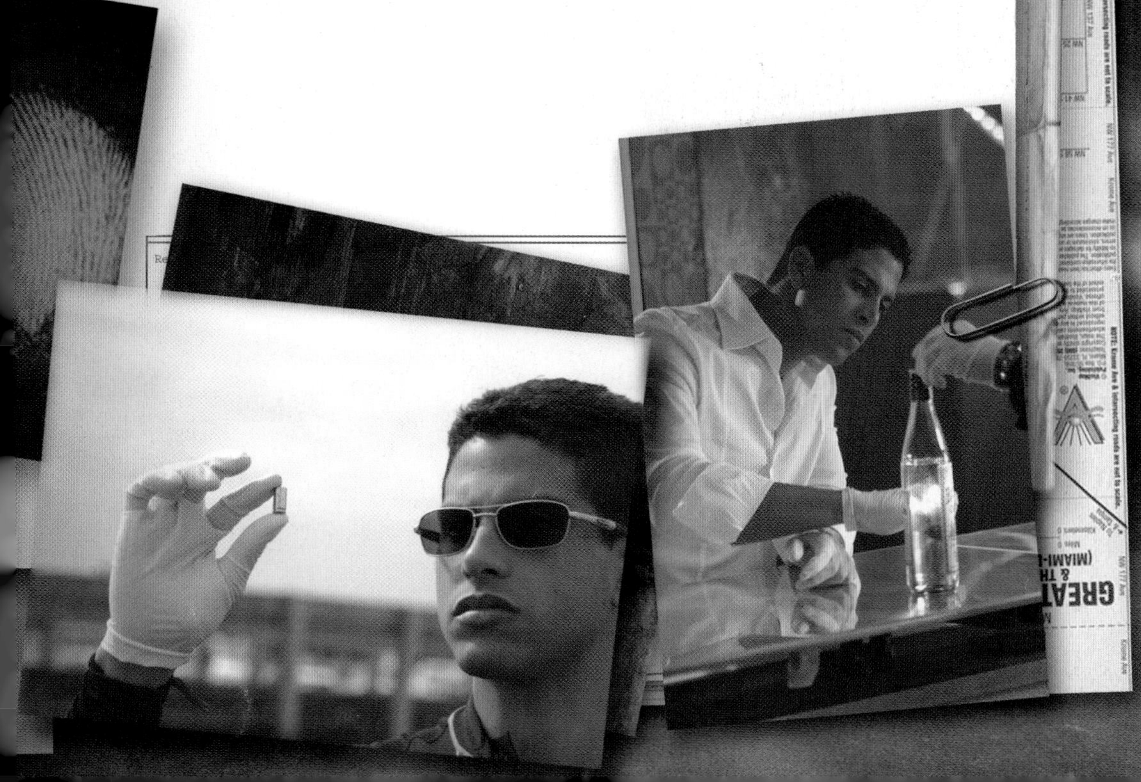

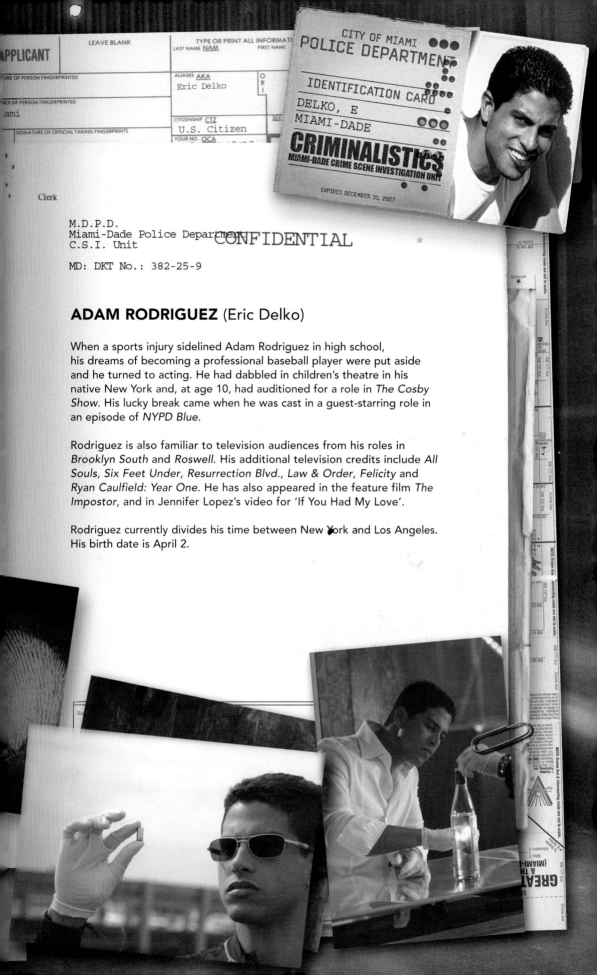

Clerk

In Replying Give Number
Of Case And Names

M.D.P.D.
Miami-Dade Police Department
C.S.I. Unit

MD: DKT No.: 382-25-10

CONFIDENTIAL

KHANDI ALEXANDER (Alexx Woods)

Khandi Alexander is probably best known to television audiences from her role on *NewsRadio*, the television mini-series *The Corner*, and her recurring role in *ER*. Alexander's additional television credits include *Law & Order: SVU*, *NYPD Blue*, *Third Watch*, *Cosby*, *Rude Awakening*, *La Femme Nikita* and *The Edge*.

Alexander's feature film credits include *There's Something About Mary*, *What's Love Got to Do With It*, *Sugar Hill*, *Dark Blue*, *Poetic Justice*, *Menace II Society*, *CB4* and *Emmett's Mark*.

Theatrically, she has performed on the stage in many roles, including Broadway's *Dreamgirls* and *Chicago* at the Shubert Theatre. Also an accomplished choreographer, Alexander has choreographed such productions as the *1992 American Music Awards* and Whitney Houston's world tours from 1989 to 1992.

She was born and raised in Queens, New York, and currently resides in Los Angeles. Her birth date is September 4.

EXC

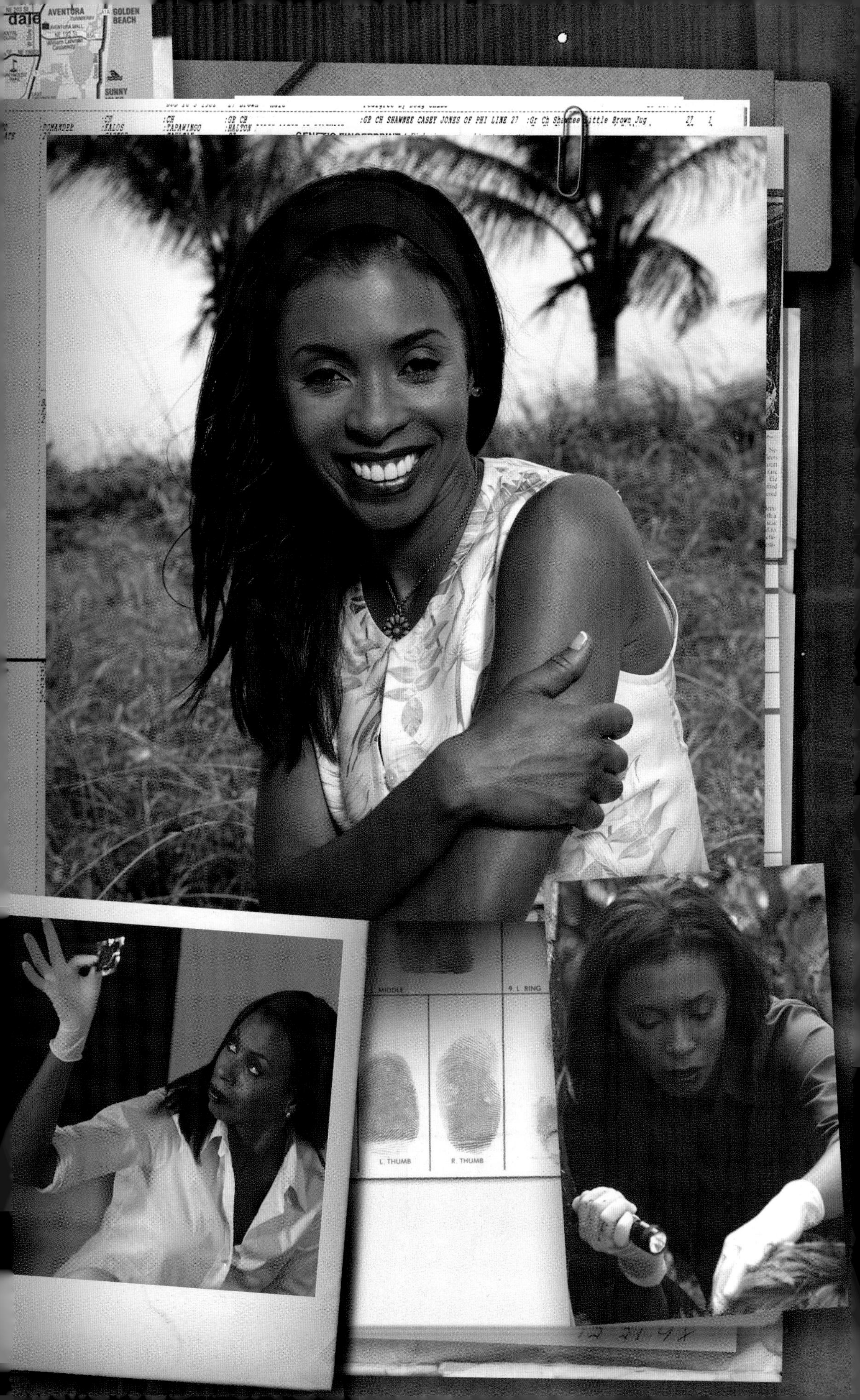
AVENTURA
GOLDEN BEACH
AVENTURA MALL
SUNNY
:GR CH SHAWNEE CASEY JONES OF PHI LINE 27
:Gr Ch Shawnee Little Brown Jug
9. L. RING
L. THUMB
R. THUMB

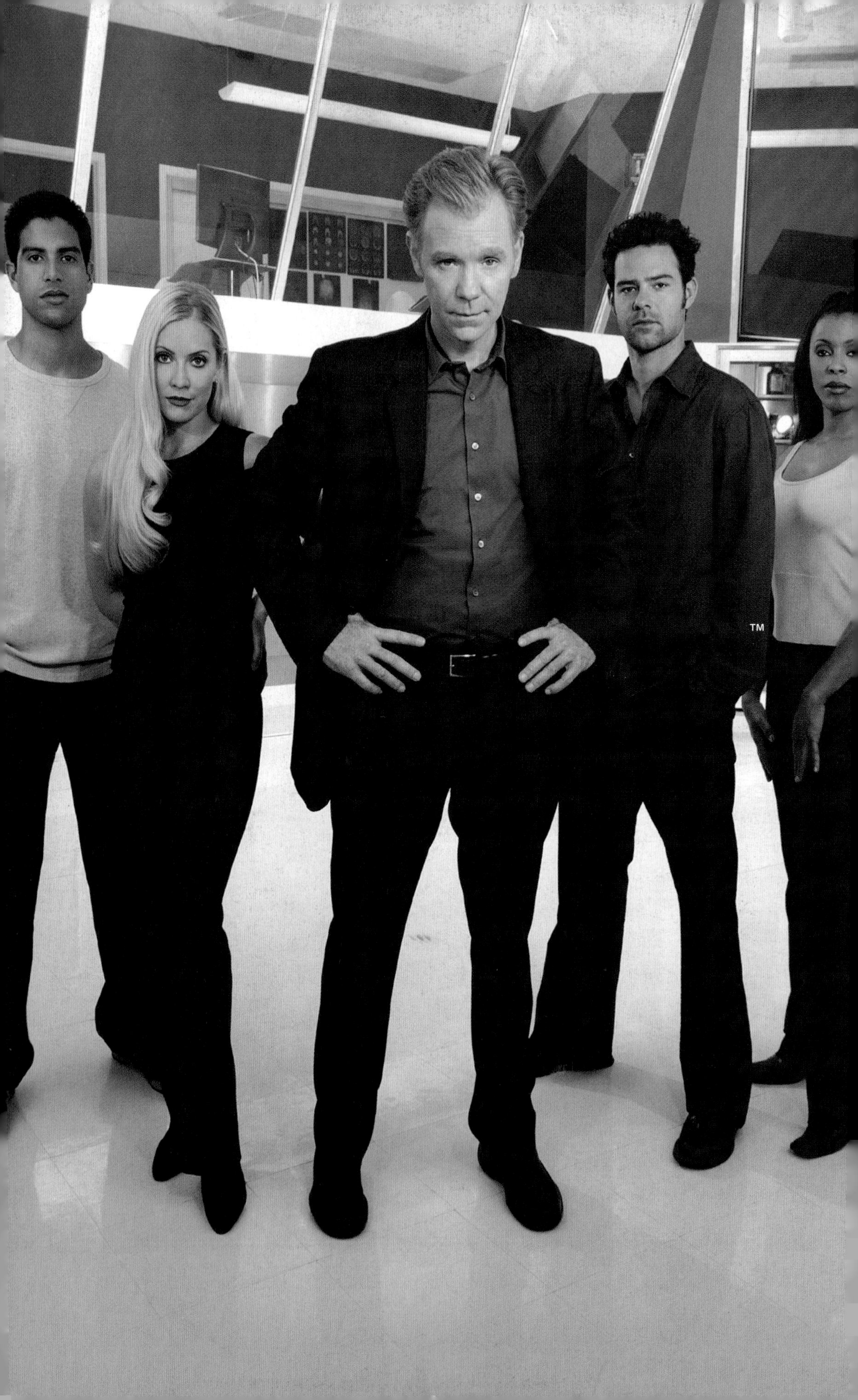
TM

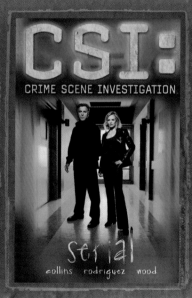